A MESSAGE

If the content in this ~~~~~~~~~~~~ of a positive impact on your life as I believe it has the potential to, it is my hope that you'll find it to be of a much greater value than the price you pay for it.

While I *can't* claim that this book will change your life for the better, I *can* promise you that if it doesn't, it isn't from a lack of effort on my part in trying to write a book that will.

Nothing in this volume has been included without considerable thought being given to the potential value it provides. While not every lesson within will be of interest or of relevance to you at the time you read it, it is likely that the contents of this book will take on new meanings and significance as you progress on your journey in life.

While the lessons within have added immense value to *my* life —and I share them with the hope of adding value to yours — my work is about presenting paths and opening doors. It is not about trying to convince anyone that any one way is better than another. *Please adapt the contents of this book to whatever lifestyle suits you best on your journey.*

And please know, that whatever direction your life leads you in from this moment forward, I'm happy that we were able to cross paths — even if it was just this once. I sincerely wish you an amazing journey.

Sincerely,

Zero Dean

If you find value in this book, don't keep it a secret.

Your positive word of mouth is not just welcome, it is absolutely essential in ensuring that this book gets into the hands of more people whose lives might be changed by it.

Readers are encouraged to share photos of this book, its contents, and meaningful excerpts with others and on social media.

Please remember to provide attribution and/or reference the book title when it isn't obvious. Feel free to tag me or use the hashtag #ZeroDean if you'd like to get my attention.

I'm happy you're here.

What you should know about this book

I'm not going to bullshit you. This book is <u>not</u> for everyone. And you may not like it.

The fact is, because everyone is different and at a different place in their journey — including me when I wrote the lessons that make up this book — what some readers find meaningful, relatable, and relevant to their lives, others will not.

It is entirely possible that many of the lessons contained within the boundaries of this book will not be relevant to you because you've *already learned* what they have to teach or you've yet to have a relatable experience.

For example, if you've never dealt with debilitating depression and still believe that happiness is a simple choice, then guess what? You're probably going to think that what I have to say on the subject is bullshit. And it doesn't make you wrong. It's simply *your truth* based on *your* life experience to date. That's just how it works.

However, I do believe that if you give this book a chance, you will find that its true *value* is not in *how many* of the lessons are relevant to you at the time you read them — or how many things you *agree* with — the value of this book is in the *one* thing you read that has the potential to change your life for the better by having read it. *Even* if that means coming across something that challenges your beliefs.

Sometimes it won't be a lesson that holds as much power for you as *a single line* within it. That single significant line can be a catalyst for meaningful connections between thoughts, experiences, and concepts that you previously hadn't considered to be related. And it is *those* kinds of new connections that create insight.

Also keep in mind that as time passes and your perspective changes in life, so too will the meaning of many of the lessons in this book.

3

This is not a "how-to" book

The contents in this book are not intended to represent the only answer or approach to a particular problem. The information within is provided as food for thought and intended to spur positive thinking and creative problem-solving — nothing more.

Many lessons (and phrases) are deliberately left open to interpretation so that they can be applied to a *variety* of different situations and circumstances.

This approach allows the contents of this book to be of *far* more value to *far* more people than if it were full of lessons with limited applications.

For example, the value in the phrase:

> *"Not everyone will understand your journey. That's fine. It's not their journey to make sense of. It's yours."* is that it means *different* things to *different* people — and even different things at different times in their lives.

For your consideration

While this book is composed of content that reflects personal opinions, insights, and experiences — and I hope that some of the content challenges you — it is not my intention to impose my views on anyone.

Your life, situation, and circumstances may dictate a different approach to those outlined in this book.

Readers are *encouraged* to *carefully consider* the lessons within and adapt the content to their individual needs. If something doesn't apply to or ring true for you and your life at this time, it is entirely possible that a different approach may be required.

This is not a book intended to tell readers *how* to live, but rather points to things that I've learned on my journey that added value to my life based on *my* personal experiences.

The lessons within this book are simply tools to use as *you* choose. How *you* connect the contents of this book to *your* own life is up to you.

An aspect of authenticity

In keeping with my mission to communicate as authentically as possible, I often write as I speak. This means that I occasionally adopt an unconventional use of punctuation, sentence structure, or word choice. Keep in mind that my point in writing this series is not to come across as an expert of the English language, but to instead present ideas and concepts in a way that allow them to "click" with people.

It is my hope that you'll not just read the words in this book, you'll also take the time to look for the multiple messages and meanings behind them and the spirit of what I'm trying to say.

Gratitude

Although the lessons in this book were prompted by personal experiences, nothing happens in a vacuum.

My view of the world and everything I share within this volume is the combined result of numerous influences — from authors to artists to educators and more. I make no claims that any of the ideas I share are original — but it is my hope that at least some of them are expressed and delivered in a way you haven't seen before.

I am forever grateful to anyone or anything I've crossed paths with that helped to broaden my perspective and provide me with knowledge worth knowing or an experience I could learn from.

Your feedback is encouraged

Whether you wish to praise, criticize, correct, or debate the contents of this book in a productive way — or in the event that something isn't clear to you — *I welcome your feedback.*

All feedback will be taken into consideration to improve future editions of this book and future volumes in this series.

You can find ways to connect with me at:
http://zerodean.com/contact

Forthcoming books by Zero Dean

Lessons Learned from The Path Less Traveled™ Volume 2

Thank you for considering what I have to offer to be of value enough to buy this book. I truly hope that some of the lessons within have as much of a positive impact on your life as they have had on mine.

— Zero Dean

DISCLAIMER

Please note that the publisher and author do not offer any legal, medical, or other professional advice, nor is this book intended as a substitute for professional advice. In the case of a need for any such expertise, consult with the appropriate professional. This book does not contain all information available on every subject or circumstance. This book has not been created to be specific to the situation or needs of any individual or organization. Every effort has been made to make this book as accurate as possible. However, there may be typographical and/or content errors. Therefore, this book should serve only as a general guide and not as the ultimate source of subject information. This book contains information that might be dated and is intended only to educate and entertain. The author and publisher shall have no liability or responsibility to any person or entity regarding any loss or damage incurred, or alleged to have incurred, directly or indirectly, by the information contained in this book. You hereby agree to be bound by this disclaimer or you may return this book to the retailer from which it was purchased according to their return policy guidelines.

LESSONS LEARNED FROM THE PATH LESS TRAVELED

VOLUME 1

GET MOTIVATED & OVERCOME OBSTACLES
WITH COURAGE, CONFIDENCE & SELF-DISCIPLINE

ZERO DEAN

First Edition
December 2018

ISBN 978-0-578-42868-0

Cover, layout, and book design by Zero Dean

M190318 C190209

FROM THE PATH LESS TRAVELED PUBLISHING
FromThePathLessTraveled.com

TABLE OF CONTENTS

DEDICATION

To Chase, for being one of the most supportive, most adventurous, and most interesting friends that anyone could have. I'm inspired by your trust, kindness, generosity, integrity, sense of humor, and how you continually demonstrate what it means to live life to the fullest. I hope that the sales of this book will eventually allow me to pay back the $130 I owe you.

SPECIAL THANKS

To Allie, for your kindness, generosity, and many the best meals of my life (and, of course, for Jax).

And to authors Garson O'Toole (Quote Investigator), Julie Guardado (Birth of a New J), Peggy LaCerra, Allie Brosh, Bill Bryson, and Bill Watterson for your inspiration.

And to Catherine Baldwin, Steph, Nancy, Doug, Rachel, Tony, Liana, Babette, Chad, Andrew, Sunny, Margi, David, Melinda, Duffy, Chris W, Vincent, Stevi, Vicki, Campa, Kaylin, Tilda, Angela, Francisco, Nigel, Chris K, Diana, Leonard, Lee, Robbie, Ari, Leah, Stormie, Joss, Susie, Vladimir, Don, Chip, Jeremy, Lowell Libby, members of 3D-PRO, and teachers and first responders everywhere. Spartan art by Freepik.

PREFACE

Who is this person?

It's a question I often ask myself of authors, life coaches, and others who offer advice for a living. While they *may* have *much* to offer, I'm always inclined to wonder *where* they came from and *how* they know what they know. Did they learn it from experience or take a class or study it in a book? Are they simply recycling *other* people's wisdom or are they offering their own personal and independent insights based on *actual* experiences they've had?

The way some people represent themselves, you'd think they sprung from the womb wearing a suit and tie — crying *not tears*, but words of wisdom. *"Yoooooou can dooooo it!"*

Yeah. *That's not me.*

I wish to neither represent myself as an expert, a perfect person, nor frankly, anyone special. This is not to say I don't have anything of value to offer you, it is simply to say that I don't want to be someone trying to get attention by making themselves appear important.

The fact is, titles & labels are not always an accurate indicator of trustworthiness, appearances can be deceiving, and one's accomplishments do not necessarily mean that what they have to sell you is something you *actually* want to buy. Marketing can be very manipulative.

It's important to remember that the quality of a book cover isn't always indicative of the quality of its contents. And it's not just people who go to great lengths to *appear* important that have something of value to offer. The most life-changing piece of advice you ever get could come from someone living on the street.

While those who represent themselves in pretentious ways *may* inspire confidence in *some*, I've found that *how* people *act* is a much more accurate indicator of character than how they *represent* themselves with words, important sounding titles, or whether they wear a fancy-looking suit or not.

One of the benefits of just being your authentic self and letting people come to their own conclusions about what kind of a person you are is that it takes no effort on your part. You don't have to *try* to *convince* people of *who* you are — because *who you are* is demonstrated by how you naturally act.

So, no, I'm not going to *tell* you who I am by listing a bunch of titles or accomplishments. Let it simply be known that, like most people, I've had my successes, but I've also had my fair share of failures too. And when all is said and done, I've learned far more from my mistakes in life than I have from the things I never had to struggle with.

Cashing in on the self-help craze

I didn't set out to write a self-help book. In fact, of all the kinds of books I thought I'd be likely to write in my life, this isn't one of them.

I resisted writing this book for *years*.

It's not that I have anything against self-help books. I've read many in my life and have found some to be quite illuminating and useful. But I've also come across many that are not — particularly those that only appear to exist because the author thought they could cash in on the self-help craze. So if that's the kind of book you're hoping to avoid, let me assure you, *I didn't write this book for money*.

And, realistically, I think there's only a .001% chance that the sales of this book will ever compensate for the personal cost of writing it and the experiences that prompted the lessons.

As cheesy as it sounds, I wrote this book to make a positive difference in people's lives — because there *are* things in life that are *far* more rewarding than money.

How this book came to be

In 2010, I began what I expected to be an incredible journey beyond my comfort zone. You'll find this explained in more detail in the eight "My Journey" chapters that accompany this book and the select journal entries that follow them.

As I traveled, I wrote about my experiences and shared them with an audience that followed along on my blog and social media.

At first, what I shared was very much like a travel journal — with simple entries that described where I went and what I did. But as the adventure I was living became less like the experiences I expected, my writing became more oriented towards problems I was having.

It was frustrating because I felt like what I was doing should be a joyful experience — and yet, from my point of view, it was just one problem or heartache after another.

I put on a happy face and hid what I was truly feeling as much as I could, but every so often my personal life couldn't help but be projected into the things I wrote about.

People called me an inspiration. But the longer I wandered beyond my comfort zone, the more I began to suffer from self-doubt.

I never really felt like the actions I took leading up to my journey were particularly inspiring. And frankly, quitting my job during the height of the global financial crisis felt more like an act of *stupidity* than an act of *inspiration*. And using my savings to pursue my passions on a cross-country adventure… *who does that?*

I wasn't exactly sure what a mid-life crisis involved, but it didn't seem to me that the actions I took were too dissimilar from those that someone suffering from one would take. Nevertheless, even as I struggled, I somehow found myself inspiring people — and I liked it. I just wasn't sure *how* I *did* it or how someone would go about doing it on purpose.

One of the fortunate benefits of time passing is that I began to learn from the experiences I was having. Many of the things that I considered difficult at the beginning of my journey became non-issues later on. Not because they became easier, but because I became stronger. A sure sign of growth — although this isn't something I would learn to appreciate until much later on.

The fact is, my life beyond comfort was providing me with challenges to which I was finding solutions. And it is those solutions that I began sharing. First, as motivational tidbits — and then as lessons later on.

And even though life was no less challenging, the fact that I could share what I learned and *help* people was encouraging. And *this was yet another lesson.*

> *Student says, "I am very discouraged. What should I do?"*
> *Master says, "Encourage others." — Zen Proverb*

The proverb above is a good example of an ancient lesson I learned *first* from experience.

Even after I'd shared hundreds of pages of lessons online, I never had any inclination to do anything else with them. I mean — why? The self-help market is saturated and nothing I shared was new.

Plus — and this was a big one — I was a nobody. What could I possibly have to say that someone with a nice title and letters after their name couldn't say better?

But I didn't see things then as I see them now. So I had no intention of writing a self-help book.

The invitation

In the spring of 2014, I was contacted by the Vice President of a large company in Orange County, California. Something I'd shared online had caught her eye and she wanted to see if I'd be interested in speaking at a seminar for the company's vast number of employees. I was intrigued by the invitation. Especially because I loved the idea of talking about my journey.

She informed me that I'd be just one of a number of speakers including doctors, writers, fitness gurus, and other important sounding people.

And that's when I did something stupid. I declined.

I *could* tell you it was because I felt unprepared, which is true. But the real reason I said no is because I was intimidated by the idea of sharing a stage with people I imagined were far more qualified to speak than I was.

I gave her the excuse that because I wasn't a speaker, I'd need more time than I had to prepare. And she accepted that — and I should have stopped talking. But I continued by saying that I felt it would make far more sense if I had some *real* credentials like the other speakers she'd lined up. Like, you know, *if I'd written a book or something.*

The next day, I realized my mistake. I'd let my fear and insecurity speak for me and had turned down an opportunity to do something that I actually *wanted* to do!

I quickly composed and sent an email expressing my desire to speak after all. But it was a message that would go unanswered. And although I suspect it is simply because she was busy, I sometimes think I talked her out of it (there's a lesson there).

Shortly after I realized my first mistake, I realized another. I'd convinced myself that my work didn't really have any place in the world beyond my blog. But clearly, if people were finding it valuable enough to invite me to speak at engagements in front of hundreds of people, then perhaps it was something I should reconsider.

I also realized that if I *really* wanted to speak, it would be really helpful if I wrote a book that contained the things I wanted to speak about.

And so I did.

Some of my rules for writing this book

I wanted to write the kind of book that *I* would want to read. That meant it had to have substance.

I've been burned by authors with important sounding credentials who appear to simply read & regurgitate what's popular at the time — or who turn a simple list of bullet points into 300 plus pages of padding.

Also, the quality of the content would need to be consistent throughout. Sometimes the best bits of a book are the first few chapters — enough to hook a person into buying it, only to discover later that the last half is nothing but fluff.

The way this book came to be — and how it's intended to be read (from any page) — means that the content on nearly any page has the potential to have as meaningful an impact on reader's lives as the content on nearly any other page. While it may only be a single thing in this book that truly connects with you, that single thing could come from *anywhere* within.

It's been said that *knowledge without experience is bullshit*. Since the lessons I share were prompted by and based on *actual* experiences I've had, the information I share is grounded in experience. *This doesn't make it more true* — but it *does* mean that I can speak as someone who has actually experienced something as opposed to a person who simply read something and assumes it's true.

The messenger matters

One thing I've learned on the journey that led to the book you're reading is that *the messenger matters*.

Although there are a lot of people writing a lot of things that revolve around many of the same subjects — *how* a person says something and expresses themselves can mean the difference between whether the person they're communicating with truly gets it or not and whether it makes a meaningful difference or not.

I spent a long time resisting writing a self-help book only to realize that that, in itself, was probably one of the best reasons to write one.

That and the fact that not being motivated by money meant that I could express myself in ways that other people wouldn't if all they were trying to do was sell books.

HOW TO READ THIS BOOK

Choose your adventure

Although the contents of this book are organized in such a way that they build upon each other, this book is written to be opened and read from nearly any page. Readers are encouraged to flip through the pages of this book and choose content based on interest or relevance to their lives or simply because it catches their eye.

Because the eight "My Journey" chapters of this book involve a continuing narrative, they will make the most sense when read in chronological order.

Contemplate the content

However you choose to read this book, keep in mind that the lessons within will only be effective if you take time to truly consider their meaning, message, and relevance to your life. Not everything in this book will be relevant to you at this time. And some of the contents will mean different things to you at different times of your life.

This is not a book that's intended to be read in a single sitting. It's a book that is meant to be dipped into and revisited repeatedly over time.

Open to interpretation

Many lessons and phrases in this book are intentionally left open to interpretation. And some are presented more as food for thought than they are as answers to questions or solutions to problems that you may have.

If it doesn't challenge you, it doesn't change you

As you navigate this book, always keep in mind that it's *not only* meant to motivate, encourage, and inspire readers, it's intended to *challenge* them as well.

It's important to understand that the best coaches, the best bosses, and the best CEOs in the world don't do their jobs effectively by telling people what they want to hear. They make the greatest positive impact by saying what needs to be said, expanding perspectives, and encouraging people to rise to the challenges of life.

Stuff you already know

Many of the lessons in this book could easily be considered common sense or ancient wisdom, depending on how you've lived your life. And much of it could be information you *already* know. Keep in mind that what's common sense to one person might be an entirely new concept to another.

When you come across things that you already know, treating them as reminders will help you see their value. Also know, there is a big difference between *knowing* something and actually *applying* it in a meaningful way to your life.

Repetition

Because the lessons in this book were written to be self-contained and read in any order, some concepts and details are presented or alluded to a number of times in different ways.

Exceptions

There are exceptions to *nearly everything*. There is no single quote, book, system, recipe, lesson, or way of life that works for *all* people in *all* situations. Some things that are of *no* value to you are of *extreme* value to someone else. Just because something doesn't work for *you* in your circumstances doesn't mean it doesn't work for someone else in theirs.

Wear it out

If you're like me and have a habit of keeping your books in pristine condition, consider making an exception with this one. It's okay to mark up, circle, highlight, or check off pieces that catch your eye. I want you to use this book without fear of making it look used.

One of the surest signs that this book is of real practical value to you will be when it no longer looks like it did when you bought it.

LESSONS LEARNED
FROM THE
PATH LESS
TRAVELED
VOLUME 1

"Life is a succession of lessons which must be lived to be understood."

— *Ralph Waldo Emerson*

"Oh crap."

— Zero Dean

Dear Self,

I am working on being a better person.

Please let me be the type of person who I would respect and admire if I saw them in action. Let me greet each new day as another opportunity to get things right. Let me be open to thinking about things in ways I haven't thought about them before. Let me find ways to make a positive difference in the world, no matter how small, and act upon them when I am able.

Let me be open to the challenge of change. Let me not shy away from things just because they are difficult. Let me face my fears and do things I would like to do, even when they make me nervous. Let me be generous with what I have to give away. Let me remember to be grateful for every second that I get to make choices in my life and act upon them.

Let me make at least one person's day brighter by having been a part of it. Let me accept my mistakes as learning experiences. Let me learn to love myself, flaws and all. Let me not care so much what others think. And let me be confident in my ability to succeed.

Thank you. -- Me

Journal Entry
Day 630

My Journey

Part 1:
Not everyone will understand *my* journey

"Restlessness and discontent are the first necessities of progress." — Thomas Edison

Once upon a time...

Spring, 2009. It was towards the end of my sixth 12-hour workday in a row — I was sitting in my cubicle staring at my monitor. This 70+ hour work week was no different than the many that preceded it.

Being on salary meant I only got paid for 40 hours, but despite this discrepancy, I enjoyed the work I was paid to do and wasn't unhappy. And I'll admit it, I was comfortable. I had a routine. And in the midst of the global financial crisis, I was grateful to not only *have* a job, but felt very fortunate to actually continue to get paid to be creative for a living.

I considered myself to be one of the "lucky ones" and assumed my life, on-the-whole, was as it should be. But as I got ready to leave work that night, I had *the* thought:

"This isn't what you're supposed to be doing".

Whoa — where did *that* come from? I responded by doing the most rational thing I could think of — I shrugged it off. But the thought came back the next day...

"This isn't what you're supposed to be doing".

And it came back the day after that, too. It was nothing if not persistent. So I decided to give it some attention. I figured if I did that, then it would go away and I could go back to living my "comfortable" life.

Needless to say, that isn't what happened — because when I started focusing on what I was doing in life, it raised far more questions than answers.

What was the point of my life? Was sitting behind a monitor in a cubicle farm for so many hours a week *really living* or had I somehow turned into a robot just going through the motions? Was I *really* directing my life to where I *truly* wanted to go, or was I just doing what I thought was appropriate for the path I found myself on? And where *exactly* was it that I was heading anyway?

With those questions in mind, I looked into my past and considered what it was I had wanted once upon a time in life. Then I examined my current life and imagined where I'd end up if I simply kept doing the things I'd grown accustomed to.

And *that's* when I realized *why* I felt like I wasn't doing what I was *supposed* to. It's because the path I was on was leading me further and further away from the kind of life I *truly* wanted. I wasn't feeling fulfilled because I wasn't fulfilling *my* potential.

I'd let my life goals fall victim to the allure of comfortable routines. I'd fooled myself into thinking that being comfortable was the same thing as being fulfilled. And as a result, I'd begun to live *someone else's* idea of the ideal life, *not mine*.

By growing complacent with comfort, I'd not only denied myself interesting and exciting opportunities for growth, I'd disconnected myself from many of the dreams, aspirations, and passions I once prioritized.

***

I daydreamed about what my future might be like if I broke away from what appeared to be a common, well-trodden path in life and, instead, made my own. The thought filled me with enthusiasm. But only briefly.

Because, I then thought about what I'd have to do *and* sacrifice to make what I wanted to accomplish happen. Nothing major really. Just comfort, security, stability and — **hang on!** Those are pretty major!

Just up and throw comfort, security, and stability out the window? Yeah, *that wasn't* going to happen.

No matter how enthusiastic I felt about the idea of breaking away, I quickly concluded that quitting a decent-paying job at the height of a global financial crisis was impractical, risky, and dumb. And so there wasn't much point in even considering it. It wasn't the sort of thing I would do. It scared the hell out of me. And then, much to my surprise, *I did it anyway*.

I *quit*. It wasn't exactly *planned*. There was an incident at work. A polite verbal exchange in which I discovered that a person I worked under was taking credit for something I'd put a lot of effort into. I calmly walked back to my desk and began tidying my workspace. It took a moment for my mind to realize what my body was *actually* doing. *Packing*.

Turns out there were more self-made surprises ahead. Two days after quitting my job, I gave 30 days notice at my apartment complex.

Suddenly jobless, with 30 days to vacate my apartment, I'd pushed myself into massive change. With *consequences*. While I didn't know *where* I would go or *what* I would do, I *did* know that when my lease was up, having an apartment full of stuff would leave me at a *serious* disadvantage.

So I started selling my stuff. Everything. And as my end-of-the-month deadline neared, I started donating it, or dragging it to the dumpster. And as I did *all* this, I considered what it was I *really* wanted in life and what my true purpose might be.

I *knew* I wanted adventure. *Real* adventure. Not the pre-packaged or manufactured type. I wanted to feel alive and less like the robot I felt I'd become. I wanted to push myself beyond my comfort zone. I wanted to connect with people in a meaningful way. I wanted to capture moments in writing and photography and share them with an audience that it mattered to. And most importantly, I wanted to feel like I was using what I had to offer in a way that had a meaningful and positive impact on others.

The (initial) context of my journey

As the days counted down towards my move-out date, I got a call from a friend in Las Vegas.

"Do you know what you're going to do yet?" he asked.

"Not exactly. But I have some ideas. I just wish I had more time to work them out."

"Well, I talked to my girlfriend. We're cool if you want to come crash with us."

It was an unexpected offer that provided me with exactly what I needed — the luxury of being able to consider my options without having a deadline hanging over my head. Granted, I was the one responsible for the deadline in the first place, but for all intents and purposes, it had worked. There were some major changes afoot. And so, I went to live with my friend.

In the time leading up to my journey, I came up with a plan that would provide me with a novel way to reconnect with five of the things I was most passionate about.

In the spring of 2010, I announced my project on Facebook — the response to which was everything I'd hoped for. People were *excited* about what I was going to do. And in early May, I released a video on YouTube.

Here's the transcript from that video:

"My name is Zero Dean. And in the audio and video segments that follow in this series, you're going to get a first-hand look at someone facing their fears and taking a leap of faith to change the story of their life. Because in order to pursue my passions, I quit my job, terminated my lease, and sold or donated everything that wouldn't fit in my 4Runner. And now, I am cutting my roots to embark on an epic tour of the United States and Canada. And I will be broadcasting the experience. But there's a twist...

Because in my quest for remarkable stories to tell, I'm leaving where I go, who I meet, and what I do, up to you to decide. This journey will be a real-life choose-your-own-adventure where your involvement will have a direct impact on the outcome of the story.

This will be one of the most challenging, and hopefully one of the most fulfilling experiences of my life. I hope you will join me and become a part of my story, and an active participant in my adventure.

I hope to see you soon!"

Put simply, by allowing the Internet to tell me where to go, what to do, and who to meet, I would become the protagonist in a real-life, choose-your-own adventure. Reality TV was huge at the time and this tapped into it.

The response I got from my video was so encouraging that I never imagined I'd have trouble attracting an audience. And with an audience, sponsors — or at least a small income from advertising I was assuredly going to get from website traffic. I was *ridiculously* optimistic.

Adventures in discomfort

On the morning of May 8, 2010, I disconnected from life as I knew it and officially began my journey. With my Toyota 4Runner overstuffed with gear and supplies, I pulled out of my friend's apartment complex in Las Vegas and headed west.

In order to make my funds last as long as possible, I decided to skip hotels, campgrounds, and couch-surfing and, instead, sleep in my car. Not only would this give me the turn-on-a-dime freedom I wanted, it also made me feel like I was sacrificing comfort to do it.

It was this sort of "planned discomfort" that I almost congratulated myself for overcoming in advance, thinking, "Sure, sleeping in my car won't be as comfortable as sleeping in my old bed, but it won't be *that* bad either."

But what I didn't realize at the time was that it wasn't the discomfort and challenges that I'd so carefully prepared myself for that would be a serious issue; It was the challenges and discomfort I couldn't see coming that *would*.

As I drove out of Las Vegas that morning, I was confident, optimistic, enthusiastic, hopeful, and entirely ignorant of how much the journey I was embarking on would change my life in ways I couldn't imagine.

Within a week of my departure, I began to battle self-doubt. Within a month, I was ready to quit. I just wasn't sure what I would be quitting to — or more precisely, I wasn't able to put it into words at the time. But it was *comfort.* I wanted my *comfort* back. I just didn't want to sacrifice the kind of life I *truly* wanted to get it. So — I kept going. And while the kind of success I originally sought was elusive, discomfort was not.

I lost friends and felt alienated by family. I had health issues, dental issues, and suffered from injuries. I had valuable things stolen from me and accidentally destroyed things that were valuable to me. I was threatened. Screamed at. Scolded. Physically assaulted. And feared for my life more than once.

And as I tried to keep my feelings — and the challenges I faced — a secret, my crumbling sense of identity, along with the bitter disappointment, isolation, and loneliness I felt manifested itself in my life as depression. It was like nothing I'd ever experienced.

And so — for a time — I lost my confidence, I lost my self-esteem, and I lost my optimism. And as a consequence, I almost lost myself. But, ultimately, the experiences I had not only made me stronger, they became the source of numerous invaluable lessons that would fundamentally change my life.

***

For nearly two years, I criss-crossed the United States on an epic road trip covering over 60,000 miles. And finally, when I was no longer able to sustain my adventurous life — and without having found a way to monetize my project — my travels came to an end. But my journey continued — in ways I didn't expect.

Rather than run to safety and away from my fears, I opened my eyes, my arms, and my mind to embrace all life experiences, not just the good ones. And by doing so, I began to gain insight from my experiences.

My priorities changed as well. I stopped looking for things that I lacked. I stopped comparing my life to others. I stopped worrying so much about the future. And as I tried to make sense of my journey, I came to realize that although I didn't end up where I thought I was going, the path I took led me to exactly where I needed to be.

> *"Do not go where the path may lead, go instead where there is no path and leave a trail."*
>
> — *Ralph Waldo Emerson*

That day

I'm standing on the edge of a cliff, thinking about jumping.

Earlier in the day...

Ding! It's the sound of an incoming message.

The words *"How are you?"* appear in the corner of my laptop screen.

"Fuck." is what I think.

I have nearly 4,000 Facebook "friends" at this point in my journey. People I've connected with, many of whom I don't know or recognize. Making my status known often leads to a chat window like this one popping up.

My online status is habitually hidden — so this shouldn't have happened, but sometimes I accidentally turn it on while posting to Facebook from the web browser on my phone.

I stare at the words "How are you?" and frown. It's not the right question.

"Are you ok?" would be a better one, but she doesn't know that. And I realize on some level, she's just trying to be nice.

Of course she's being nice. She's a nice person. Like people think I am.

But I'm not *thinking* nice at the moment. I'm just staring at the words. Annoyed. And I kind of don't care — about almost anything.

I feel like such an asshole. *I am an asshole, asshole!*

I put my hands on my keyboard and type an answer in the only way I feel I can at this particular moment without being offensive or setting off alarm bells.

"Can't complain."

And then I add my reflexive, "How are you?"

I think I'm *so* clever. I'm good at hiding what I'm going through. People think I'm happy. No one has a clue.

A few hours later...

I'm standing at the edge of a cliff face overlooking the ocean.

And I'm thinking about jumping.

This reminds me of a song lyric I can't quite think of. Which bugs me, but it probably shouldn't. Not if my life is about to end. It's a stupid thing to be thinking about while also contemplating death.

In any case, I only climbed up on this wall to take a picture from a perspective that few people do. And it is a truly beautiful view.

But as beautiful as the view is, I'm now perched upon this wall pondering my demise.

But I'm also thinking about my hat. The one I'm wearing — and the one I lost when I was here before — standing on this wall in almost the exact same place. But, at that time, I felt so much better than I do now. And there was much more wind. That's how I lost my hat.

A gust of wind came by and ripped it right off my head — as if the Nike logo offended Mother Nature. She then tossed it *not* down, but *up* — into the air — where it floated like Wile E Coyote for a moment before plunging several hundred feet to the rocks and surf below.

The hat I'm wearing now — while standing on this wall — bears the letters ZERO. It's a skateboarding company that conveniently named themselves after me. I don't mind because it means I get to buy gear with my name on it.

They should sponsor me.

I'm wondering what would happen if I stood closer to the edge and just sort of fell. Studying the landscape now, I imagine I'd probably hit the cliff and tumble. It wouldn't be a direct drop. I'd really have to jump for that — and even so, there's no guarantee of a safe fall down.

A safe fall?
A safe fall down to my *death*?
What the hell am I thinking?

Well, I'm *thinking* it would suck to bounce off those rocks. That would probably hurt. Plus, there's the slight chance the cliff would catch me and I'd just end up lying in a seagull crap covered crack with a broken back or something.

That would suck.

I'm amazed they have places like this along PCH (Pacific Coast Highway). *So* beautiful. *So* dangerous.

You know… someone should really put a barrier here to keep people from the edge.

Oh. Wait. *I'm standing on it.* **Duh**.

"Well, *that's* not safe", I think, "I could just fall and it would be *'game over'.*"

I gotta be careful up here. I could lose another hat.

*** *

It's true. I'd been thinking a lot about death. Maybe as much as I once thought about it as a kid, back when I didn't want to feel *anything*. Even when I imagined all of the creative ways in which I might do it, I never *wanted* to die. Not then. Not now.

A desire to rush to death was *never* actually *the issue — even when I obsessed about it.* And here's why: I think suicide is just — well — dumb. Like, *really* dumb.

It's *not* because of any of the numerous ways in which society considers it offensive or wrong. I think it's dumb because it's a missed opportunity to get the most out of life beforehand.

At some point, in my childhood, I decided that if I ever wanted to kill myself, I'd empty my bank account, max out my credit cards, and do everything I'd ever wanted to do until I had nothing left. I mean, if you're going to die, then you might as well do it on empty. There's no sense in ending it all with a full tank of gas.

I thought of it as a *suicide ride*. It's where you finally do the things you always thought you couldn't — or wouldn't — let yourself do when you were too worried about how much things cost or the risks involved.

Skydive? Sure. I mean, if you're going to *die* anyway.

Perhaps you'd take out a loan or sell whatever you owned to make it all possible.

*** *

So I'm standing at the edge of a cliff overlooking the ocean. And I'm realizing my life over the past several months has been a sort of perverted version of my suicide ride.

And if that's what it was, I was completely fucking it up. Because — in a weird way — it was supposed to be *way* more fun than this.

And I always thought it was sort of brilliant, because I imagined that there was always the possibility that t*ruly living* before rushing to death might actually curb my desire to die.

So I'm standing at the edge of a cliff overlooking the ocean and I realize I really don't want to die.

Not today.
I just want something to live for.
But I haven't found it yet.

And with this in mind, I jump off the stone wall.

My Journey

Part 2:
The window

I remember sitting in my cubicle looking at the window on the nearby wall. I say looking *at* the window and not *out* of it because, from where my desk was situated on the second floor, there wasn't much to see *out* that window. Just the sky. Which, being based in southern California, meant it was typically blue. So it wasn't the *view* that drew me to the window — it was what it represented.

The window was a gateway to the great "out there". Another world. A place where *"real life"* happened.

Because as much as it *appeared* as if I was alive, my life didn't feel natural. The number of hours I spent sitting in my cubicle staring at a computer monitor certainly didn't.

And yet, I *enjoyed* what I did. I loved being creative. And I felt fortunate to get paid to do the work I did.

But as much as I enjoyed it, I also felt like the life I was living was an artificial construct that was keeping me from the life I *actually* wanted.

Which was on the *other* side of that window.

And so, at times, as I sat in my chair under the fluorescent lighting playing the role I was paid for, I felt like I was living a lie. Not least of which because the life I led was out of sync with *who* and *what* I wanted to be.

I *didn't want* to live a repetitious and predictable life that left me feeling like a robot. I *didn't want* to be a paint-by-numbers person.

I wanted to color outside of the lines and feel like what I did truly mattered — or at the very least, feel like the life I lived was allowing me to maximize my potential, not keeping me from it. But I'd grown comfortable with my routines and addicted to my stability. The repetitive nature of my life had created a rut in which I was deeply entrenched.

In the same way that it can be difficult to get out of a soft, warm bed in a cold room on a brisk morning, so too is abandoning the comfortable routines of one's life in order to take a chance at something better.

Because that's what life on the other side of that window would provide, just a *chance* — *not* a guarantee — at a more fulfilling life. Perhaps the life I was living was as good as it would get. But then again, perhaps not. I didn't know then what I know now.

The fact is, comfortable routines are what keep people from growing, stretching, and truly knowing themselves. They limit a person's exposure to new experiences and by doing so, instill people with a false sense of security.

Comfortable routines lead people to believe that they're far more capable of handling what life throws at them because their routines limit what they're exposed to.

It's easy to feel like one is the master of their domain and everything is under control when their domain is a comfort zone in which everything that happens is within the realm of what's *expected* to happen. It's far less easy to face uncertainty and the unexpected, but these two things are at the root of some of the greatest gratifications in life — like mystery, wonder, possibility, and new discoveries. And it is *precisely* these things that I wanted more of in my life.

The longer I played the role of a robot, the less I was challenged and, consequently, the more I drifted from many of the things I truly desired.

Without a steady stream of new experiences that challenge us, we don't grow. And this lack of growth can cause people to feel like they've lost touch with who they are and what they want in life — and as a result, they're often left feeling unfulfilled.

Which is how I felt — like I was just going through the motions of life. And *I was*. My comfortable routines essentially locked me into a loop that wouldn't change until *I* changed them.

As long as we are actively engaged in living an unfulfilling life — comfortable as it may be — we greatly limit our ability to lead a fulfilling one. This is because it is extremely difficult to go from one kind of life to the other, without first letting go of the things that are holding us back. And that often means letting go of the routines we've learned to rely on to keep us comfortable.

It may seem self-evident, but *change requires change*. It requires abandoning the comfort of the known for uncertainty and ambiguity. And focusing more on what you wish to *gain* by moving forward than what you must give up to do so.

Life loses its wonder when it's predictable. The moment we stop challenging ourselves is the moment we begin to die inside.

And I wanted to *live*, not just *exist*. And that meant exploring a life on the *other* side of that window.

> *"Take risks: if you win, you will be happy; if you lose, you will be wise."* — *Swami Vivekananda*

My Journey

Part 3:
A means to an end

Prior to quitting my job, I'd saved money with the idea of eventually opening a photography studio somewhere in Southern California.

But *after* quitting my job and re-evaluating what I *truly* wanted to do with my life, it seemed like such a safe idea — and one that would once again commit me to something I wasn't certain I was supposed to be doing with my life.

Sure, I loved photography, but even when I loved what I did, every job I'd ever had always left me feeling like my potential was being wasted. I had yet to find a profession that allowed me to truly take advantage of what I felt I had to offer.

I realized that if I couldn't find a job that helped me fulfill my potential, perhaps I could *make* one. And the money I'd saved gave me the freedom to try.

So I did.

I created an interactive, social-media-based project that combined my love of writing, photography, adventure, travel, and connecting with people.

If I was careful about how I spent it, the money I'd saved would support my travels for more than a year, if necessary, but I was certain I'd be able to find a sponsor to help offset the costs well before then. After all, everyone I spoke to about the "choose-my-adventure" aspect of my journey thought it was awesome.

Giving people the opportunity to influence my travels and make decisions for me pushed me to do things — and go places — that I wouldn't necessarily choose on my own. This ensured that I had new and unusual experiences and didn't just stay in my comfort zone.

Additionally, the more that people got directly involved with — and emotionally invested in — the outcome of my adventures, the more meaningful the experience became for them. And by the same token, the more meaningful what I did became for me.

A Means to an End

When it came down to deciding how I was going to travel around the United States for an indeterminate amount of time — I considered a lot of options — and then threw most of them out the window.

I wanted to make my savings last as long as possible — so staying at hotels was out. And camping, while cheaper at $10 to $30 per night, was still way too much to justify.

I considered couch-surfing, which is free, but it requires knowing where you're going to be, when you're going to be there, and how long you plan on staying. The interactive nature of my journey, and my audience's involvement in choosing where I went and what I did, largely ruled that out. Plus, I didn't want to sacrifice the turn-on-a-dime freedom that my new lifestyle would allow. So couch-surfing was out.

For a time, I even considered purchasing a cheap, used camper or RV — but realized that I wouldn't be able to really get off the beaten path if I ever wanted to.

That's when I came to the conclusion that I *already* had a low-cost solution to lodging. And one that would also allow me to traverse all kinds of terrain, if necessary. My Toyota 4Runner. And so, I chose to sleep in my car.

As it turns out, sleeping in one's car doesn't really hold a person back from accomplishing most things. Granted, it *does* take some getting used to.

For starters, I had no stove, no refrigerator, no bathroom, no running water, no WiFi, no overnight climate-control, limited electricity, limited airflow, and an even more limited amount of space. But all of these things were predictable issues that I was eventually able to adapt to.

And, although I didn't know it at the time, of all the challenges I would eventually face on my journey, the issues associated with living in my car were some of the easiest to overcome.

My Journey

Part 4:
Beyond comfort

When I originally envisioned my journey, one of the things I wanted to do was explore what it meant to *live beyond comfort*. I'd read that pushing yourself beyond your comfort zone was a catalyst for personal growth, so I deliberately set up certain aspects of my life in a way that would force me to do that.

It wasn't just about sleeping in my car or living without many of the amenities that people take for granted. It was *also* about taking a leap of faith, following my intuition, and living life without a road map.

When I got in my car and made my way west out of Las Vegas, I considered myself prepared for this journey and looked forward to the challenge of what my new life had in store for me. But the massive changes that I initiated were *not* just *difficult* to deal with, they were *far* more difficult than I imagined they'd be.

Between facing my fears, hosting a persistent, interactive social media project, starting a blog, constantly traveling, living in my car, accepting challenges, doing what people suggested, and trying to keep my audience interested and entertained, I was overwhelmed.

In fact, I was *so* overwhelmed by the challenges I'd created for myself, that I had little time to really make sense of my life. I'd bitten off more than I could chew and was choking on it.

As the weeks went by, and the initial excitement I felt at the beginning of my journey faded, I struggled with a persistent feeling of failure and frequently felt as if nothing I was doing was living up to anyone's expectations — *especially my own*.

As things I hoped *would* happen *didn't*, my expectations led to disappointment and self-doubt. *Was I putting my time, energy, and resources into something that would never pay off?*

Some days I couldn't shake the feeling that I'd made a mistake and that this was the worst decision of my life. And until I was forced to face my own self-doubt on a daily basis, I never really understood what it meant to battle one's demons. The fear of failure can turn a person's mind into their own worst enemy.

If a person is treating you poorly, you can leave the situation. When your mind is treating you poorly, you can't just walk away.

To make matters worse, the more I traveled from one unfamiliar place to the next, the more isolated and alone I felt. And as much as I interacted with people online, it failed to ease my sense of solitude.

As I struggled with the new life I'd chosen — that many people said they envied — I put a positive spin on everything, knowing that being negative would likely turn people off — especially the sponsors I so desperately wanted.

The price I paid for putting on a happy face is that when people said they were jealous of what I was doing or suggested that I was "living the life", I felt like there was something wrong with me because I wasn't enjoying myself as much as everyone assumed I should be — including *me.*

The more I conformed to what I thought other people expected of me, the more I felt like I was living a lie. But I didn't know how to fix it.

I was so far beyond my comfort zone that I was unable to see that the experiences I was having would lead to some of the most valuable lessons of my life.

> *"Adversity has the effect of eliciting talents, which in prosperous circumstances would have lain dormant."*
> — *Horace*

My Journey

Part 5:
Be careful what you wish for

When I first toyed with the idea living beyond comfort, it was almost an abstract concept. I wasn't entirely certain what it would entail.

At the time, the challenges I expected to face on my journey had more to do with living without common amenities than anything else. I didn't really expect to be uncomfortable, per se, as much as I imagined having to work a little harder to accommodate my basic needs.

In my overconfidence, optimism, and naivety, I figured that any discomfort I faced could be quickly managed and ultimately overcome.

Not only was I wrong, I greatly underestimated the impact that even short-term discomfort can have on disrupting one's well-being, balance, and sense of control.

It's easy to overestimate your abilities from a state of comfort and a stable position. But the fact is, when a person's world becomes unstable, even simple problems can quickly be compounded to create situations that feel impossible to overcome or escape from.

One of the things about heading into unexplored territory is that we don't know what we'll encounter until we encounter it.

And no matter how prepared we think we are, we can never account for every conceivable experience or problem we may have at any given time in life.

I eventually discovered, however, that the more frequently one is forced to face and overcome unexpected challenges, the more confident they become in their ability to deal with other obstacles they encounter.

While confidence doesn't necessarily make new challenges *easier*, believing in one's ability to succeed can make the discomfort easier to bear because one knows it will only be temporary.

My Journey

Part 6:
A double-edged sword

Regardless of whether my journey was playing out as I'd hoped or anticipated, I was getting an education — even if the lessons I was learning would take weeks, months, or even years to process. I didn't yet realize that while insight is often gained in an instant, that instant may be far removed from the experience that triggered it.

If I'd been able to see what the experiences I was having would eventually teach me, it would've made them easier to bear. But then, that's life — we live it forward and only make sense of it in reverse.

At the time, I failed to see that every experience I had — and every challenge I faced — would eventually provide me with the tools I needed to handle whatever came next in life. But because I hadn't yet learned to have faith in the fact that all life experiences are valuable, I often feared that nothing I was doing was getting me closer to where I wanted to be.

One of the biggest lessons I had yet to learn on my journey — and one of my greatest sources of suffering at the time — had to do with expectations.

One of the problems was, I'd set up my expectations in such a way that it was only if certain things went as well as — or better than — I expected, that I'd feel as if I was successful at what I was doing — or, at the very least, making progress. Anything that I didn't perceive to meet my expectations — particularly within a specific time-frame — would be considered a failure.

And so, because nothing was going quite as well as I'd hoped it would, I felt like I was failing at *everything*. When the fact is, I wasn't. I was simply using the wrong things to measure my success by and making myself miserable by what I chose to focus on.

***

Expectations are a double-edged sword.

On the upside, positive expectations are more likely to yield positive results than negative expectations — because people who believe they can do something are far more likely to succeed at it than those who expect to fail. Confidence often plays a major role in the outcome of a person's efforts.

On the downside, high expectations and overconfidence can lead a person to be unprepared for unexpected challenges and especially failure. The disappointment resulting from unmet expectations can be demoralizing and have a debilitating effect on a person's ability to push forward.

Such was the case when — within weeks of my departure — several things that I expected to happen, didn't, I felt like I was failing. This made it very difficult to focus on the positive and maintain my enthusiasm. While my intuition was telling me that the journey I was on would be worth it, it only made the question of what I should do more difficult, because my intuition often said one thing while my common sense said something else. This often resulted in a vicious cycle of self-doubt.

So, although I was doing exactly what I wanted with my life — and it would be reasonable for anyone to assume that I was having a blast — my high expectations kept me from fully appreciating much of what I was experiencing. I was so focused on the difference between where I was and where I wanted to be that I lacked the perspective necessary to truly appreciate things as they were.

Another issue was the manner in which I measured my progress. I took a leap of faith, hoping that the path I chose for myself would lead me to a life that was better than the one I'd left behind.

Success could have been anything that felt like a significant and desirable milestone in my life — from connecting with my soul mate, to ending up with a job I was happy at, to attracting an extraordinary opportunity.

The problem is, these were mostly open-ended and subjective-based goals that relied on events happening that I had little to no control over — nor did they provide me with any means to actively track my progress towards them over time. They were simply events that would happen — or not.

Unfortunately, many of my more immediate goals were no better. For starters, I wanted a larger audience, more engagement, more likes, more shares, and a sponsor. While there was much I could do to encourage these things — and I tried — there was little I could do to truly control them.

Also, being new to nearly everything I was doing — and especially the manner in which I was doing it — I had nothing to compare it to. I had no reliable way of knowing if the results I was getting were good, bad, or typical — all I knew was that it seemed like every few days someone's site, content, or Facebook page was going viral — and I wasn't. And every time it happened, rather than see it as an encouraging sign of something that could just as easily happen to me, it left me feeling frustrated and bitter.

The flawed ways in which I measured my progress left me feeling as if nothing I was doing was getting me any closer to achieving my goals. So, even as I was making progress, I often couldn't see it because I was using the wrong means to measure it by. Had I known better, I would've seen how often I confused the results I was getting with failure instead of feedback. I hadn't yet learned that the route to whatever goal we seek is rarely a straight line. The path to success sometimes requires us to move in ways that are contrary to where we believe our goal ultimately lies.

Taking the path less traveled requires a kind of blind confidence in that, as long as you are consistent in your effort to make progress towards your goals, things will ultimately work out in your favor. But it also requires patience and flexibility. Because sometimes the positive aspects of what we consider to be a negative experience don't become apparent until long after an experience has passed.

The twists, turns, dead-ends, and obstacles we encounter on our journey through life are often an integral part of our successes.

What sometimes feels like failure can be exactly what we need to experience in order to gain the perspective necessary to succeed. Even if that means ultimately failing at one thing in order to succeed at the next.

Remember, life is a *journey*. What often matters most is the direction we're consistently heading in life, not the number of missteps we make along the way.

My Journey

Part 7:
Fear

As much as I tried to learn from the experiences I was having and course-correct along the way, it wasn't clear if the path I was taking would eventually lead me to where I wanted to go or not. That's one of the consequences of taking the path less traveled. Without a well-defined roadmap to follow, one must often rely on one's intuition as a guide.

While listening to one's intuition can be helpful, it not only isn't infallible, it can be susceptible to one's state of mind — and especially self-doubt. In fact, for the person burdened with an abundance of self-doubt, simply determining the difference between the voices of intuition, fear, and common sense can be a trying task.

Self-doubt feeds fear. And fear has a way of distorting one's judgment and disconnecting them from what they truly want. Fear and self-doubt destroy dreams by turning people who are completely capable of achieving their goals into quitters, comfort seekers, and underachievers.

At nearly six months into my journey, I was still nowhere near knowing if what I was doing was a mistake or not.

An excerpt from one of my public journal entries from around this time begins like this:

"This may just be my worst idea in a history of bad ideas — I know this. And no one is more invested in what I'm doing than I am. And nearly six months into my journey, I can assure you that no one has thought about or questioned what I'm doing more than I have.

Am I an idiot for abandoning security, comfort, and what's tried and true to take the path less traveled? I don't think so — but have I gotten what I wanted out of this? Yes and no.

If mistakes were medals, I'd be fully decorated. In fact, my medals would probably have medals by now. But with each mistake I make comes experience — and with experience, insight. So, regardless of whether I consider what I've done to be a success or not, I cannot deny that this is a valuable learning experience."

While I still wasn't confident of whether what I was doing was a mistake or not, something had changed. Because, in an almost counter-intuitive way — and despite my self-doubt — I was becoming increasingly resistant to the idea of quitting. And not because I'd learned to ignore my fears, but the opposite.

In an attempt to manage my mental state, I began focusing on my fears in an effort to understand them. I figured if I understood exactly what it was I was afraid of, I could find ways to work with it or work around it.

For example, one of my fears was that I was spending a great deal of money on something that would never provide me with a return on my investment — especially after my bikes were stolen. The process of identifying and understanding this particular fear allowed me to inoculate myself against it.

I told myself that while it is true that I may never see a return on my financial investment, abandoning my journey without seeing it through to some kind of "end" made it almost certain that I wouldn't.

Understanding my fear allowed me to define its boundaries. It was no longer this ominous abstraction, but something I could manage. In this case, I did so by countering one fear with another. Because in my analysis, I came to realize that I was more afraid of living with regret for the things I didn't do, than I was of spending my savings to take a chance at a better life.

Any time I felt like quitting, I focused on something I was even more afraid of — missing out on experiences that were still well within my reach, just as long as I didn't give up.

I repeatedly reminded myself of the fact that there may never again come a time when I would have as much freedom to go after what I wanted in life as I currently had. I had no job that I needed to show up for. No apartment I had to pay for. And no girlfriend, wife, or children that I needed to devote time to. And, at least for the time being, I still had savings.

And so I continued to push forward.

It wasn't until later in my journey that I came to understand that familiarizing ourselves with our fears — as I had done — reduces the power they have over us.

Ignorance feeds fear. By truly understanding what we are afraid of, we learn to accept it, manage it, or transform it.

My Journey

Part 8:
Personal development

When I quit my job, I wasn't acting on any grand plan. At the time, the last major goal I'd set for myself is the one that led me to get hired at the company I just quit. So I wasn't following some carefully crafted blueprint for my future. It was simply that the artificial nature of my life had left me feeling like I was just a cog in a machine — and I wanted to change that. I wasn't sure how I was going to do it — I only knew that I wanted to.

My first inclination was to take a trip. To travel. To simply get away. I wasn't sure *where* to, or for *how* long, but I wanted it to be long enough for me to feel alive and more connected to the things I'd felt myself slipping away from. It wouldn't necessarily provide me with the answer to what I was supposed to do with my life, but if I did it right, it might just help point the way.

It was a simple thing. But then — as I realized that the changes I'd already made in my life had created an opportunity that I should take advantage of — this "simple thing" grew.

Before long, what could almost have been mistaken for a vacation evolved into a personal journey. I wanted to have the kind of experiences that I'd read about others having when they went off to find themselves. I wanted to do something that had the potential to reinvigorate my soul.

And this was the plan for a while. It had nothing to do with social media or sharing my travels with an audience. Nothing to do with finding a sponsor. And nothing much to do with anyone but me and those I crossed paths with as I traveled.

But then my desire to connect with people changed all that. And suddenly my "simple thing" wasn't so simple anymore.

And although I loved the idea of not only sharing what I did with an audience, but doing it in a way that allowed others to participate, I had a nagging concern. I worried that when what I originally envisioned as a personal journey evolved into a public one, it might be at the expense of something I sought: room for personal growth.

I needn't have been concerned. The rapid-fire succession of new experiences I had continually left me on the brink of being overwhelmed. The frequency at which my new life presented challenges — and the amount of time I spent out of my comfort zone — made personal growth nearly inevitable.

At one point in my journey, it became clear to me that the experiences I was having were changing how I perceived the world and even my perception of myself was evolving. Although I didn't know what to call it at the time, this was a sign of the personal growth I was seeking.

At first, the progress I made along my path to self-improvement was simply a byproduct of life — as it tends to be. Things would happen. I would react to them. And, if I was lucky, I'd learn something in the process. But the ever-changing environment I negotiated on my journey — along with the challenges that accompanied it — increased the rate at which I developed.

Of course, at the time, I didn't equate what I was experiencing as personal growth. I just knew that my journey was more challenging than I imagined it would be and I was often left feeling exhausted, overwhelmed, or confused. I considered these things a sign of weakness and nothing to feel particularly proud of. Little did I realize that these symptoms are typically triggers for, or consequences of, personal change.

In an effort to manage my mental state and give the onslaught of thoughts I was having an outlet, I downloaded a note-taking app on my phone and started using it to take notes. This process allowed me to record things I felt were important — as they happened — and defer my thinking about them to a time of my choosing.

At first, my recordings were mostly related to my travels. Things written down with the intention of relaying them to my audience. But as time went by, my notes became more of a reflection of my inner journey than my outer one.

I recorded comments and criticisms about encounters I had, observations about my mental state and general well-being, and questions I wanted answers to. I no longer had to think through every thought, answer every question, or solve every crisis in the moment. And this had the desired effect — it took some of the burden off my brain.

But it also had an unexpected consequence — one that would dramatically change my life.

By putting aspects of my personal journey into words, I gave substance and structure to my thoughts in a way that went well beyond the mental meanderings I was accustomed to. My thoughts were no longer just a stream of frequently forgotten mental associations, but something I could revisit and actively work through.

And when that happened, I became a proactive participant in my personal development. And thus, my progress along my path was no longer just a byproduct of my journey, but something I began to take an active role in.

Select Journal Entries

Day 68:
The river

I'm driving north towards Yellowstone National Park. It's been a couple of days since my last shower, so I'm feeling kind of gross. Wet wipes and washcloths work in a pinch, but they're never as refreshing as running water.

But I'm in luck. There's a river running alongside the highway. And I've never actually bathed in a river before — not on purpose — so the idea appeals to me.

I find a place that's suitable for what I have in mind and pull over. It's a sort of secluded launch-spot for boats — probably for some of the rafters I've seen floating down the river.

With soap in hand, I walk across the pebbly shore and into the water. It's mid-July, but the river is freezing — far colder than I expect it to be. But the urge to finally be clean pushes me forward — along with the thought,

If c-c-cowboys c-could d-do this, so c-can I!

Finally, standing waist-deep in water, I take a deep breath, dunk once, gasp involuntarily, and then wipe the water off my face. But the sudden shock I feel in that moment isn't from the ice-cold water, but from the fact that my hands are covered in blood!

My nose is bleeding.

Now, I don't ever get nose-bleeds, so it takes a moment for my mind to make sense of what's happening — or why. My first thought is, "I'm dying!" — and in that instant, I'm convinced that it's the truth.

As I walk back towards the shore, I rinse the blood from my hands and face. The bleeding has nearly stopped which eases my mind. Because, although I still may be dying, I probably have at least a few minutes to think about it.

So I do. I think about death. And I quickly come to terms with it. I realize that if I'm dying, there's only so much I can do in this moment — and certainly nothing I can do to change the past.

No, I haven't done everything I've wanted to do, but I've lived a decent life — and not everyone has the good fortune to live as long as I have. Besides, everyone dies eventually.

It's been a good run, Zero.

A few minutes passes, my nose stops bleeding, and I'm still not dead. That's when I realize that there's a possibility that I might not be dying. At the very least, I probably have a little more time than I initially thought.

Maybe I overreacted?

But since I don't get nose bleeds, perhaps it's just the first sign of some other serious issue? I can't help but think about how odd and interesting that would be.

I mean, I recently chose to live my life in such a way that it isn't entirely different from how I'd choose to spend my remaining days if I'd found out I was dying.

I'd want to travel, see the world, and have new experiences. I'd want to feel like I was directing my life and not just drifting through it. And, above all, I'd want to feel alive. And I do.

No, my life over this past two months hasn't played out as I imagined it would. And it's been a lot harder than I thought it would be. But I chose this path, I'm doing what I wanted, and I own it.

If a doctor told me I had only six months to live, I think there's really only one thing I'd want to change — and that would be to spend more time with family and friends.

But not *too much* time.

I mean, how much "We're so sorry you're dying." could one actually take?

So I'd want to be out celebrating the remainder of my life, not prematurely mourning my death.

And, as I have this thought, it hits me. I *really* am dying. Like, *for real* dying. We all are.

Whether it's today, tomorrow, or twenty years from now, we all have an expiration date — we just don't know when it is.

I just happen to be living my life in a way that is similar to how I would choose to if I knew my expiration date was near.

Are you?

Day 186:
Room for improvement

One of the many things I didn't anticipate when I began this journey is how much uninterrupted time alone I would have. In the past six months, I've had more time to think, more time to watch, and more time to wonder about the world, and my place in it, than I have ever had at any other time in my life.

The unexpected consequence of being able to give my questions and curiosities undivided attention is that I've been exposed to new thoughts, and come to new conclusions, at a rate unlike any other time I can remember.

In the many days since — and precisely because — I disconnected from conventional life, I've been forced to focus a massive amount of attention on myself, my relationships, and my interaction with others.

I've continually searched for signs that I'm on the right path and looked for meaning in everything. And in doing so, in a way, I've become a student of life experience.

I've studied people and how their actions affect those around them. I've seen how smiles spread from one person to another. And how acts of kindness encompass far more than the moments in which they occur.

I've watched parents reprimanding their children, husbands berating their wives, and owners yelling at their pets. And I've witnessed the adverse reactions of those affected. Including myself.

I've noticed how I let my observation of others affect me.

I've felt happiness, sadness, and anger from nothing more than watching people — let alone interacting with them. And I question that. Because if I'm not in control of my emotions, who is? And do I really want to live a life in which other people so easily pull my emotional strings?

But it isn't just people to whom I've inadvertently given power over my mental state.

I've noted how my brain automatically responds to things like traffic, waiting in lines, or the weather. And I see how ridiculous it is to let things I have no control over adversely affect my mood.

Over the course of 186 days I've come to see how many of my actions, reactions, or lack of action are based on fear. Fear of the unknown. Fear of rejection. Fear of being judged. Fear of failure. And fear of causing or experiencing pain.

And while that may be the person I am, it isn't the person I want to be. So I'm focusing on not just being good, but being better than I am.

I haven't yet learned how to let everything in my life just flow without resistance. Or learned how to not let my fear of what other people may think affect my choices.

I haven't yet learned how not to be controlled by my ego in some situations or my emotions in others. But I *want* to.

Because I can see the value in these things. And maybe that's what this journey is *really* about.

So while I've been thinking about how to become a better person, I decided to make a list of things I can do to help facilitate that.

I can't say it's perfect. And I can't say it's complete. But I can say it's a start.

From this day forward…

✓ I'm going to stop giving so much weight to what other people think or to my fear of being judged by others. Not because I don't care, but because I believe in myself and who I am as a person. I am not what other people think.
✓ I'm going to stop being held back by my fears or the fears of others.
✓ I'm going to be confident in my abilities and use my intuition as a guide.
✓ I'm going to go after my goals — no matter how lofty — with enthusiasm and a sense of purpose.
✓ I'm going to strive for excellence, but not be held back when I fall short. I will not be discouraged by my mistakes, I will simply use what I learn to push forward.
✓ I'm going to stop trying to have power over things beyond my control.
✓ I'm going to stop reacting negatively to things I know I cannot (or will not) change.
✓ I'm going to be grateful for everything in my life and what it teaches. Grateful for my health, my friends, and my family. Grateful that I am breathing and able to experience a traffic jam — as much as I may not want to be in one. And I will be grateful that I am alive and able to feel embarrassment or pain versus the alternative. Grateful for each and every day I am alive.

- ✓ I'm going to have faith that I am exactly where I am meant to be at this moment. I will appreciate and be grateful for my life journey.
- ✓ I'm going to look for places where I can make a positive difference — and do so — without being manipulated by social pressures or guilt.
- ✓ I'm going to have faith that everything will be ok and is as it should be at this moment, no matter how different it may be from my expectations.
- ✓ I'm going to be the best person that I can be. I will not strive to be perfect, but consistent. And to make consistent progress towards these goals.
- ✓ And I'm going to continue not taking myself or life too seriously.
- ✓ Oh yeah — and I'm gonna not be such a prefectionist.

Day 414:
The car thief

Jackson, Wyoming.

I'm parked for the night in a hotel lot — the sun has just gone down, but there's still plenty of light in the sky. I see a man walking around the lot — he's looking at cars and occasionally pausing and peering in as he strolls by. Then he stops at a car, takes a long look inside, and —

— he tests the driver's side door handle.

"THIEF! THIEF!" my mind is shouting as I'm suddenly having a flashback to an earlier experience in my journey —

I'm in rural town, USA. Parked in a dim hotel parking lot.

It's late. And I've just woken up, but I don't know why. As I lay in the dark in the back of my 4Runner, I stare at the ceiling and listen for anything out of the ordinary.

And then I hear it.

Rattle ... rattle ... rattle ... rattle.

And now silence.

What the hell was that!?

Rattle — wait, there it is again! — rattle ... rattle ... rattle.

Silence.

Rattle ... rattle ... rattle ... rattle.

What *is* that!?

Silence.

With a jolt of adrenaline, I realize what it is — it is the sound of someone checking — rattle — all — rattle — four — rattle — doors — rattle — of every car in the parking lot to see if they're locked.

And the sound is getting closer — Wait! Did I just see something move in the darkness?

YES!

There's a shadow at my passenger side door — my mind is pleading: "Oh please! Please let me have remembered to lock all my doors."

RATTLE!

My passenger side door is locked.

Oh please. Please be locked. Please be locked. Please be locked.

I feel a vein in my neck throbbing.

RATTLE!

My rear passenger side door — the one I am looking out of as this happens — is locked.

RATTLE!

My other rear passenger side door — is locked. I feel like I'm in a horror movie.

This is it. The last door — and the one I am most likely to accidentally leave unlocked.

I'm holding my breath. My head and my heart are pounding. Everything slows down. He reaches for the handle...

So it was *this* terrifying experience that's running through my mind as I get out of my car — in that hotel parking lot in Jackson, Wyoming — and shout to the man who just tested the door handle.

"Hey!" — he turns around. He's an older guy. Grey hair. Potbelly. Hawaiian shirt. Slightly taller than I am.

He seems surprised to see me. Very surprised. And I think I would've been, too. There was no one else around and I just popped out of nowhere.

"Why are you checking car handles!?" I ask — trying to remain calm, but not doing a very good job of it. I just created a confrontation.

"I wasn't." he says with a German accent.

Whoa — wasn't expecting that — but I'm committed now. "Yes. You. Were. I *saw* you.", I say.

"I wasn't.", he replies.

"Sir, I *saw* you walking around the parking lot looking into cars—"

"No sir, I was not." he interrupts.

"—then you stopped and checked the door handles of this one."

There is a momentary pause as he considers the fact that I actually saw him do it. I'm waiting for him to change his story. And then:

"That's my car," he says, "*Myyyyyy* caaaaaar!"

Shit. I wasn't ready for that.

Maybe it was his car. It's plausible. Man, how much of an ass would I be — but then…

"Why were you checking the handles?" — Ha hah! Got you there, you shady car thief!

"I don't know."

I suppose I could've gone with the I-caught-you-red-handed-buddy! look — but instead, all I could muster was a "What?"

"I'm telling you it's my car. Look I'll get my keys. I'll show you."

At this point, I've calmed down. But now — and this is also a surprise — now he's getting fired up. Fired up and in my face. Agitated. Well within the no-go-zone of my spacial bubble. So much so that I can smell the beer on his breath as he speaks.

And he's moving and speaking in such a way that — at that moment — I would not have been at all surprised if he pushed me.

He didn't.

So he's talking — borderline shouting — in an exasperated fashion, but not exactly "angry", but it's hard to tell. I'm definitely not picking up everything he's saying because of his accent and the fast manner in which he's speaking.

But I get the gist of it — and it's this: "I'm telling you the truth." and "I'll go get my keys."

Shit. I'm not sure what to do.

I was trying to do a good deed — but suddenly I realize, *I'm* the one who *isn't* supposed to be there. I'm the one being shady by sleeping in my car in a hotel parking lot.

But — what if this guy is just trying to get away by going inside? I'm not going to escort this man into or out of the hotel — the hotel I'm not a guest at.

This has gotten really weird fast. And what if he's telling the truth? I don't know. One thing I do know is that he needs to get out of my face. He's too close and he's agitated. And possibly drunk.

I don't believe in violence. I'll defend myself, but I won't hit anyone. But I feel like this is a test now — and I walked into this situation as the alpha male, I won't let him take the role from me, so I'm standing my ground.

"Back off." I say calmly but assertively — something I learned from the Dog Whisperer.

"What?"

"Step back. You're too close."

Now it is he who is looking surprised. He waves his arms — says something about Americans. Was it "silly Americans"? — I don't know. But he steps back — and as he does, he appears calmer. He continues speaking.

He's here with his wife, he says. They're on vacation from Belgium for 10 days. And he'll just go get his keys... This is all happening fast — it's a rollercoaster — either this guy is testing me — or he's telling the truth.

What the hell is going on with my life? I'd tried to do the *right* thing, but now — I don't know. *I'm the one who isn't supposed to be there.* Is he telling the truth or not? Am I the bad guy here? Am I!?

"No." I say, "You don't have to get your keys."

"Nein, nein! I'll get my keys. I'll show you. I'll *show* you", he says while nodding.

It seems like he needs to prove something at this point — and I'm thinking I would, too, if someone had just accused me of being a car thief.

So he walks inside, peering back to see if I'm still standing in the parking lot. What do I do? Stay? Leave? Is he lying? Will he come back? Or is he telling the truth and I'm an asshole.

You want to know?

That night. In that parking lot.
In Jackson, Wyoming…
I was an asshole.

Day 540:
The hell with paradise

It's the Saturday before Halloween. I'm in Key West. It's one of my favorite places and one that I've referred to as "Paradise" more than a few times. I've been driving across the country from Las Vegas for a week to get here. And I'm exhausted.

The long days of driving — compounded by sleeping poorly and the loss of 3 hours — due to time zones — have really done a number on me.

But hey! — I'm back in Key West on the one-year anniversary of my first visit here. And because it's paradise, I've not only just witnessed a spectacular sunset of red and gold, but a rainbow at *the same time*. I didn't even know that sort of thing happened until tonight! This world is *amaaazing!* I should be feeling great!

No, I appear no closer to solving any number of the problems I'm facing right now. And the love of my life hasn't shown up yet — out of nowhere — laughing and lobbing water balloons at me while shouting, "You looked like you needed to get wet!" (Oh, how I love you fictional-girl-of-my-dreams.)

But, despite any of my issues, I could at least be feeling good about the fact that I've once again followed through on something I said I would do — I drove to Florida. I'm here. But as the sun sets and the rainbow fades, all I'm thinking about is sleep. And how I can get more of it.

I need sleep like Gollum needs his ring. And much like that ring, the lack of sleep is twisting my mind — turning me into a grotesque creature.

My journey has made me intimately aware of the fact that the less sleep I get, the less optimistic I become. Which is a good thing to know about one's self, but a difficult thing to deal with. I consider my optimism to be a great asset when I have it. It helps me deal with the challenges of the life I've walked into. And without my optimism, those challenges always seem so much bigger — and my confidence in conquering them so much smaller.

So it's a holiday weekend and Key West is swarming with people. I think I read somewhere that there are an additional 60,000 visitors on the island to celebrate — and there's a parade going on in town.

"Hey, that's a great opportunity for some street photography!", says the voice in the back of my head. But it isn't going to happen — my "inner Gollum" won't have *anything* to do with *anything* that doesn't directly involve sleeping. I walk from the beach back to my 4Runner to begin my search for a place to get some much-needed shut-eye.

Key West is a very small island. As such, parking on the island is limited and difficult — even for residents. But it's not *impossible*. But sleeping in cars is (allegedly) not allowed. And I know from experience that there's an obvious police presence on the island and parking lots are patrolled and offending cars are towed.

I also know that hotel lots — at least some of them — require dashboard guest passes. And if you think you can get away with sleeping in your car in a hotel parking lot without a parking pass in Key West, you will likely be in for a rude awakening. Literally. That was a lesson I learned a year ago and not something I wish to repeat.

There's just something *more-than-a-little* unpleasant about being woken up from a sound sleep by someone shouting and shining a flashlight in your eyes.

Fortunately, it's something I won't have to deal with. Because, after a bit of driving, I find a spot that I'm confident won't get me into trouble. Mainly because I parked here *last* year without issues. So that's comforting. But what *isn't* comforting — which I haven't really been paying attention to until now — is the heat.

I effectively skipped summer this year by spending the hottest months in the northernmost parts of the United States where it was considerably cooler than it is now. It was an intentional strategy that worked.

I didn't want to have another incident like the one I had in Lexington, Kentucky where it was so hot and humid, I literally slept on bags of ice in an attempt to avoid being baked alive. I survived, but it wasn't as brilliant of a plan as I imagined. Waking up soaking wet isn't really an experience I'd like to repeat.

After parking, I crawl into the back of my car. After months of travel, I've gotten into the habit of keeping my windows shut to either keep people from peering in or to keep mosquitos out. I *do*, however, leave my sunroof open since it's discreet and provides a source of fresh air, even if my enclosed car doesn't really allow it to circulate much.

At the moment, it doesn't matter. I'm so tired that, even being the light sleeper that I am, I ought to be able to pass out easily.

And I do.

But I awake an hour or two later at the sound of two guys on a moped shouting at the top of their lungs as they drive by. And I'm not at all surprised. It's a Saturday — a party night on a holiday weekend. People are in a festive mood and the roads are busy.

What *is* a surprise, however, is the rain pouring in through my open sunroof. *Dammit!* — I already learned this lesson last year when everything in the front seats got soaked. I'm getting sloppy. Forgetting things because I'm tired.

I reach in front, put my keys into the ignition, and start my car in order to put my sunroof in the "pop up" position — which is barely cracked. It keeps the rain out, which is good, but it also restricts air flow to almost nothing.

Hopefully it won't be a problem. I try not to think about it. I just want to sleep. I flop back onto the foam pad I use as a mattress.

There must have been sand stuck to the bottom of my shoes as I was getting ready for bed the first time. I didn't notice it before, but now my shuffling around has scattered it all over my sheets — and because I'm hot and sweating, it's sticking to my arms and legs. I feel like I'm wearing sandpaper. It's not the most comfortable sensation, but after a few attempts at wiping it away, I'm too exhausted to deal with it in any way that would be effective.

Instead, I just roll onto my side, close my eyes, and surrender to the darkness. I'm thinking, "And some people still say they envy me" as I fall back asleep.

Only to awaken shortly after.

Something — *no. Many* things — are *biting* me. My arms and legs. *What-the-fuck?*

Whatever they are, they're small — and they're not mosquitoes. They don't make any noise. I can't tell in the dark if they fly or not. All I can tell is that they bite. And after they bite, it itches.

I try to use the screen of my cell phone as a flashlight to see if I can spot whatever they are, but I don't see anything. The little bastards are either too fast or too small to be seen by cell phone light. I spend the next few minutes swatting and scratching. And I wouldn't have known I somehow managed to fall asleep if it wasn't for the unpleasant sensation of waking up again.

Traffic is really picking up now. Bigger vehicles are driving by and every time they do, my car shakes with the "whoosh!" of their passing. Others have their music blaring with enough bass to wake the dead — proven by the fact I keep seeing ghosts and zombies go by — or wait — it's Halloween. Ok, that makes sense now — I'm not crazy.

And in the midst of all of the above — every so often there's a police siren — people getting pulled over. I know from the sirens that lots of people got pulled over that night.

And I'm lying in the back — soaked. My shirt is wet to the touch, but it's not water — it's sweat. And I don't know if it's the heat, the sweat, the sand, or the bug bites, but I'm itchy everywhere. It feels like things are crawling all over my skin — or maybe there really *are* things crawling all over my skin. But if there are, at least they're not biting me. Wow. A positive thought. I have managed to find something to feel good about.

It is a small and short-lived victory.

"WHOOSH!" *shake* — there goes another car. There has been debate in courts over whether sleep deprivation is a form of torture. Well, in my mind there's no question.

"WHOOSH!" *shake* — music — shouting — moped — "WHOOSH!" *shake* — motorcycle — screaming kids — police siren…

I thought the traffic would die down as it got later, but it's only getting worse — or maybe it just *seems* worse because all I want to do is sleep. But every time I near unconsciousness, I'm disturbed by the sound or shake of a passing vehicle. I can't sleep. So I just lay in the back in the back of my 4Runner sweating and wait.

Time passes. It must be after midnight now. Is the traffic dying down? No, it's worse. In a flash of inspiration, I remember some foam earplugs I have stowed away. But they're not enough. They help cut down the sound of passing traffic, but they do nothing to keep my car from shaking as it goes whooshing by.

I'm irritated with the world at this point. "Paradise my ass!" says Gollum, "This was a *baaaaaad* idea." He pushes me up and into my driver's seat. I start my car, and pull into the very traffic I aim to get away from.

It's a little after 2 am when I finally find what I hope will be a suitable and semi-safe place to park for the remainder of the night. I pull into the spot, turn off the engine, and once again flop down onto my wet and sandy sheets.

I'm so irritated, so uncomfortable, and so tired at this point that I begin to think that if I do end up having to deal with law enforcement, sleeping in jail would probably be a lot more comfortable than I find myself now.

"Jail." — *sigh* — "Wouldn't *that* be nice?"

I take a deep breath. I *know* I'm just tired. And I *know* that as challenging as this night has been, "it too, shall pass". Even if it doesn't *seem* like it. I've been in many difficult situations in the past 18 months — and I've survived them all. And I'll survive this one as well. I just need some sleep. That's all. I know this. And so, I once again aim to get some.

But as I'm lying there, I become aware of something.

"What the hell is that smell?"

It's my dirty laundry. Surprise! A week's worth of sweaty gym clothes stuffed into a bag in the back is now fermenting in the heat and humidity. It wasn't noticeable with the sunroof open, but now... it's an issue. I don't like smelly things. And I don't like feeling gross. I'm sticky. I'm itchy. I'm sleeping on sheets sprinkled with sand. And I've got what I hope are just imaginary bugs crawling all over my skin.

"Life is tough!" Wait — *what*? "Life is tough!", says Gollum.

It reminds me of something. Earlier in the day, I'd shared a motivational video with a friend. It was called, "This is how winners are made." And it starts with the line, "Life is tough. That's a given."

I mainly shared it because I knew my friend could use some encouragement, but now I'm thinking something in that video connected with me on a deeper level. Because, in this moment — as my mind flashes back to that video — I'm determined that I can fix my life. *All* of it. Not later. *Right now*.

For starters, I'll just toss my dirty laundry into my roof cargo bin, I'll remake my bed, I'll—

"Nooo!", says Gollum. "I don't care about the sand, the stench, or the sensation of bugs crawling all over my skin. I'm just too tired to deal with it. Just. Let. Me. Sleep!"

And I do. Sleep comes as a welcome reprieve from everything that currently ails me. But then, at 4am — 3 and a half hours before sunrise! — the many roosters inhabiting the beautiful island of Key West start to crow.

As such, I'm not writing this from Key West or even the Florida Keys. I had to go somewhere I could actually sleep. Somewhere that didn't leave me feeling like a night in jail would be preferable to a night in my car.

I'm rested now. And thinking more clearly. And I've searched for the lesson in this experience and I believe it's this: "Paradise" can be hell and jail can be "paradise" — it's just a matter of perspective.

And living beyond comfort means that you don't always get what you want, but it often means that if you work with what you get, you will likely learn something worth knowing.

As awful as this experience was at the time, it's something I'm grateful to have had the opportunity to experience. Not just because it gave me a different perspective, but because it really helps me appreciate so many of the things I rarely think about and frequently take for granted.

Day 631:
The jerk

9:45 pm

He was still there. Leaning up against the wall in the dark. I pulled up one space over and parked. Then I stepped out of my car and walked up to the man…

"I was a jerk. I'm sorry. I didn't let you finish. What were you going to say?"

He didn't seem surprised to see me, but it was dark and I couldn't really see his face very well.

He said, "I live outside. And I'm hungry. I was going to ask if you had anything you could give me so I could eat."

I reached into my pocket for the 5 dollar bill I'd separated from my wallet…

"Here's 5 dollars," I said as I handed it to him, "Again, I'm sorry."

There was a change in his voice, "It's ok. Thank you, sir."

In an awkward gesture, I reached forward and patted him on the shoulder — then I turned back towards my car and started walking. And then stopped and turned around.

He was still looking at me. I wanted him to know something. It felt important.

"There are good people in the world."

I felt compelled to say it. I didn't want him to think that everyone was like…me — how I was.

"Keep your chin up," I finished. And again, felt awkward and self-conscious.

"I will." he said. And then he stepped five paces to the front door of the sandwich shop and walked inside.

I got back into my car and drove to where I was originally heading. And then I took out my laptop and wrote what you just read.

10 minutes earlier...

I'd just finished eating my sandwich and stepped out of the sandwich shop and towards my car parked in front.

"Excuse me, sir—" began the black man with a backpack on.

"I'm sorry man. I can't help you."

He stopped talking — defeated. He may have said "Ok.", but I was too busy getting into my car. Then I sat there for a minute looking out the window at the man. I didn't feel good, but I started my car and drove out of the parking lot.

At the stop sign before turning onto the road I hesitated, but I was already in line and there was nowhere else for me to go but forward. Still, it didn't stop me from thinking about what I'd just left behind me and how I acted.

I'd said so little, but I'd said so much. And I didn't like it.

I pulled out onto the road and started driving away from the place where I had just disrespected a man simply because I thought he was going to ask me for money. I couldn't even be certain of that because I didn't even let him finish what he was going to say. I'd acted like I just didn't care.

But I *did* care, but nothing I'd done had said that. In fact, I was a jerk to the guy.

This isn't who I want to be. This *isn't me*. Is it? — *IS IT?*

***

I remember the first time I ever became intimately aware of a homeless person and how it made me feel. I was waiting at a red light just before the Bangor Mall in Maine. A young woman and her son were standing in the median. The woman was holding a cardboard sign. And as I stared from the comfort of my car, I saw myself standing in that median — first as the mother and then as her child. It made me sad.

I remembered hearing that it wasn't good to give homeless people money — that they would often just buy drugs or alcohol with it — so I didn't give her money. Instead, I drove to a grocery store half a mile away and bought two bags of food.

I didn't know what I was doing. I didn't know what "homeless people" ate. I just grabbed stuff off shelves and tossed it in my cart. "If I was a homeless person, this is what I would want to eat.", I thought.

And then I drove back towards the median and parked nearby. I then grabbed the bags, walked across the street, and handed them to the woman and her child. She said thank you, but she wasn't happy. I wasn't sure why. Still, I felt like I'd done a good thing.

***

As I continued driving away from the sandwich shop, I thought about how living first in San Francisco and then Santa Monica, California changed my perception of the homeless. For one, it was a much bigger issue than I'd ever realized while living in rural Maine. They were everywhere. They would go through your garbage. They would beg for your leftovers outside of restaurants. They'd scream at imaginary people as you passed.

When I first moved to San Francisco, I used to give homeless people dollar bills and change whenever I walked from work to my car or back. But after a while it began to have a significant impact on my income. It also felt unfair.

Why give to *some* people and not others? What if some are just good liars? What if I was giving money to the wrong types of people?

And what about me? I can't give money to every homeless person who asks — I won't have anything left to give. So I just stopped giving. I didn't know if that was the answer, but it seemed fairer somehow. And at least none of them would use what they were given to buy drugs or alcohol.

My intentions were good, but somewhere along the way, my reflexes took over. Rather than consider someone's circumstances or treat people like human beings, I simply deflected them. And tonight, I'd shut down another human being without even giving him the chance to say what he wanted to say.

It wasn't sitting easy with me. He didn't deserve to be treated as I had treated him. And that wasn't how I wanted to be. And even if I had nothing to give, he's still a human being — and I hadn't shown him any compassion. It made me sad. It made me disappointed in myself.

But I was already driving away — what's the point of turning around? I'll just "fix myself" for next time, I thought. I'll react differently next time.

But then I thought about the man again. And I thought about how I always say "I want to make a difference" and how hypocritical it was for me to say that while driving away from an opportunity to do so. And even if I didn't have anything to give the guy, it wasn't about money.

I was a jerk to the man.

And I didn't have to be rude.

And I could at least apologize.

So I did.

Day 678:
I told myself I wasn't
looking for love. I lied.

Part one

I looked for you before leaving Las Vegas in May 2010. And again in San Diego, Los Angeles, San Francisco, Sacramento, Portland, Seattle and Spokane.

It's possible I held the door for you and your parents in Salt Lake City — or perhaps I let you pull out in front of me on a street in Phoenix. You may have served me Mexican food in Tucson or Santa Fe... or — who am I kidding — any place I've traveled to.

I looked for you in the book aisles of a bookstore in Albuquerque. And I may have smiled at you in Denver or Colorado Springs or Boulder or Billings or Boise or any of the few dozen stops I made in between.

We may have crossed paths on the walkways of Yosemite or Yellowstone or Mount Rushmore — or perhaps at the Devil's Tower, The Field of Dreams, or in the hallways of the UFO Museum in Roswell.

We may have exchanged polite greetings at a rest stop in Dallas, or Austin, or Houston, or New Orleans. I may have helped you plug in your laptop at a café in Kansas City or accidentally bumped into you while standing in line in for food in Indianapolis (sorry about that).

You may have served me coffee in Memphis or St Louis or Atlanta or Palm Springs. Or perhaps you were one of the women who laughed at me while I posed my stuffed animals for photos in Raleigh or Charlotte or Knoxville or Virginia Beach.

I may have called after you when you dropped your sweatshirt while leaving the gym in Miami. You may have been on the cardio equipment next to mine in Tampa. Or perhaps we made eye contact on a pier in Key West while watching the sun slowly melt into the horizon.

All the while, I told myself I wasn't looking for love.

So — I wasn't looking for love in Washington DC or Baltimore either.

I wasn't looking for love in Philadelphia — and I wasn't looking for love in Hartford or Albany or Troy.

And all that time I was telling myself that I wasn't looking for love…

I was lying to myself.
I was lying to myself because I was looking for *you*.

For 678 days I looked for you. Through dozens and dozens of cities coast to coast. I looked for you — and for opportunities to meet you. But it never happened.

And so despite all my searching and all my effort at seeking you out — or because of it — I missed you.

I missed you in Columbus.
I missed you in Chicago.
I missed you in Madison and Des Moines.

And I missed you in every other of the dozens of cities I've visited. I thought of you every. single. day. as I searched — and every single day I missed you. Again and again and again and again — for 678 days.

Well no more. I'm done. I'm done looking for you. I'm done looking for love.

Part two

One of my goals for this journey when I began it 678 days ago was to make myself more "visible" — and yet for all my efforts and activities in that area — from promoting my website or seeking (and getting) press — I've remained largely invisible. And you have remained hidden from me.

And for all I've done to try to get people to look into what I'm doing, the people who are most interested in my story and my travels found me independently of my efforts — and I think that's a sign.

And these people — these kind, generous, open-minded, and truly amazing people who have become the most active and most emotionally invested in my journey — they are the same people who have also had (and continue to have) the greatest impact on my life during my travels.

And they found me — or were drawn to me — on their own.

As much as I am grateful for what I have in my life, the fact is that as I have searched for all the things that have remained elusive to me, I have felt a sense of loss for those things. I have felt a sense of loss and emotional frustration for things I've never had — for things I have absolutely no control over.

And for all the things I've actually gained during my journey — the life lessons, the kindness of others, a better understanding of the world and my place in it — choosing to continue focusing on what I don't have just doesn't feel right.

I've even managed to feel a sense of loss for you — a woman that I've never met — and may *never* meet. And even if I did meet or cross paths with you — the fact is, one cannot make another person love them. And even if I could, I wouldn't want to because it wouldn't be real.

So all this time — it's as if I was fishing — hoping some unknown catch would go for the bait I set — when in actuality, it's not the bait I want my catch to fall for — it's me.

I have to be my own bait — by just being me. By just being true to myself and the best person that I can be — and not searching for *you* in every city I visit. I need to let you find me — as I once wrote you would.

And the fact is, I may never meet you — it may turn out that I'll reach my expiration date before that happens. And when I think about it — when I really think about it — I'm actually ok with that. I really, truly am.

And that's a realization that rather than make me sad, actually brings me comfort. Because as much as I relish the thought of your companionship — or as much as I relish the thought of starting a family and raising happy children — you are not something I need. You are not a missing piece of my life needed to complete me. I'm whole without you. I am comfortable with myself. I like who I am.

And I like who I'm in the process of becoming. And I like my life. And I like the challenges that have been set before me. And I like the positive impact I've been able to have on people.

And when all is said and done — when I let go of my desires for the things I don't have, including you — I am even more grateful for what I do have, the life I lead, and those who are in it. And that's enough. It really is.

No — I'm not "giving up" — this is not a defeat. It's a victory. It's a step in the right direction. I'm not going into hiding, I'm simply letting go of my obsession of seeking you out. And I'm letting go of my desire for things that I don't have.

I'm putting my energy and focus on the things I do have — the things I am grateful for — and the things I am capable of giving away. And if — or when — you finally find me, I hope to be a better person when you do. Because until the fateful time when that happens — or it doesn't — that's what I'll be working on — myself.

And as I do so, I'll be continuing my efforts to make a positive difference in the world. One laugh, one smile, one positive thought at a time. Because that, too, is enough for me. It really is. And that's no lie.

"Your task is not to seek for love, but merely to seek and find all the barriers within yourself that you have built against it." — Rumi

Day 730:
Three simple words

Flashback to December of 2010.

I'm sitting with Peggy LaCerra in a café in San Francisco, California being interviewed for an article in the March/April edition Spirituality & Health Magazine.

As we near the end of our conversation, I say in a moment of self-doubt, "But in all of this. I don't know. Perhaps someone else is better suited for what I'm doing than I am. Perhaps I'm not the guy—"

"You're the guy."

"But—"

"*You're. The. Guy.*"

I didn't realize it at the time, but those three simple words of encouragement would help carry me in times of darkness.

Three simple words.

Three simple words have helped me to believe in myself in times of doubt. Three simple words have helped me to continue to face my fears. Three simple words have continually told me that "I can do this."

And when I finally saw the significance of those three simple words, and the effect they had on me, I finally understood the power of encouragement.

And I realized that if three simple words could have such a profound and positive impact on me, perhaps it was possible that my words could have that kind of effect on others.

And so I resolve to try.

I resolve to share not just the experiences from my journey, but the lessons I learn as a result of those experiences. And by doing so, I hope to provide the encouragement that others can use to help assist them in their own journey.

Never underestimate the power of three simple words.

> *"I hope that my achievements in life shall be these — that I will have fought for what was right and fair, that I will have risked for that which mattered, and that I will have given help to those who were in need that I will have left the earth a better place for what I've done and who I've been." — Carl Hoppe*

CHAPTER 1

BREAK ON THROUGH

> ⓘ *This book is a toolbox. And like a toolbox, not everything in it will be of interest or of relevance to you at this time. Readers are encouraged to flip through the pages of this book and read whatever catches their interest and skip anything that doesn't.*

⚡ Don't squander your potential living a life that amounts to far less than the one you are capable of living.

Congratulations

Congratulations. You made it. You're here.

You've survived all the hardships. All the heartache. All the criticism and rejection. Every challenge. Every disappointment. And every plot twist of your life.

This shouldn't be taken lightly because this isn't a *small* achievement. You are not just undefeated in the game of life, every adversity you've faced and every obstacle you've overcome has made you stronger. And every mistake you've ever made, a little bit wiser.

The path that got you here hasn't always been easy — and at times, it may have seemed damned near impossible — but the fact that you're here — still breathing — makes you a survivor of every challenge you've ever faced.

Remember this whenever life gets hard and you doubt yourself. Because every time you've been forced to face the absolute worst thing that has ever happened to you, you have survived and pushed forward.

And because of this, you my friend, are a force to be reckoned with. And while you may not yet have the vision needed to see it or the perspective necessary to believe it, it doesn't mean it isn't true.

So I, for one, choose to celebrate you and all that you've accomplished to get here. And I sincerely hope that you will join me.

Maximizing the effectiveness of what you read

Because not all words are written to be read in the same way, maximizing the effectiveness of what you read, particularly anything written with the intention of providing you with potentially meaningful information, may require a different approach than the one you are used to.

Many people read and forget what they've read while still giving themselves credit for having read it. But in order for something to make a meaningful and lasting difference in your life, it must be integrated into your mind and your life in a meaningful way. Reading something repeatedly or regularly revisiting something that impacts you may help you integrate it into your life.

Also, be mindful of the difference between having a superficial understanding of something and having a meaningful one. There is a big difference between understanding the words you read and understanding a concept they are trying to convey. Some of the things we read and interpret as simple have a significantly deeper message and meaning than we initially see.

Many of the techniques that students use to study in school are abandoned once they are no longer in the education system. It is a mistake to think these things are no longer needed or of value in life.

Don't underestimate the value of highlighting or underlining phrases or passages that strike you as important. And don't underestimate the value of taking notes or recording the thoughts that the content you read helps trigger. Your thoughts can result in insight that can be even more valuable to your life than the content that causes them to occur.

Also, note that discovering things you disagree with can be as important as the things that make you nod in agreement. Just because you disagree with something you read doesn't mean you should immediately disregard it (and yet, people often do).

Understand that discovering things that someone else believes, but you don't agree with, can be an important opportunity to see things from someone else's perspective. Thinking about what you believe and *why* you believe it will either help you reaffirm what you already believe or allow you to update your beliefs to reflect new information and new insights you've made as a result of that information.

The potential for greatness

You are stronger, smarter, and more resilient than you think. You are capable of achieving far more than you believe. And you have the potential for greatness — like all of those who have achieved it.

Within you lies the power to transform your health, your wealth, your education, your relationships, your attitude, and nearly any other area of your life that you wish to improve. But freeing yourself from the constraints that are holding you back in life requires persistence. And determination. And the courage to confront your fears.

It requires a readiness to face and initiate change. And a commitment to continue towards your goals no matter how many obstacles you encounter, challenges you face, and setbacks you experience.

If you want to achieve greatness, you must rid yourself of the notion that shortcuts will get you there. You must devote yourself to doing that which is hard and necessary, instead of seeking that which is quick and easy. And you must shed the notion that there is a better time than now to begin making progress.

The rescue party isn't coming

One of the biggest mistakes people make is thinking that they will be rescued from whatever direction they find themselves heading or whatever undesirable situation or circumstances they currently find themselves in.

It's important to understand that no one cares about you, your life, your health, or your circumstances *more* than you do. And if you want any of these things to change, you must make them a priority, take action, and change them yourself.

Life is forever providing you with signs as to what actions are in your best interest and what actions are not. These signs are reflected in every aspect of your life — many of which literally come with *warning* labels. By that same token, your life is littered with clues on how to make it better, but you have to look for them.

If you truly want or need something in your life to change, you need to take action and change it yourself. The rescue party isn't coming.

Letting go of what is

If the way things *are* no longer reflect the way you want them to be, and you're no longer making steady progress towards your goals, then it's time to come to terms with the fact that how you've been doing things *isn't* working.

It's important to understand that *you can't have it both ways.* You can't have things as they *are* and as you ultimately *want them to be* at the same time. You cannot elicit positive changes in your life without *making changes.* And this means letting go of the way things currently are in order to reach for the way you want things to be.

One of the reasons so many people resist letting go of something they're not entirely happy with, in order to reach for something better, is that they fear the worst possible outcome. They fear that they'll lose something they already have in the process of striving for something better. But *that's* the point. Real growth in life requires people to face their fears, deal with uncertainty, and take action.

If you truly desire change, you have to be willing to give up the habits and routines that have stopped you on your path to a better and brighter tomorrow. Stop using your current habits and methodologies as an excuse to get out of making the changes necessary to get you to where you want to go.

This is the day

What's happened up 'til now in your life is far less significant than what you do moving forward. Because it's *not* about where you've been or what's happened to you in life, it's about *where* what you're *doing* is taking you.

You can sit there and do nothing or you can stand up and proclaim that *this is the day* you finally take steps to initiate lasting, positive change in your life.

Because, despite whatever you've been telling yourself, you *can* change. You *can* make a positive and permanent difference in your life — and *other people's lives*. And you *can* end up in a better place than where your current lifestyle is leading you. And you don't need me to tell you this because it's something you *already* know.

What can you do?

Let's face it, even if you're happy with where you are and where your life is taking you, there are still things you can do — starting today — that have the potential to influence your life in a significant and positive way. Give yourself some time to think about your current life, what you want to improve, and what steps you can take to do it. No matter where you are on your journey, there are things that you can begin doing to help bring your life more in line with a future you look forward to.

✓ You can work on your weaknesses
✓ You can identify things that are draining you and find ways to fix them
✓ You can reduce the amount of stress in your life
✓ You can re-evaluate the things you are committed to and find exit strategies for those that are no longer adding value to your life
✓ You can adopt good habits and break bad ones
✓ You can further your education
✓ You can learn new skills
✓ You can begin to save more money
✓ You can sell or donate things that are just taking up space in your life
✓ You can get more organized

From honing your skills, to increasing your knowledge, to improving your health or fitness, nearly everything you do to actively develop yourself will reward you in immeasurable ways throughout your life.

Life isn't fair

No. Life isn't fair. But how you deal with life being unfair is *a choice*. You can *choose* to play a victim and live from a position of weakness. And you can lay blame for whatever negative situation, circumstance, or condition you currently find yourself in on factors that are beyond your control, but this won't do anything but perpetuate your problems.

Alternatively, you can choose to take personal responsibility for your life and the challenges you face and use your adversities as a catalyst for growth.

Refuse to quit

No matter what life throws your way, no matter how unfair it may seem, refuse to play the victim. Refuse to be ruled by fear, pessimism, and negativity. And refuse to quit.

Be a warrior and work through whatever challenges you face in life with courage, love, and positivity. And continually push forward. Because you are a survivor of the unfairness of life. You are stronger than you think. And you are capable of achieving far more than you believe.

Broken vs. unsolved

We don't look at a box of puzzle pieces or a bag of building blocks and think "What a shame!". Nor do we look at a scrambled Rubik's Cube and call it broken. This is because we know these things are simply in a state that requires effort to either assemble them or solve them.

When a person learns to recognize the difference between something that's actually broken and something that is simply unassembled or unsolved, the manner and attitude with which they approach that thing can have a dramatic impact on its outcome.

If you've ever referred to yourself or someone else as broken, understand that the same concept applies. Every person is a puzzle and every person's life is a bag of building blocks.

Focus on what you can do

The journey to one's goals will always be susceptible to challenges, obstacles, and setbacks. At any given time, there will be things you simply cannot do — but by the same measure, there will always things that you *can*.

Refuse to concern yourself with what you can't do for any longer than is necessary to put you on a path doing what you can. No matter what the challenge may be, train yourself to always look for the positive actions you can take to aid yourself on the path to your goals.

Find your own limits

"You won't get very far..."
"A person your age..."
"Won't you feel embarrassed..."

Find your own limits. Don't become a victim of the limits that people place on you. You are not a stereotype or a statistic. You are a unique individual with unlimited potential.

You don't have to constrain yourself to other people's expectations. You don't have to accept life as other people know it. Your life is as unique as you are. And you are as unique as you choose to be.

The heroes

Be careful not to get so caught up at looking at the darkness of the world that you fail to see the heroes who are doing whatever they can to fight it. Every single day, countless heroes wage war against darkness with light. And with each battle they win, the world becomes a little kinder, a little more friendly, and a little more peaceful.

And while the heroes that fight these battles are everywhere, people are naturally more drawn to drama, famous people, politics, and displays of bad behavior than they are to unassuming individuals performing acts of kindness for no other reason than it's the right thing to do.

So rather than being reminded regularly of those who battle darkness with light, we are bombarded and sometimes overwhelmed with dark messages that disappoint us, divide us, or make us angry or fearful instead.

We are blasted with bad news so frequently, and see displays of bad behavior so often, that it can be easy to forget and recognize how many of these heroes are out there and how many battles they are fighting in support of what we believe in.

And while just knowing these heroes are out there can be encouraging and being mindful that they exist can be all it takes to make our day a little brighter, lending your support to and actively finding ways to appreciate these people, or better, becoming one of them can mean all the difference in how many more battles against darkness are won and how many people's lives become better as a result.

Always look for the heroes. And if you are so inclined, become one of them.

Archive your thoughts & ideas

With very little awareness on your part, a tremendous number of things you *think* every single day are quickly forgotten and lost forever. The sad thing is that some of these things could have a direct impact on the direction of your life if only you could recall them.

Many of people's most interesting thoughts and ideas pass into oblivion simply because the human brain is better at processing information than it is at remembering it.

One thing that every person can do, which can have an immediate and lasting effect on their lives, is to get in the habit of keeping track of the noteworthy things they think by taking notes. It doesn't matter whether you do this digitally from your phone or scribble things into a notebook, the important thing is that the thoughts you fail to keep a record of will often be forgotten. You won't just remember the specifics of something you thought, you'll forget that you thought it at all.

This will eventually be evidenced by the fact that once you get in the habit of keeping track of the noteworthy things you think, when you revisit them later you will often have little recollection of having ever written them. *Your own thoughts* will appear *new* to you.

Once you get in the habit of keeping track of the noteworthy things you think, you will likely be surprised at how quickly they add up. And because the things you think come directly from your brain, they are catered to *you* as perfectly as they can be.

Notes vs. diaries & journals

While diaries and journals can be helpful, not everyone has the discipline to maintain them; nor do they replace the efficiency of storing noteworthy thoughts and ideas close to the time they are conceived.

> *This book is a direct result of years of taking note of the things I was thinking by using voice-to-text to dictate them into my phone and collecting these notes in the cloud.*

Energy awareness

If you frequently find yourself at odds with others, it's important to be aware that people often receive a reflection of the energy they project. People who project *positive* energy are far more likely to receive it than those who don't. And, of course, the opposite is also true.

If you are constantly finding yourself in conflicts with random people, it is very possible that the kind of energy you're carrying isn't congruent with how you see yourself. You may be justifying your actions and blaming others for the friction you experience while being totally blind to the root of the problem which isn't so much other people as it is *you*.

Remember, people respond to facial expressions, tone of voice, body language, eye contact, and even word choice. It isn't always *what* you say as much as *how* you say it. It is entirely possible that the manner in which you communicate is at odds with what other people are comfortable with or accustomed to.

When you are consciously aware of the kind of energy you project, you're more likely to act and communicate in accordance with what you truly want out of your interaction with people.

Know that if you don't like the kind of energy you're receiving from the world, a large portion of it is entirely within your control to change. And often, it is as simple as adjusting your attitude and what you communicate as a result of that attitude. Yes, negative things may happen in your life, but with the right attitude, it's possible to deal with them in a positive way.

Minor adjustments to how you communicate may be all that is needed to reduce the recurrence of negative encounters you experience while increasing the possibility of positive ones.

CHAPTER 2

ARE YOU AWAKE?

⚡ **Refuse to be an extraordinary person trapped in an ordinary life.**

Remember this day

Remember this day as a fresh start. A new beginning. A clean slate. An optimistic look forward.

Remember this day as a day of hope. A day of unlimited possibilities. A day of immeasurable potential.

Remember this day as an occasion to learn. A day to improve. A day to get things right.

Remember this day as an opportunity to make a positive difference in someone's life. A day to have a lasting positive impact on those you come in contact with. A day to lead by example.

Remember this day is a symbol. Because this day, this moment, and every moment that follows is an opportunity to not only be the type of person you want to be, but the type of person you want to be *remembered* as.

This day is not just a fresh start that comes but once, it comes *every day* — every moment that you exist. This day is your life. And this day and all the days that follow are your legacy.

Remember this day. Because no one has more of an impact on *this* day and every day that follows in your life than *you* do.

> *Originally written as New Year's Day sentiments, this lesson is applicable to life no matter what day or time of year it happens to be.*

From this day forward

Nothing you do from this day forward will ever change the past, but *everything* you do from *this moment* on can change the future.

By making a few simple decisions and *acting* on them, you can literally change the trajectory of your life. You can put yourself on a path towards a future that's even greater than you can imagine.

Do it.

Are you awake?

If you don't want to be someone who loses sight of the things that you truly want to get out of life, it's important to be mindful of where your present actions, lifestyle, habits, and relationships are leading you.

Far too many people allow themselves to drift so far from where they really want to go in life that when they finally assess where they are and how off-track they've gotten, they lose the courage, determination, or desire to do anything about it.

Taking the time to periodically stop and assess where you are and if your lifestyle is leading you to where you *truly* want to go allows you to correct your course as necessary — but doing so requires that you be present, proactive and *awake,* not asleep at the wheel.

By failing to pay attention to the direction in which life is leading you, you are far more likely to end up in a place you don't want to be.

Someone that you used to be

Does the life you currently lead accurately reflect the person you are *today* or has it become a reflection of someone you *used* to be?

Think about it. *You've changed.* You're a different person today than you were last week, let alone y*ears ago* when you made decisions without the knowledge and experience you have at this moment.

By taking the time to recognize the things in your life that are no longer serving you — and letting go of those that are simply taking up time, energy, or space — you create space for things of higher value.

The more that you incorporate things that you *truly* value into your life — from knowledge, to skills, to people, to activities — the more value you not only bring to *your* own life, the more value you bring to the people and places you encounter on a daily basis.

Between a rock and a hard place

Sometimes we find ourselves in personal or professional relationships that inadvertently turn sour. And then we stay in these relationships due to a lack of options or the feeling that leaving would put us in a poor position.

When we rely on things that are beneficial to us in one way, but bad for us in another, we can become trapped. And this feeling of being trapped can leave us miserable and indecisive because we convince ourselves that there's nothing we can do. And while it is true that we may not be able to immediately quit a job or leave a dysfunctional relationship, one thing we can do is plan an exit strategy.

If you know you are in a relationship that you need to leave, but feel like you don't have any options, planning your exit strategy will likely leave you feeling empowered and hopeful. Remembering that you are in the situation you are in by choice — and only staying until you can leave on your own terms — can provide you with the strength necessary to survive unsavory conditions without being miserable.

You can't always go where you want to go when you want to go there, but you *can* begin planning the path you'll take when the time is right.

Beware of monsters

People will often go to great lengths to ignore obvious warning signs, red flags, and common sense in order to have what they want to believe fit the narrative they wish to follow.

They will even do so at their own peril.

People can believe so strongly that they are right that they are blind to all that is wrong. All the while, their condition worsens and the life they want crumbles.

From addiction to domestic abuse, obesity, stress, debt, self-injury, eating disorders, and more. Don't make excuses for the monsters in your life. Don't normalize them. And certainly, don't ignore them. Because sooner or later you'll see what you've been blind to.

Better *sooner* than *later*.

 The longer we tolerate things that we find unappealing or unacceptable, the more normal they seem and the less those things shock us. This is how "I can't believe it." becomes "That's just the way things are."

Who do you think you are?

Know that *whoever* you *think* you are, *that person* only exists in your mind. To every other individual you've ever met or crossed paths with, you are a *different* person. And the person that other people *see* you as can differ greatly from the person you picture yourself to be.

Everyone makes sense of life through the lens of their own personal experiences and biases. And because everyone's experiences are entirely unique, so too, are their interpretations and assessments of others.

While we are always influencing what other people think about us, we can never control it. But one thing we can control is what we think about ourselves. And we can continually take steps to ensure that the person people see in their lives is as close as possible to the kind of person that we picture ourselves to be.

This is your life

This is it. This is your life. *Here. Today. Right now.*

It's important to recognize that your life is *in-progress*. This *isn't* a dress rehearsal. Regardless of whether you live a long life or a short one, every day that passes is another day closer to your expiration date.

Life isn't about what you say you're going to do *tomorrow*. It's about what you do *today*. The actions you take today to improve your life are the only thing standing between where you are and where you want to be.

Have you taken a good hard look at yourself and your life lately? It's important to do this from time-to-time because it's the only way you can accurately assess whether the path you're on is pulling you closer to or pushing you further away from where you truly want to be. If you haven't done this recently, *do it today*.

What's your trajectory in life? *Where* are you heading? If you stay on the path you're on, without changing course, where will that leave you a year from now? What about five years? Where will you be, both personally and professionally in five years? What about ten?

Do you see yourself happy and healthy in the future that you imagine? If you don't change your habits, will you be in a *better* place, worse place, or the same place? — and if the *same* place, is that *really* a good thing?

It's important to take the time to consider *where* you are, *what* you want out of life, and *what* you're willing to do to get it because the truth is, no one cares about — or has as much control over — *your* life as *you* do.

Stuck in a rut

Sometimes we get stuck in a rut because something that no longer works for us is so deeply integrated into our lives that we are blind to it. Even when we are open to change, we literally overlook this thing because we never consider it as something that needs to change. When, in fact, it may be the very thing holding us back from where we want to be.

Always keep in mind that as we move through life, some of the things we do at certain times in our lives not only lose their effectiveness, they can begin to work against us by keeping us from moving forward.

When we are stuck in a rut, sometimes what needs to change is exactly the thing we've grown so accustomed to that we don't ever consider changing it. Not because we aren't willing to, but because it never crosses our minds as something that needs to change. We simply accept it as a given in our lives.

Always remember that routines can be very powerful, but they can also work against us if we're not careful. Not everything that works for us at one point in our lives works in another. Sometimes it's necessary to let go of something in order to accommodate something better.

And sometimes it's necessary to step sideways or even backwards in order to ultimately move forward. As you consider making changes to your life, be sure not to overlook the obvious.

Priorities

Every day you make choices based on your priorities. And every day those choices are leading you closer to, or pushing you further away from what you truly desire in life.

Priorities not only have a dramatic effect on everything from your health to your wealth, your relationships, career, and how respected you are, your priorities will ultimately create the backbone of your *entire* life.

If you truly wish to make positive, long-lasting changes to your life, it's important to have a very clear understanding of what your priorities are and to arrange them in a way that they consistently and persistently push you towards what you want in life. Because it is not a question of *if* you will ever be tempted to deviate from the path to your long-term goals, so much as *how* you will respond when you are. Because no matter who you are and where you come from, the temptation to seek instant gratification or comfort is always lingering.

The difference between success and failure in many endeavors is often determined by how one chooses to respond to the allure of something they desire *in the moment it's presented,* versus what they desire *overall*. So by having a clear and consistent understanding of your overall priorities, it becomes easier to make the choice that is most conducive to achieving your long-term goals.

Take the time to determine what your most important goals in life are and then sort your priorities in a way that aid you on your journey to achieving them. Because when you change your priorities you will change your life. It's *not* easy, but it *is* simple.

- ✓ You can quit — or you can continue
- ✓ You can choose healthy — or unhealthy
- ✓ You can sleep in — or you can get up early
- ✓ You can seek progress — or you can seek excuses
- ✓ You can set high standards and meet them — or you can settle for mediocrity
- ✓ You can follow the path of least resistance — or you can challenge yourself to do more, be more, and get more out of life

> *"Things which matter most must never be at the mercy of things which matter least." — Johann Wolfgang von Goethe*

Do something

Refuse to sit back and watch your life pass you by thinking, "If only..." and regretting all the things you *could've* done but chose not to.

How you spend your time is *a choice*. And the fact is, there are things you can do *today* that will increase your chances of attracting what you desire tomorrow.

- ✓ You *can* get focused
- ✓ You *can* release yourself from your self-imposed limitations
- ✓ You *can* commit yourself to positive, life-changing actions
- ✓ You *can* prioritize your life in a way that attracts more of what you truly desire
- ✓ You *can* live a life congruent with your beliefs instead of the constraints of other people's expectations

You can put yourself on a better path in life starting today, but it requires you to actually *do* some things.

You must stop perpetuating your own dissatisfaction with yourself, your career, your relationships, or your life by doing *nothing*. You must commit to no longer settling for the path of least resistance. You must commit to working towards your goals instead of relying on wishful thinking. And you must be willing to deal with life's challenges without allowing yourself to be overcome by them.

It is a fact of life that you will suffer setbacks on the way to your goals. *Everyone* does. If you truly want to live a life you are proud of, you must never use your setbacks as an excuse to abandon your path to a better future.

Toxicity

Be mindful of prolonged exposure to toxic conditions and dysfunctional relationships. Even an outhouse will appear to lose its smell the more time you spend in one.

Just because something seems to stink less than it did in the beginning doesn't mean you should expose yourself to it any more than is necessary.

Self-awareness

The difference between having self-awareness and not having self-awareness is the difference between someone who inconveniences you *on purpose* and someone who has *no idea* that they're doing it.

You may not always be aware of *how*, but the fact is, your existence impacts other people. And the *less* you consider how your actions impact others, the *more likely* the results of your actions will inconvenience one or more people.

While it's true that *some* people are just hypocritical, disrespectful, self-serving, egotistical assclowns, *most* people who inconvenience others *don't* do it on purpose.

If you don't want to be the source of someone else's inconvenience, always consider how your actions will impact other people. And if something you're considering doing will affect someone else in a way you wouldn't appreciate if it was done to you, then *don't do it* — no matter how hard you try to justify it. (i.e. "Just this once", "I'm in a hurry", "No one is looking", "It's a stupid rule", "I've seen other people do it").

Doing unto others as you would have them do unto you means *not being an assclown when you can help it* (and you can nearly always help it).

It means considering the needs of the many over your own personal needs. It means not blocking traffic, not making yourself an exception to laws, not disrespecting the environment, or trying to make other people pay for your own mistakes.

Gravitation

People have a tendency to be influenced by those they spend the most time with. Friends and coworkers with bad habits, for example, can influence you to adopt attitudes, behaviors, and habits you wouldn't naturally acquire.

But it works both ways — and with good habits and bad.

Always be mindful of who you are spending your time with and if those people are helping you or hindering you from being the kind of person you want to be.

Try to surround yourself with people that influence you in positive ways. And if this doesn't include your friends, you may want to reconsider your friendships.

Just because it sounds good, doesn't make it true

Just because it sounds good, doesn't make it true. Always seek the whole truth, not just the version that pleases you.

Remaining closed to factual evidence that contradicts what you believe doesn't make the truth less truthful, it simply supports a distorted view of life, based on limited information, half-truths, or outright lies. People are often content to believe lies as long as those lies fit the narrative they wish to follow.

Always remember that people naturally seek evidence to support what they already believe. It doesn't make them bad people. It does, however, make them impressionable to those who use this fact against them.

People are happy to root for the bad guy if the bad guy repeatedly reaffirms what they already believe. It doesn't have to be true. It just has to fit the narrative that they already believe.

When seeking the truth, be sure to consider evidence that challenges your beliefs. Otherwise, it isn't *the truth* you seek, it's simply confirmation of what you already believe.

CHAPTER 3

LIVING WITH INTENTION

⚡ Never stop seeking meaningful ways to improve yourself and you will be rewarded with a life that attracts and reflects more of the things that are meaningful to you.

If the results of your habits don't make you a better, stronger, or healthier person, it's time to consider new habits that do.

A reason for being

While you still may not know what you want to be when you "grow up", knowing how you want to live your life can be equally as significant (if not more so).

Finding or giving your life a purpose can be one of the most rewarding and fulfilling things you ever do because it not only makes it easier to prioritize your life, your purpose gives you direction.

And when you have a purpose, it makes it much easier to determine whether the path you are on is the right one or if the actions you're taking are of genuine value on your journey.

If you haven't found or given your life a purpose yet, one of the most effective substitutes you can make is to choose "doing good for others" as a default to get you by. Because it is by adding value to other people's lives that you will likely find your purpose

Expiration date

By failing to face the fact that life is limited, we run the risk of wasting enormous amounts of time getting caught up in things that ultimately add very little substance to our lives.

It is simply a fact of life that every day that passes is one day closer to our expiration date. While we can never get more time, we *can* manage it more effectively by living with intention and learning to appreciate the value of a single day.

There are more things to do and more places to see in the world than any person could possibly experience in a single lifetime. So already, our lives and *what we choose to experience is a compromise.*

If you want to maximize your potential to experience life, it's important to not just *know* what you want to get out of your life, it's important to prioritize how you spend your time.

Reminding yourself that every day has value and every day that passes is another day closer to your expiration date, can provide the perspective and motivation necessary to help you prioritize your life in a way that reflects the kind of person you truly want to be.

If you want to love your life

It is important to realize that if you want to love your life, you need to *really live* it. Don't just exist and wonder why your life isn't that interesting when you're bored.

A typical lifetime may seem like a significant amount of time, but we experience life in the context of the various *stages* of our lives *only once*. Desires, perspectives, priorities, and physical capabilities change over time. We only experience life from the perspective of our teens once, our 20's once, our 30's once, and so on.

The amount of time that anyone has to do certain things at certain times in their life is *limited*. A journey to a foreign place, for example, is a very different experience from the perspective of someone in their early 20's versus someone in their early 30's.

Refuse to live the kind of life where you look back and wish you'd taken advantage of the opportunities you had available to you when you had the chance.

If there are things you want to do, don't waste the time you have to make them happen by doing things that are not adding value to your life.

What it means to live life to the fullest

Living life to the fullest means continually reaching out for newer, richer, deeper, life-changing experiences. It means using those experiences as a means for personal growth and pushing the boundaries of yourself mentally, spiritually, and intellectually for the betterment of yourself and the world at large.

Living life to the fullest means taking an active role in your own development. It means steering the rudder of your own life and taking advantage of your unique and powerful potential as a person.

It's about how the things you do in your life motivate and inspire others to do something motivating and inspiring in theirs — and, if you're lucky, it means leaving a legacy that long outlasts you.

To live life to the fullest means maximizing your capacity to experience what life has to offer around you. This, in turn, expands your consciousness, allowing you to see and take advantage of even more opportunities that result in an even broader range of life experiences.

"Opportunities multiply as they are seized." — Sun Tzu

To live life to the fullest means facing your fears with bravery, an open mind, and a lack of prejudice. It means making the most of what you have, refusing to complain about what you don't, and never settling for less than the life you are capable of living.

To live life to the fullest means not just rising to the challenges of life, but continually seeking out new ones — because if you're not being challenged, then the experiences you're having are no longer fostering growth, or leaving you as prepared as you could be to handle the trials and tribulations of life.

Living life to the fullest is about acquiring strength and wisdom from the challenges one has overcome and having experiences that alter how one perceives the world.

If you really want to live life to the fullest, make a habit of always reaching for new experiences that push you to grow. And when you're growing, and your growth is having a positive influence on others, you'll know you're truly maximizing your life. You'll *know* you're living life to the fullest because you can feel it.

 If you aren't at least occasionally taking calculated risks, challenging yourself, or living beyond comfort, you aren't really living life to the fullest.

It's your life

As you live your life, you will encounter people who will offer advice or make judgements about how you spend your time. While it can be beneficial to consider feedback (even negative feedback), as a way to make sure you haven't gotten off-track, it's important to remember that *your life is your own,* and how you spend your time and, ultimately, what you do with your life is up to *you.*

Be very careful to not fall into the trap of living your life according to someone else's ideals. Always keep in mind what you ultimately plan to achieve during your time on the planet.

Remember, it's your life and how you choose to spend your time should be a reflection of what *you* wish to do with it, not what someone else wishes you would.

Busy is easy

Be careful not to fool yourself into thinking that being busy or having a full schedule is the same thing as living life to the fullest. It's not.

Being busy is *easy*. Prioritizing your time in a way that allows you to truly enrich your life with experiences that allow for personal growth is *not*.

The quality of the time you spend matters.

Do your thing

We are all not only driven by a combination of values and priorities that are as unique to each of us as our DNA, we all draw from a very unique set of personal resources, life experiences, and circumstances that can never truly be replicated. So although some people's paths may, at times, resemble others, no two people are on the same journey through life. And because every person's path through life is unique, it makes no sense to let the perceived successes of others on *their* paths discourage you from walking *your own*.

Always remember to concern yourself more with what *you* want to do on *your* path in life and less about what others are doing on theirs.

By focusing more on what you wish to accomplish in *your* life and less on what others are doing in *theirs*, you will be rewarded with an authentic life that fits you and not a poorly-fitting imitation of someone else's.

Be inspired by the greatness of others on their paths, but don't ever let the accomplishments of another person deter you from your own.

Use your free time wisely

What you do in your free time determines how much of your life will be spent being told what to do by other people. If you're not using your free time to direct your life where you want it to go, you are far less likely to get to where you want to be.

There's a big difference between being able to *choose* how one spends their time and having to act out of necessity due to a lack of options. The more you do things that you don't necessarily *have* to do — such as better yourself in some way — the more in-control of your life you will feel, because you are exercising your power of choice, versus being told what to do or having to act out of necessity or obligation.

By being proactive and using your free time to direct your life where you want it to go, you won't just increase the likelihood that you'll get to where you want to be, you'll also increase the number of options and opportunities that present themselves to you along the way.

Always remember that everything you do today influences what you can do tomorrow — and over time, your entire life. You can't just wish for what you want to happen — you have to *work* for it. And that means taking action when you're *able* to, not just when it's convenient.

Work/play balance

Taking time to relax, play, and enjoy life is *vital* to a person's emotional and physical well-being, but when done excessively or as a way to procrastinate, it can lead people astray from where they want to be in life.

Enjoy yourself, but always be mindful of where you want to go in life and remember to take consistent steps forward if you want to have the pleasure of getting there.

Whether you use your time to work or play, always spend your time in such a way that when tomorrow comes, you will be thankful for what you did today.

Be mindful of your time

Be mindful of where you invest your time. Try to focus more on things that add value and less on things that simply make moments go by. Time is one of the few things in life that we can never get more of. Be diligent in determining when it is in your best interest to avoid situations and activities that do nothing but put off things you could be doing that actually make a positive difference in your life (or someone else's).

Remember, by changing your priorities you change your life. When you prioritize your time to those things that add *real* value to your career, your education, your relationships, and your mental and physical health, your life responds by giving you more of the rewarding things that you seek and fewer of the negative things that you don't.

Is it useful?

Whether it's an activity you're participating in or an item you own, there is a big difference between something that is simply taking up time and space and something that is actually adding value to your life.

Every now and then ask yourself, "Is this useful and adding value to my life?" If the answer is no, it might be time to move on to something that does.

 Be mindful of the discrepancy between what you intend to do and what you are actually doing. The person who acts only out of habit, and not desire, is a puppet.

Stop wishing for more time

Anyone who ever accomplished anything great in life had exactly the same number of hours in *their* day as *you* do in yours. Today we have more ways to solve more problems and get more done in a single day than have ever existed before, in the whole span of history. A "lack of time" isn't really a *time* problem as much as a *priorities* issue.

If you wish to better manage your schedule, always commit more attention, time, and resources to those things that add value to your life, while minimizing the amount of time you spend on the things that don't.

Learn to prioritize your activities based on the value they add to your life and others and how effective they are at moving you closer to your goals.

We don't get more time by wishing for it. We get more time by making better use of the time we already have.

"Those who make the worst use of their time are the first to complain of its brevity." — Jean de la Bruyere

Beware a lack of evidence of your efforts

Be very careful about pouring yourself into things that provide very little to show for the time and energy you put into them. Sometimes this is a sign that what you are doing or how you are doing it isn't the best or most efficient use of your time.

What you consistently do

Always be mindful of the fact that even the smallest things you do consistently can alter the path you're on. And if those things are continually pushing you in a positive direction, then the outcome of those actions will likely be of great benefit to you.

But by that same token, if the things you are consistently doing are giving you results you don't want, those results when repeated with enough consistency can eventually lead to undesirable consequences. And in some cases, those consequences can be irreversible.

 If you want to feel more in control of your life, get in the habit of taking action and making things happen instead of being a person who simply reacts to whatever happens.

Appreciation of the effort

Let this be the year that you work towards something you desire and consider the struggle to be a *positive* part of the process. Because if you're struggling to achieve something you want, it means you're pushing yourself in ways you haven't pushed yourself before. And it is through this process that we get stronger.

Find appreciation in the effort it takes to make progress on your journey and commit to earning honest results without seeking shortcuts, instant gratification, or waiting for the perfect time or circumstances to get started.

Don't cheat yourself out of the experience of true growth on the way to your goal because the growth we experience is often far more valuable than the goal itself.

Maximizing output

If you want to maximize your output, learn to recognize the times you are most productive and typically able to get the most amount of work done in the least amount of time. Try to set up your schedule in such a way that you are routinely able to work at this time.

Intentional vs. reactionary

Distractions are the enemy of productivity. If you want to live with intention, it's important to segregate your time in a way that you're able to focus on what you wish to accomplish without being needlessly distracted or tempted by other things.

Set up your time in such a way that it allows you to do things on your own terms rather than in a reactionary way. The time you set aside to get things done must be one of the most important parts of your day. Resist the urge to be at the beck and call of notifications, emails, and phone calls. Whenever possible, disconnect and turn off anything that keeps you from being productive. Your time is sacred. And the less distracted you are the more productive you will be.

Riding the waves of momentum

There will be times in your life where things seem to happen easily or you're able to *do* things more efficiently or be much more productive than usual. Try to take advantage of these times as much as you're able to and don't assume that what you're experiencing will last forever. Things that happen in life are often cyclical and wave-like instead of steady.

By recognizing times in your life when you are experiencing a wave that is having a positive effect on your life, you can multiply its benefits by actively taking advantage of the momentum it provides instead of just experiencing it passively.

"Never do it for free"

There is a deceptive saying that suggests, "if you're good at something never do it for free". It's deceptive because it fails to recognize that some things provide benefits that are as valuable or more valuable than money.

Always keep in mind that money isn't the only form of currency and remember to balance the pros & cons of a potential opportunity before making a decision one way or the other.

While there may occasionally be times when people try to take advantage of you by attempting to get something that they could easily afford for free, there will also be times that the experience you gain, the connections you make, and the relationships you develop as a result of doing something for free *will* be worth your time — *especially* if you *enjoy* it.

There's no rule that says you can't do what you love in your "free" time out of enjoyment of the task and the benefit it provides to someone who could truly use what you have to offer.

How you choose to spend your time is up to you. Don't conform to someone else's standard simply because *they* value money above everything else.

Having expressed the above, I want to make it clear that I am not suggesting that anyone work for free when doing so doesn't provide any benefits.

And even if you don't feel as if your skills are as good as they could be — especially when you compare yourself to those who inspire you — never forget the amount of time energy and effort you put into becoming as skilled as you currently are. If someone is seeking your skills, that means your skills have value.

Whether you choose to work for free, for pleasure, or something else of value is entirely up to you. But never let yourself be taken advantage of by people or companies who could easily afford you, but instead, try to get you to give them your work or services for free. This kind of behavior from these kinds of people and companies should not be rewarded or supported. Remember, if the people who want you to work for free are getting paid, then you should, too.

Also, don't let someone negotiate for your services by paying for them with "exposure". Exposure often provides very little benefit and, in many cases, is worthless. What isn't worthless are relationships with people and companies and future opportunities for paid work (if these future opportunities are *actually likely* and not just used as a tactic of negotiation).

Regardless of the circumstances, if you decide to provide your services for free, always make sure to do so on your own terms and are comfortable with your decision.

A ticket to anywhere

A boring or uneventful life is not only a sign you've stopped trying new things, it's evidence that you've stopped growing as well.

Saying you're bored is like holding a ticket to anywhere you might want to go and saying you have nothing to do. Don't just exist. Do new things and *evolve*.

CHAPTER 4

TAKING ACTION

⚡ You have exactly one life to live to do everything you ever wanted. Stop wasting it caught up in things that don't matter.

The "do" in "just do it"

The results of your actions speak louder than words. You can read a million motivational sayings to pump yourself up — or echo them to others until you're blue in the face — but that won't change anything unless you take action and consistently change your behavior.

Don't just read it or preach it and expect it to make a difference in your life. *Knowing* something is not enough. Knowing what you *should do* is not enough. You have to *use* what you know and *take action*.

This is the **do** in *just do it.*

 It's better to be the indispensable lead of your own life story than a dispensable part of someone else's.

Why not today?

Of all the things we get in life, we can never get more time. And yet, people often let days, weeks, months, and even years go by without ever taking action on the things they *intended* to do.

Obviously, it takes more than intention to get things done. It takes more than a dream, a vision board, and a strong desire to *do*, *be*, or *have* something. It takes *action*.

If you don't take steps towards overcoming the things that are holding you back in life, when will you? *Why not today?*

If you don't get back on the path to living a healthy lifestyle, when will you? *Why not today?*

If you don't start tapping your potential to do more than simply exist, when will you? And *why not today?*

Far too many people spend far too much time yearning for things they don't have without ever doing anything to get what they want. Refuse to be one of them. Refuse to let what

123

amounts to nothing more than excuses deter you from the kind of life you could have, if you chose to take action and work for it.

Commit yourself to taking action on whatever it is you wish to do, be, or have. Commit yourself to making progress toward your goals. And commit to achieving them.

Not tomorrow. *Today.*

The next step

It is important to not lose sight of the framework of your life. Always keep in mind that life is a journey. A single event in your life, although it may be significant, is just that, a single event in a *lifetime* of events.

Your future has much less to do with where you've been, what you've done, or the mistakes you've made along the way than it does with the direction that your steps are consistently leading you.

Every action we take and every mistake we make is not an end. The actions we take and mistakes we make are simply an ever-evolving part of a process by which every step we take either maintains, reinforces, or weakens the action made prior. A person can make numerous mistakes that are directly responsible for leading them to exactly where they want to be. By that same token, a success can ultimately lead a person astray.

Refuse to get hung up on mistakes you've made in the past. And refuse to be discouraged by where you are if you're not somewhere you truly want to be. Because the fact is, your life is a journey. It's not about where you are at this moment. It's about the next action you take that will get you closer to where you want to be or push you further from where you want to go.

Always remember that the *next step* is always the most important step in your life. And after you take that step, it's the *next* step.

Do something

The only thing that some people are certain of is that they aren't happy with where they are, but they don't really know what they want or where they want to go. And this can be frustrating. This often causes people to resist taking action out of fear of making a mistake or doing something that leads them in the wrong direction.

At times like this, it's important to remember that doing *something* is far more conducive to creating change than doing *nothing.* And that a person doesn't have to pick their final destination at the onset of a journey. Often, it's the act of taking action that is important.

People who don't take steps never get anywhere. But those who take steps and correct their course as they go can ultimately end up where they want to be, regardless of how many missteps they make along the way.

Sometimes you won't know where you want to go until you start moving. Stop waiting for the perfect job or perfect conditions. Start moving and you will naturally be drawn to or attract into your life that which you seek.

Action and opportunity

It's important to understand that, more often than not, opportunities present themselves to us as a result of an action or actions we've taken in some area of our life. Those actions are what lead us to be in the right place, at the right time, in a state of preparedness that allows us to take advantage of them.

If you want to attract more opportunities into your life, refuse to sit back and think, "I've done my work." or "I've tried everything." These expressions are frequently used as an excuse for inaction. We use them to wrestle ourselves out of feeling responsible or guilty for no longer putting in effort towards getting something we desire.

Even if you truly believe that you've done everything you can, doing nothing — when you *could* be doing *something* — is the surest way to keep opportunities at bay. Because, the fact is, there's always *something* you could be working on to make yourself more valuable to the world.

By focusing your energy on bettering yourself in some way — or by taking the time to assist others — you keep a channel open to the numerous opportunities that exist around you.

By making a conscious effort to add value to other people's lives, you not only increase the likelihood of attracting opportunities you had no idea existed, you create a tremendous amount of goodwill in the process. While you may not always see the results of your work right away, no amount of effort you expend to improve yourself or the lives of others is ever wasted. And doing this is far more productive than sitting around waiting for opportunity to knock.

Never forget that opportunities are attracted to *actions*.

More or less vs. all or none

Always consider the benefits that doing *more* or *less* of something will provide versus the feeling that you need to do *all* or *none* of it.

Doing more of something you need to do, rather than waiting until you can do *all* of it, generates results you wouldn't otherwise be getting by waiting. Conversely, doing less of an undesirable thing can provide immediate benefits over waiting until you are able to eliminate it from your life completely.

Every little bit of effort you put into something adds up and anything you do consistently can be life-changing over time.

The master of your destiny

Whether it's to lose weight, get fit, save money, or some other worthy goal, people often have a pretty good idea of what they need to do to get the results they want, but then fail to get those results because of the inevitable discomfort that stands between where they are and where they want to be. They either give up during the struggle to achieve, or perpetually put off making progress with the hope that what they want to do will eventually become easier.

People who avoid the challenges of today, hoping that the challenges of tomorrow will be easier, fail to see the folly of their ways. It isn't a lack of effort or action that makes us strong.

Strength isn't built within one's comfort zone or developed from a lack of resistance. One's strength is manufactured in the moments when one decides that the struggle to achieve something is more important than the temporary discomfort that comes from achieving it.

Every challenge we face and overcome today provides us with the strength and knowledge necessary to overcome the challenges we face tomorrow. It is because of this that one's goal should not be to avoid challenges or to seek out the *easiest* life possible, one's goal should be to develop the strength necessary to handle a difficult one. And that comes from taking action and working through challenges.

You have it within you to be the master of your destiny by resolving to bravely face the challenges necessary to get the positive results you want in life. But you must also make a commitment to yourself to take action and get through the process without giving up.

"Can't" vs. "Don't want to"

If you truly wish to be a person of action and accomplishment, refuse to rely on "can't" as an excuse for inaction. Avoid using the word "can't" when what you *really* mean is you "*can*, but don't want to".

There is a *big* difference between being incapable of doing something and simply not wanting to do it. And there is a big difference between "I can't" and "it just isn't a high priority."

Refuse to say one thing, when what you really mean is the other.

"It's too late"

Far too many people use the phrases "It's too late", "I'm too old.", "It's been done.", "I already know what will happen." or "Why even bother?" as an excuse to *give up* on something without ever putting in any effort to see if they're mistaken.

It is a disservice to your life to imagine your limits without ever making an attempt to see where they *truly* are. The vast majority of people on the planet are capable of achieving far more than they let themselves believe. Refuse to minimize the amount of time that you potentially have left in life.

If you've always wanted to do something, **do it**.

It is simply a fact of life that the time between this moment and your death is going to pass *regardless* of how you spend it. You might as well spend it going after something you want and doing something that you *truly* want to do.

The time spent learning new things or setting new goals and achieving them is never wasted. Even if you don't ultimately get what you aim for, by artificially restricting your options, you deny yourself from having what could be some of the best experiences of your life.

 Try to anticipate future problems in a way that allows you to plan and prepare for them before they arrive. If you know a bridge is broken, don't wait until you get to it to plan how you're going to cross.

It doesn't have to be perfect

Always remember that it is often better to take action and start getting results at something — regardless of what those results initially look like — than it is to try to have the process go perfectly or to wait until the perfect conditions.

Learn to recognize the value in getting results and then working on improving upon those results versus having such high standards or expectations that you never make any progress.

Knowledge isn't power

- It's important to balance work and play
- Junk food is unhealthy
- Smoking causes cancer
- Eating processed meats is linked to cancer
- Balancing nutrition and exercise is the key to weight loss

What you know isn't doing you any good if it hasn't *changed* how you live. Knowing something doesn't get you results until you apply it. Knowledge is only *potential* power. It doesn't become true power until it's *applied*.

One of the quickest ways to make dramatic, positive changes in your life is to stop ignoring what you know and to start using it in ways that improve the quality of your life.

If you don't know what to do

If you don't know what to do, do something to make yourself, your life, or someone else's life better. One of the easiest ways to make a difference in someone else's life — and potentially a new friend — is to appreciate people for something they've done or are doing.

"I could do that"

"I could do that," you say. And maybe you *could*. But as long as you *don't*, you **won't**. It's not what you *could* do that matters. It's what you *do*. The sooner you start making progress towards your goals, the sooner you'll start getting results you can work with.

You'll never get a "yes" if you never ask. You won't get the job if you don't apply. You can't win if you don't play. And you'll never do great things unless you **make the effort and try**.

Stop sitting on the sidelines and get in the game of life.

"I could do that." is a start. But "I did it." sounds so much better.

- ✓ Write that book you've always wanted to
- ✓ Climb that mountain
- ✓ Travel to that place
- ✓ Set that record
- ✓ Learn a new language
- ✓ Play a musical instrument
- ✓ Start that endeavor
- ✓ Run that marathon
- ✓ Get in the best shape that you are physically capable of at this time in your life

⚡ Struggling for things that you want is far more rewarding than continuing to struggle with things that you don't.

CHAPTER 5

LIVING A LIFE YOU'RE PROUD OF

 Be the person you want to be remembered as.

What it means to live a life you're proud of

The only person who truly knows what it will mean to live a life that *you're* proud of is *you*. But more likely than not, it will involve seeking ways to improve yourself and the lives of others in a way that the ripples of your existence linger long after you're gone.

With every bit of value that you add to the people and places you encounter, the impact of your existence expands in ways that you may rarely witness, but is felt by those through which your positive energy touches and travels through.

Looking back on your life

Knowing how you want to look back on your life can not only influence how you act from this moment forward, it can put you on a path towards a future you *look forward to* and a past you can be proud of.

If you've never considered what it means to live a life you're proud of, take a moment to do so — because the fact is, it isn't up to anyone to decide but *you*.

- *Are you happy with your efforts in going after what you want in life — and if not, where is there room for improvement?*

- *Will you be content wondering what might have happened if you went after what you really wanted, or will you feel better knowing that you had the courage to try?*

- *If making a positive difference in other people's lives matters to you, how is that reflected in your life?*

- *If you grade yourself on your current mental and physical health and how well you take care of your body, is it a grade you're proud of?*

Always remember that whether or not a person is proud of themselves often has as much or more to do with the amount of *effort* that a person puts into their endeavors than the results.

Not everyone is capable of *being* the best, but everyone is capable of putting in their *best effort*.

What it means to "be awesome"

Being awesome doesn't mean simply existing. Being awesome means acting in a way that contributes something of value to the people, places, and things that you connect with throughout your day. Because if your presence doesn't add value, your absence won't make a difference. And if you're not making some kind of positive difference, that's not "being awesome."

So if you truly want to be awesome, always strive to contribute something of value, wherever you may be and to whoever you come in contact with, by doing more of what you'd like to see in the world.

Collect value by contributing value

Your *true* value as a human being is not in the things you own. It's not in your bank account. It's not in the accolades or awards you've won. You can chase money your entire life and still be worth very little, because it's not what you *get* in life that creates your value, it's what you *give*.

The real measure of your worth is how much value you add to the world by being a part of it — by how many lives you touch in a positive way — and how many of *those* lives, in turn, add value to *other* people's lives.

Because you create your value by *being* valuable, if you truly want to make your mark in the world, always strive to make your presence matter in meaningful ways. The more that you make a habit of adding value to the world, the more the things you seek in life will naturally fall into place on your path.

Collect value by contributing value.

Making a difference

While you may want to change the world, never forget the world of difference you can make for a single person.

It takes far less time to see progress and make a meaningful impact on one person (or a few people) at a time than it does trying to change the habits and patterns of a large number of people.

The more of a positive impact you have on individual lives, the more noticed you or your influence will be. And as the effects of your influence expand, so too will your ability to have an even greater impact on a greater number of people.

Everybody wants to be a superhero

Everybody wants to be a superhero, but if you're not already using the tremendous powers you already have to do good in this world, then why would anyone expect superpowers to make any difference?

If you use the powers you *already* have to their maximum potential, you will likely discover that you already have the ability to make a real and lasting, positive difference in the world.

You don't need superpowers

You don't need superpowers to stand up for what you know is right, to maintain your integrity, or to be a source of encouragement.

You don't need superpowers to take the time to truly listen to people, to keep your word, or to live with honor. You don't need superpowers to lead by example or be the change you'd like to see in the world. And you don't need superpowers to see that there's *nothing* stopping you from doing any of these things.

Wearing a cape is optional.

How to be a superhero in real life

- ✓ Encourage others
- ✓ Be the change you wish to see
- ✓ Give without expectation
- ✓ Observe without judging
- ✓ Be authentic and genuine
- ✓ Clean up your own messes
- ✓ Be upfront and honest
- ✓ Give thanks and be sincere
- ✓ Be kind
- ✓ Appreciate without comparing
- ✓ Live with intention
- ✓ Take the time to truly listen to people
- ✓ Pursue excellence
- ✓ Strive to add value wherever you may be
- ✓ Smile sincerely and generously
- ✓ Seek ways to be helpful without waiting to be asked
- ✓ Treat people with respect and dignity
- ✓ Do what you know is right, even when no one is watching
- ✓ Keep your word
- ✓ Live with integrity and honor
- ✓ Be the kind of person your heroes would be proud of
- ✓ Treat the world as if those you want to impress the most are the ones who have to clean up after you.
- ✓ Take personal responsibility for your actions and your life
- ✓ Be patient with people
- ✓ Lead by example
- ✓ Be tolerant of others
- ✓ Treat people well, regardless of how you feel
- ✓ Honor your commitments
- ✓ Be brave
- ✓ Appreciate differences
- ✓ Be reliable
- ✓ Share
- ✓ Let your actions be congruent with your words
- ✓ Live without prejudice
- ✓ Act as if what you do makes a difference (it does)
- ✓ Be polite
- ✓ Inspire others
- ✓ Be humble

- ✓ Honor your relationships
- ✓ Be compassionate
- ✓ Be someone you respect and admire
- ✓ Be open to new ideas
- ✓ Share your enthusiasm
- ✓ Respect your body
- ✓ Try new things
- ✓ Focus on what you can do, not on what you can't
- ✓ Let go of what you can't control
- ✓ Be solution-oriented, not problem-focused
- ✓ Don't let others dictate your sense of worth
- ✓ Strive for progress, not perfection
- ✓ Don't be afraid of failing, be afraid of not trying
- ✓ Focus on what you have, not on what you don't
- ✓ Forgive yourself and others
- ✓ Let go of your emotional baggage
- ✓ Act with confidence
- ✓ Admit when you are wrong
- ✓ Put things back where they belong
- ✓ Spread hope
- ✓ Make peace
- ✓ Generate joy

Not *once*. But as often as you can.

CHAPTER 6

ATTITUDE & APPROACH

⚡ Anger and hate dig holes. Love and kindness move mountains. Choose your motivation wisely.

Exceptions abound

Always keep in mind that even some of the wisest and most valuable pieces of advice or general rules of life have exceptions. Just because a statement can be applied to one or more situations or circumstances doesn't mean it applies to all situations, all circumstances, and all people.

Great quotes and clever sayings, for example, can often summarize complex concepts in ways that allow people to easily understand them, but they should not be treated as if they have no exceptions.

Always keep in mind that everything has a context in which it was originally expressed. And many times, short statements are simply a single component of a larger piece of information that provides context.

Also understand, that people interpret information in different ways depending on where they are in their lives, the experiences they've had, what they're feeling, and what their priorities are. It is extremely rare for a single simple piece of information to be universal or interpreted in the same way by everyone.

Always be mindful of the fact that advice, quotes, and clever sayings are simply *tools* to use as *you* choose. And if you don't have a hammer, sometimes a wrench or a rock will do.

Attitude and perception

It's important to understand that what we perceive in the world is influenced by what we believe and the attitude we harbor as a result. When we believe we are stuck, lack opportunities, or otherwise can't do something, our reality often becomes a reflection of those beliefs. We literally limit what we can achieve because of what we believe.

By adopting an attitude that reflects a belief in not only ourselves, but in positive possibilities — whether we can see them or not — we heighten our awareness to things that might otherwise go unnoticed because we failed to believe in their existence.

Those who keep an open mind and believe that opportunities or solutions to problems exist are far more likely to find them than those who don't.

Difficulty is not a standard

Always keep in mind that difficulty is not a standard and what's difficult for one person may be easy for another. Consider, for a moment, the common video game. When a person begins a game at level 1, the character they play has a limited number of resources and a limited amount of experience. Characters gain experience points by meeting challenges, fulfilling missions, and overcoming obstacles. And as a player journeys out into the world, they also acquire valuable resources, in the form of assets, that make them more effective at playing the game. As time passes, characters acquire new skills and grow stronger while players become wiser to how the game is played and get even better at playing it.

Eventually, a character gains enough experience to reach a new level in the game. And they do this repeatedly. And while each new level is always accompanied by increasingly difficult challenges, it also brings with it additional skills, resources, and experience points to help players push forward.

Now, although the challenges in the game grow increasingly difficult from one level to the next, from a character's point-of-view, the perceived difficulty and effort required to overcome obstacles and the threat that obstacles present is often perceived to be very similar from one level to the next. And yet, a level 100 character is immensely more powerful than a level 1 character.

Now, imagine taking a level 100 character and going back to level 1 and playing. What was originally perceived as difficult at level 1, and what is genuinely difficult to a level 1 player, isn't at all challenging to a level 100 player.

I may have described a video game, but this is how life works as well. Except that the players and the character they play are the same person.

Don't disparage level 1 players simply because they're facing challenges that are no longer difficult to you. Just because a person is having a difficult time doing things that are easy for *you* doesn't diminish the fact that things are hard for *them*.

What makes one person miserable may be a walk in the park for someone else. Always remember that everyone is at a different level in the game of life and not everyone perceives things in exactly the same way that you do.

Contrast is good

You may not always like what's happening in your life, but nothing provides a person with as much appreciation for the high points in life as the lows. Everything we experience in life helps provide us with the lessons and perspective necessary to be able to better handle whatever comes next.

When one learns to appreciate contrast in life and accepts challenges as *learning experiences,* one begins to see the value in *all* life experiences, not just the "good" ones.

Learning how to effectively cope with life by channeling your thoughts and feelings into positive, life-enhancing actions is one of the most rewarding things you can do for yourself.

Plot twist!

How we *think* about adversity and the way we react to it can have a dramatic effect on the extent to which it ultimately impacts our lives. The stress associated with setbacks and disappointments alone can have a significant impact on both our mental and physical health.

Because we can't see the ultimate outcome of any series of events until after they've passed, it doesn't make sense to see things in your life as "falling apart" so much as simply rearranging themselves for alternate and potentially better outcomes.

Always remember that not everything that appears to be a "bad" thing ultimately is. The plot twists that reroute us from one path to another in life always have something to teach us. And what we learn from, or how we respond to these experiences can be *exactly* what we need to place us on a path that far more suits who we are and where we want to be, than the one we were on.

Whenever life presents you with a challenge, remind yourself, "There is a lesson in this" and realize that it will likely not become evident until after the experience has passed. Because most of life's lessons are not labeled as lessons until one has learned what they've had to teach.

We rarely learn what a difficult experience is *truly* teaching us *as it happens*, but reminding ourselves that there is *value* in it can make it easier to bear.

 If you want to see more of the things you appreciate in life, it's important to make a conscious effort to be grateful for what you already have and to focus on finding things you admire versus constantly tuning into things that you don't.

Don't judge, but if you must...

Don't judge. But if you must, always be mindful of the fact that unless you know the context of someone's actions or what they're thinking, you are simply making an uninformed assessment. And you will never know what anyone is *truly* thinking or why they did what they did unless they *tell* you.

The happiness of your life

How you *think* affects how you *feel*.
How you *feel* affects how you *live*.
How you *live* affects your *life*.

Improve *how* you *think* to improve *how* you *live*.

> *"The happiness of your life depends upon the quality of your thoughts."* — *Marcus Aurelius*

Something good

Each day you awake, assume something good is going to happen to you. And if a whole day passes and nothing good happens, realize it's *not* that nothing good happened, it's that you missed it.

Not everything good that happens to you in life comes with bells and whistles attached. Sometimes the good in our lives is composed of very simple moments that we take for granted.

If you don't see the good in your day-to-day life, look more closely. Because if you're *alive*, it's there.

It's not what happens to you

Always remember that the quality of one's life is *less* dependent upon *what* happens than it is upon how a person chooses to *think* about what happens and the *actions* they take as a *result of that thinking*.

Many things are beyond your control, but how you choose to react to them isn't one of them.

⚡ If you're not happy, a healthy attitude is far more likely to lead to happiness than an unhealthy one ever will.

Extraordinary isn't normal

Opportunities and catalysts for positive change often arrive in disguise. They appear as investments in time that we're unsure we want to commit to, as people we don't consider our type, or as something that deviates from the norm.

Our initial response is often to resist the things that we are unfamiliar with. And yet, in order for something to be extraordinary, it must be beyond what is considered usual. And that means *different*.

Before you close the door on anything that appears unfamiliar to you, be sure to take some time to make certain it isn't something that you are, in fact, seeking.

If you want something "spectacular" or "extraordinary" you either have to make it happen, go out and get it, or let it into your life when it knocks on the door. If it feels the same and looks the same as everything else, it's not extraordinary.

By remaining open to the unfamiliar, you might just find that the extraordinary opportunities you seek in life have been in front of your eyes — and simply in disguise. Extraordinary *isn't* normal. It's *different*.

 Learn to embrace challenges. The most significant sources of satisfaction in a person's life will often stem from things that were difficult to face or accomplish.

Why you should give a damn

There's a misleading message being spread over social media. It looks something like this:

"Stress is caused by giving a fuck." or "The less you give a damn, the happier you will be."

These statements are fallacious, at best — and at worst, simply false. First, stress is not caused by "giving a fuck".

Stress is caused by trying to have power over things that are beyond your control.

There's a big difference between *not* caring and actually *caring*, but accepting that one's ability to influence a particular outcome in life is limited to the things that one has control over.

It's *not* the *caring* about things that's an issue so much as people becoming emotionally attached to outcomes that they have no control over. If you have no power over something, there's no use trying to control it.

To encourage people to not care about things is a step in the wrong direction. This mode of handling things is a dysfunctional extreme — in much the same way that caring *too much* tends to be. The world doesn't need people to care *less* — or people who sit by and do nothing when they have a chance to make a positive difference. What the world needs is more people who know how to *effectively* channel their energy into strategies that work.

Adopting an "I don't care" attitude about everything is *not* an effective strategy. The fact is, a lack of caring, a lack of focus, a lack of priorities, and a lack of positive role models don't make the world a better place.

It's not people who *don't* care that change the world for the better. It's people who do.

People are far more likely to reap the rewards of their efforts by focusing intently on what is within their power to change for the better than they are by not caring. The world needs more people who care — and care passionately about the things that matter.

Saved by criticism

Not caring what people think or say about you is one thing. Not letting others have control over your sense of self-worth is another. Of the two, having the ability to listen to feedback and not let it adversely affect your self-image, is far more conducive to personal growth.

As we go about our lives, people are constantly providing us with valuable feedback. This feedback is a reflection of how effective we are at interacting with the world and others. It's what allows us to know if we're acting and communicating in the manner we *think* we are. And if we're *not*, it provides us with the opportunity to correct our behavior to be more representative of the person we want to be.

While one shouldn't change who they are for the sole purpose of being liked by people — or cave-in to social pressure at the expense of their identity and values — not caring what people think is not the answer. There is a *big difference* between compromising yourself to please people — or confining yourself to their expectations — and being open to the feedback you receive, considering that feedback, and moving forward accordingly.

It is simply a fact that we are sometimes blind to our own behaviors and how our actions and attitude adversely affect others. This is because we judge ourselves based on our *intentions* and *not our actions*. We don't always recognize or give weight to the annoying or offensive things we do because the reasons we choose to do them are *always* justified from *our* point of view.

Most of the people who inconvenience others in the world don't walk around with the intent of doing so. But because they've learned to tune-out or disregard the feedback they get in life, they often don't realize when they act exactly like the type of person they *don't* want to be.

> *"Critics are our friends, they show us our faults."*
> — *Benjamin Franklin*

Remaining open to feedback

If one is to remain open to feedback in life, it's important to have or develop a strong sense of self. A person with a strong sense of self has a fundamental understanding of who they are and who they want to be. They realize they're a work-in-progress and that making mistakes and occasionally acting in undesirable ways is a part of life. But because they *know* who they are, they don't live in fear of what other people may think or say.

This approach to life allows them to consider criticism (or praise) without letting it adversely affect their sense of self-worth. And if they discover they've acted in a way that isn't a reflection of how they want to be, they can use this feedback as a means to correct their behavior.

Allowing yourself to be open is a sign of confidence, and it's a strength that will get you much further in life, and provide you with the ability to weather more storms, than simply pretending that storms don't exist.

You can't please everyone

Because you can't please everyone, sometimes you will act in a fashion that upsets people or makes them uncomfortable. And sometimes it is completely warranted. Expressing yourself in an authentic fashion can sometimes attract those who disapprove of how you choose to do so.

Just because you get a negative response to something you do, doesn't mean you *shouldn't* do it. But it also doesn't mean you *shouldn't* care about the response you get. Because that response has the potential to provide you with valuable feedback. You simply shouldn't be afraid of it or let it affect your sense of self-worth.

Not letting what other people think bother you is one thing, not caring is another. It isn't that we shouldn't care what other people think, it's that we should seek to develop a strong enough sense of self to not let what others say or think about us diminish (or inflate) our sense of self-worth.

While you may not always agree with what people think or say about you (and some would say it's none of your business), if you believe in bettering yourself as a person, it's important to allow yourself to internally acknowledge and be aware of the feedback you get in life.

Be confident enough in yourself to listen to criticism and explore views you don't necessarily agree with — because those who always agree with you will rarely push you to improve as much as those who don't.

A life without problems

People often make the mistake of thinking, "If only I reach this next phase of my life, then I won't have to deal with the problems I'm dealing with now." But the fact is, no matter what stage one is at in life, there are always challenges that accompany those stages. It's important to note that just because a person reaches a certain level of success doesn't mean that all the problems in their life disappear. They don't.

It is a far better strategy to develop the ability to deal with challenges effectively than it is to hope or expect to ever reach a point in your life that is entirely absent of issues.

How to reduce the size of your problems

How large or insurmountable the challenges in one's life appear, is in direct proportion to how well one has learned to handle the challenges they've previously encountered. For example, dropping an ice-cream cone or spilling some milk can seem like a *serious* problem as a child. But to most grown adults, it isn't. This is because the process of encountering and overcoming challenges in life builds strength, discipline, and perspective.

The trick to reducing the size of one's problems — and how much challenges set them back in life — is not in magically making them disappear. The trick to reducing the size of one's problems is to develop the attitude and mental discipline necessary to positively and productively handle whatever challenges arise, regardless of their size.

The more one adopts an, "I can and will handle this" attitude, the smaller one's problems appear. Complaining about problems — or actively resisting challenges — doesn't diminish them, but the act of facing them productively does.

"A clever person turns great troubles into little ones and little ones into none at all." — *Chinese proverb*

Level of difficulty

The degree to which difficult tasks *feel* difficult has a lot to do with the attitude one harbors while doing them. The more we focus on the difficult, negative, or undesirable aspects of whatever challenges us, the more challenging our challenges become.

By repeatedly telling ourselves (or others) how hard something is, how much we dislike doing it, or how bad we are at it, we not only set ourselves up to have a negative experience that has a greater likelihood of failure (or inferior quality), we inhibit our personal growth as a result.

It is very difficult to get better at something, or find pleasure in the process, if you are constantly telling yourself how bad you are at it, or focusing on how much you dislike doing it.

By harboring a positive mental attitude that finds value in challenging experiences, we allow ourselves to flow more easily through them on our way to wherever we wish to be. And often, the more progress we make, the more encouraged we are to continue to completion.

By focusing on progress — and successes rather than failures — we strengthen our resolve and rally ourselves through challenging experiences. Not only does a healthy attitude reduce the perceived discomfort associated with a challenging task or experience, it also reserves our mental energy for the act of pushing through it.

If you wish to reduce the perceived difficulty of tasks and challenges, discipline yourself to maintain a positive mental attitude, look for the value in the experience, and focus on how much progress you've made.

Someone should do something

If you've ever thought: *"Someone should do something!"* Remember, *you're someone.* You may not be able to do everything, but you can always do something. Don't let what you *can't* do stand in the way of what you *can* do.

Fortune favors the flexible

Be very careful about relying on anything in your life happening exactly as you imagine it will. Every second that passes brings into existence countless potentialities and a person's situation and circumstances can change in an instant.

Take the actions necessary to move your life in the direction you desire, but remain flexible in the manner in which things play out. The person who is capable of adapting to new information, circumstances, and change will always fair better than the person who isn't.

Phone. Keys. Wallet.

Phone. Keys. Wallet. Have you ever gone looking for something, only to realize you had it with you the whole time?

Happiness. Contentment. Inner peace. It's like *that.*

The hard sell

How much a person genuinely wants to help you is often inversely proportionate to how many things they're trying to get you to buy.

Be cautious around people who spend more time talking about the things they are trying to sell you than they do demonstrating the value that those things can potentially provide.

The direction of your life is a reflection of your priorities and the choices you make as a result of those priorities.

If "Plan A" doesn't work

It has been said that, If "Plan A" doesn't work, don't worry, you still have 25 letters left.

The *truth* is, you don't always get a second chance, let alone a third. But every mistake or failure provides valuable lessons to learn from.

- ✓ Re-think where it went wrong
- ✓ Seek help where you need it, and
- ✓ Take everything you learned from the experience and use it to strategize a new plan for success.

When things are bleak

It is simply a fact that not everything in our lives will work out as we want it to and there will be times when, despite our initial enthusiasm or expectations, something we hoped would happen no longer appears likely.

It is important to remember that even though things may seem bleak, not to adopt an attitude that automatically determines failure by blocking what you want from happening.

Quit when it's necessary and makes sense, but refuse to burn bridges that don't need to be burned. Because sometimes, as bleak as things may seem, there still remains the remote possibility that they will happen, but *only if you let them*.

Sometimes the deciding factor between getting something that you want and not getting it is the attitude you adopt when things are bleak.

CHAPTER 7

FOCUS & ATTENTION

⚡ Be a person who believes in the possibility of positive change because it is often the belief in something that creates the possibility.

The power of attention & beliefs

It is what we've habitually paid attention to in our lives that has created our beliefs. And it is the interplay between our beliefs and our attitude that shapes our perception of the world.

When a person believes something, they set themselves up to be more attentive to evidence that supports that belief. The more attentive someone is to something, the more likely they are to find it. And the more often they find it, the more it reaffirms what they *already* believe — *even if there exists an abundance of evidence that suggests what they believe is false.* (This is called *confirmation bias.*)

For example, if we believe the world is cold and hostile, we set ourselves up to pay *more* attention to evidence that supports our belief, while at the same time discarding evidence that contradicts it. As such, it's important to always keep in mind that what we choose to pay attention to — the good or the bad — has a dramatic effect not only on our view of the world, but on our sense of well-being as a result of that view.

Because the types of thoughts we hold in our head have a direct impact on the reality we perceive, it's important to always be mindful of where and how we direct our mental energy.

Attitude determines energy flow

Because energy flows where our attention goes, we stimulate whatever we choose to focus on in our lives. It is our attitude — and what we believe to be true at any given moment — that determines whether we give energy to or take energy away from whatever we choose to focus on.

For example, with a positive attitude, we are much more likely to focus on the progress made in an endeavor than we are to dwell on or worry about how far we have left to go. Focusing on progress is *encouraging* and *adds* energy that we can *use* to continue, while dwelling on how far we have left to go often robs us of it.

This is why it's important to be mindful of not only what you choose to focus on in life, but the attitude you harbor when you do. A negative attitude causes us to see *more* negative because it's what we train ourselves to pay attention to (whether we mean to or not).

The more we pay attention to the negatives in our lives, the smaller and less frequent the positives seem to appear. It's not that they don't exist, it's simply that while the negatives take center stage of our lives, the positives have little where else to go than a place where we're less likely to see them.

A *positive* attitude not only allows us to see *more* of the positives in our lives, it robs the negatives of much of their power. We may *see* them, but because we choose to focus on the positive, we give ourselves the energy and strength needed to deal with the negatives without letting them drag us down.

EXAMPLES OF
THE POWER OF ATTENTION, ATTITUDE & BELIEF

SUCCESS

Harboring a positive attitude that reinforces our belief in our ability to achieve channels energy into our efforts and increases our chances of success — and when we harbor a negative attitude, the opposite is true.

This is the premise Henry Ford's famous quote: *"Whether you think you can, or you think you can't—you're right."*

PEOPLE

When we focus on what we *like* about someone, we tend to like them *more* because we are adding energy to that which we appreciate and admire. When we focus on what we *don't* like about someone, we make those things appear far more significant than when we don't.

GRATITUDE

The more we pay attention to what we lack in life, the more what we *lack* expands in our consciousness. The more that we pay attention to what we appreciate and are grateful for in our lives, the more *this* expands in our consciousness.

RELATIONSHIPS

Relationships often grow sour when potentially negative factors that were often ignored at the beginning of a relationship (honeymoon phase) are given so much attention (sometimes unfairly) that they overshadow the positive traits that lead to the relationship being formed in the first place.

If this happens often enough, it rewrites an old belief ("this relationship is awesome") with a new one ("this relationship is terrible"). This is why it's important to never lose sight of the things that caused a relationship to bloom in the first place.

NEGATIVE STEREOTYPES

When one holds a negative expectation of a person or group of people, they heighten their sensitivity to the traits they find offensive without giving equal attention to those that they don't.

Because we remain far more ignorant of things we don't give our attention to than we do to the things that we do, we overlook evidence that has the potential to prove our belief to be inaccurate.

Complaining vs. encouragement

You can be someone who looks for and complains about what they *don't* like — or you can be someone who looks for and encourages the things they *do* like. One of these things will nearly always leave you feeling better than the other.

You can wish that more people did a certain thing — or you can actively begin showing appreciation to those who already do that thing. And once again, one will nearly always leave you feeling better than the other.

The fact is, how we approach and seek to overcome problems can leave us feeling better or worse. Combating a negative situation with more negativity is rarely effective. But seeking ways to fight negativity in a positive and empowering way often is.

Encouraging the types of things and behaviors we want to see more of not only leaves us feeling more empowered than complaining does, it helps set a positive example for others to follow. This, in turn, helps to create more of the type of people and behaviors we want to see more of and less of the type of people and behaviors we don't.

Encouragement is extremely powerful in that it not only nurtures the people you give it to, it nurtures the very thing you are encouraging. And this, in turn, brings into the world more of what you would like to see.

And remember:

It's ok to show appreciation for things that you feel should be or are relatively common. People love recognition for the good things that they do.

- ✓ You can thank someone for returning their grocery cart to the carousel
- ✓ You can thank someone for cleaning up their mess in a public place
- ✓ You can thank someone for holding the door for someone else
- ✓ You can thank someone for any positive action you see them perform

Perception isn't always reality. Just because you think someone appears successful or isn't the type of person (or company) that could use positive feedback doesn't mean your assessment is accurate. When everyone assumes their feedback won't be significant to the people (or companies) they give it to, few people provide feedback. So instead of the perception that someone is being buried with praise, the opposite is true.

The point is, always take the time to show meaningful appreciation for the things that you like regardless of how "liked" you think they are.

We always miss what we don't pay attention to

Our entire lives are shaped by what we've experienced. And these experiences are shaped by what we've *paid attention to* — not by what we haven't. Whatever we choose to focus on in our lives is always at the expense of *not* being aware of something else that may be present, but isn't visible to us because we either aren't looking *at* it, aren't looking *for* it, or it isn't glaring enough to grab our attention.

This is how attention works. We find the kinds of things we're looking for because they are what we *pay attention to*. This is how two people can be in the same place at the same time and have two entirely different experiences. Our perception creates our reality.

This is an important concept to understand because, from the moment we are born, every experience we have in life provides us with information that either reaffirms something we already believe, alters a belief we already have, or creates a completely new belief.

The things we've paid attention to throughout our lives have helped create our beliefs because, unless we know we are being deceived, *we believe what we perceive*. But because what we perceive isn't always accurate, the beliefs we adopt aren't always a reflection of reality. And because who we are and how we act is a reflection of what we believe, when what we belief isn't accurate, it can have life-changing consequences.

By holding onto negative or false beliefs, one often denies themselves the possibility for positive change by limiting their ability to discover their delusions. Those who fall victim to self-limiting beliefs not only severely restrict what they're capable of achieving by mistakenly believing they're incapable of achieving it, they often hold onto their beliefs so strongly that they're incapable of being proved wrong.

"I could be wrong"

Remaining open to new views and information and evolving one's beliefs as a result of new experiences is essential to personal growth. One doesn't grow from what they already know.

The moment one is so certain that what they believe is true that they refuse to consider additional information is the moment they leave no room to learn that they're wrong. And if they're *not* wrong, they miss the opportunity to reaffirm that they're right.

Always remember that our beliefs are personal assumptions based on our *interpretation* of life experience. And our interpretations are not necessarily accurate or contain all the information required to come to an informed conclusion. Our brain is always telling us stories that help us make sense of what happens around us. And we readily believe these stories without verification. This is why as one journeys through life, it's important to consider alternatives and make an effort to see things from different angles.

Whether viewing things from different perspectives ultimately alters one's beliefs or not, it's a good mental exercise in maintaining an open mind and leaves one open to gaining knowledge beyond the perimeter of one's comfort zone.

The little things

Too many times — in the process of getting from where we are to where we want to be in life — we fail to linger on or even acknowledge positive moments of our journey. And, as a result, these moments pass without recognition and are quickly forgotten.

Because what we habitually direct our attention to in life — the good or the bad — has the power to shape our perception, it's important to be mindful of what we have a habit of paying attention to because what we *perceive* can have a dramatic effect on how we *feel*.

A great many people have a habit of dwelling on anything that's even remotely negative in their lives without ever giving equal time to the positives. For example, people are far more likely to disregard a compliment than they are a criticism. So while a compliment or act of kindness may be quickly forgotten, a criticism or act of aggression often is not — and because of the disproportionate amount of attention typically given to negative things, a person's perception of reality can become distorted.

Good things happen, but if a person doesn't acknowledge them when they *do*, the good things that happen fail to have an impact on that person, let alone remain in their memory.

To make matters worse, people are often inclined to discuss negative events — and the simple act of discussing something creates *another* memory which is then linked to the original.

If you wish to see more positives in your life, heighten your sensitivity to them by actively seeking evidence of their existence, acknowledge positives as they occur, and linger on them long enough to make a memory.

By consciously taking the time to dwell on the positive moments in our lives — no matter how small they may seem — we not only give the positive the attention it deserves, we add to our list of things to be grateful for.

Anytime *anyone* ever does something nice for you, is considerate to you, makes you laugh or smile, or otherwise just makes you feel good, always take an extra moment to acknowledge the gesture and highlight it in your mind.

And when you see signs of beauty, selflessness, and kindness in the world don't just disregard these things as meaningless moments on your way to where you want to be. Because life is far more about *the journey*, than it is about a destination.

By taking the time to dwell on the good things in your life, you change what would otherwise be fleeting, quickly forgotten moments into potentially long-lasting memories. Memories worth keeping.

Starting today, always make an effort to always dwell on the positive moments in your life. Because the more you do, the more likely you are to discover that the things that ultimately matter most to you in your life were there all along and you simply weren't paying attention.

Beacons of hope

With acts of unthinkable aggression and terror highlighted in the news at an alarming frequency, the world can sometimes seem like a dark place dominated by hostile people.

At times like this, it's important to remember that there are always far more people performing acts of love, acts of kindness, and acts of altruism in this world than those few who seek to disrupt it.

You may not always see them, but the world is full of countless individuals who perform positive deeds and add value to other people's lives without expectation or a desire for anything other than the satisfaction of knowing they made a positive difference when they were able to.

Remember these people when the news gets you down. Look for them when you can. And, most importantly, be one when *you* are able to.

It is by spreading your light that your actions become a beacon of hope and a source of inspiration for others in need of exactly what you have to offer.

Love. Not fear.

Refuse to let a non-stop cycle of negativity and bad news divert your attention from all the good that takes place around the globe on a daily basis. Remind yourself that the world is *not* just a stage for conflict no matter how much the media makes it out to be.

When the news makes you anxious and fills you with fear or xenophobia, remember your friends, your family, and the kindness of strangers. Make note of those doing good, seeking peace, acting selflessly, or going out of their way to make a positive difference in other people's lives.

Don't let the acts of *a few* contaminate your view of the whole. The vast majority of people all over the planet, regardless of their race, religious beliefs, political party, or skin color, would *much* rather make *friends* than enemies. And like you, they'd much rather live in peace than disharmony.

Refuse to be manipulated into thinking that the world is mostly made up of people seeking conflict or living their lives at the expense of others. Because it's *not*. Don't let the 24/7 coverage of bad news make you cold and hateful.

Remember that leading with love is far more effective than leading with fear — and that light extinguishes darkness in no way that darkness ever can.

The answer to the world's problems is not *less* love, it's more.

Beware blind optimism

Optimism is what allows a person to look at things in a positive light, regardless of the circumstances. It provides a person with the ability to face and adapt to reality in a positive way.

Blind optimism, on the other hand, involves ignoring facts and data in order to fool one's self in feeling better about one's circumstances.

Both *can* be effective depending on specific situations, but the nature of blind optimism makes it far more prone to problems. For example, ignoring health issues that progressively get worse by fooling yourself into thinking they are not that serious can be life threatening.

In addition to exacerbating a person's problems, blind optimism can leave one vulnerable to being exploited by others or knocked off balance when something they didn't see coming happens.

As such, optimism is a better choice because it allows a person to live with their eyes open and *acknowledge* what they can't control — while directing their attention to what they *can* — without pretending that the things they don't wish to see don't exist.

Always remember that by staying optimistic *without* putting blinders on, you give yourself the ability to direct your energy to where you want it to go, without losing sight of the bigger picture or remaining blind to things you could have avoided.

More to life

There's more to existence than most people experience. Another dimension. We're so busy paying attention to the clock, the TV, the internet, and our phones that we miss out on life as it happens. We're so busy rushing to get somewhere and so preoccupied with superficial thoughts and distractions that we miss a myriad of moments that *could* add value to our lives, but never do.

We miss the sound of leaves rustling in a breeze. Miss the sun sparkling off morning dew. Miss the scent of ozone in the air after a thundershower.

We miss the sparkle in the eyes of the person who holds the door for us. And the sound of sincerity in the voices of the people who give us a compliment.

We miss the signs of stress as it approaches. We miss how our muscles tighten when we think about what troubles us.

We miss how good our meals taste because we eat them in a hurry. And we miss how our body feels after we consume junk food.

We even miss the significance of our own internal dialogue, how it affects our mood, and how we let it run rampant with our thoughts, feelings, and emotions.

We let our minds wander so much that we are often mentally disconnected from our environment and life experience.

Few people ever actively take the time to just pause. To listen. To feel. To breathe. To use the full extent of their senses. And as a result of this, far too few in the world are actively aware of, or are fully immersed in, the experience of life.

By failing to be mindful of our thoughts, feelings, surroundings and senses, we miss out on an enormous number of potentially meaningful and magical moments in our lives. We miss out on much of the experience we call life and the true beauty that often goes unnoticed and unappreciated because we're not paying attention. Just taking a moment to truly tune in to the world around you in an intimate way is enough to help create new perspective, new insights, and to experience the interconnectedness of all things.

It's enough to realize that we are all playing background characters in each other's lives — and if we wish, we can not only play a larger role in those lives, we can choose what kind of impact we have.

It's enough to realize that we can have a positive influence on someone's day. That we can make a difference that ripples from one person to the next. And that there's more to life than what most choose to see.

If you wish to tap into another dimension of existence, remind yourself every now and then to take a moment and truly immerse yourself in life experience. Breathe slowly. Use all of your senses. And try to see the things that have escaped you because you weren't paying attention. Because there's more to life — and it can be amazing to experience — but it isn't coming to a TV, phone or computer screen near you.

So stop. Listen. Feel. Breathe. And be mindful. And when you finally do, you will be thankful that you did.

> *"It's not what you look at that matters, it's what you see."*
> *— Henry David Thoreau*

CHAPTER 8

PERSONAL RESPONSIBILITY

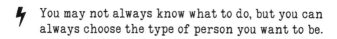

⚡ You may not always know what to do, but you can
always choose the type of person you want to be.

Life happens.

Life *happens*. Sometimes it's good. Sometimes it's bad. And sometimes it dumps a pile of shit in your path.

What matters is *not* whether life is fair (it often isn't). What matters is how one chooses to deal with it.

We can spend time complaining. We can spend time pointing the finger. We can spend time blaming others for the situations we find ourselves in. And we can learn to identify as a victim of the unfairness of life.

Or — we can take personal responsibility for our lives and use our ability to seek out more favorable options — including learning *how* to cope with life's challenges and push forward in spite of them.

How we deal with adversity is a *choice*.

Every single person on the planet is forced to deal with hardship and misfortune at one time or another. Sometimes it's because we make bad decisions. Sometimes it's because we tolerate things far longer than we should. Sometimes it's because we're in the wrong place at the wrong time. And sometimes we're simply thrust into situations we don't want to be a part of.

But that's life. *Challenges are inevitable.*

It's important to understand that one doesn't improve their life by complaining about the life that they live. One improves their life by taking steps to change it for the better. And often, the first step to changing one's life for the better is taking personal responsibility for it.

Taking personal responsibility means no longer blaming others for any and all aspects of your life. No longer complaining about the things that are holding you back. And no longer making excuses for why things are not the way you wish them to be.

It means taking action to change the things that you can, learning to recognize the things that you can't, and continually pushing forward towards the life that you want, regardless of the obstacles you encounter along the way.

Taking personal responsibility for one's life — and taking action to change it for the better — is *far* more effective and leads to *far* greater things than complaining about the way things are and doing nothing.

Because our lives are a direct reflection of our priorities, if we don't like where we are in life, we can change it by changing our priorities. Because when our priorities change, so too does our focus. And whatever we choose to focus on, we give energy to.

- ✓ Want to be healthier? Focus on your health.
- ✓ Want to be smarter? Focus on your education.
- ✓ Want to be a better person? Focus on self-improvement.
- ✓ Want to be more resilient? Challenge yourself.
- ✓ Want to get over your fears? Face them.

Complaining about, or making excuses for our lives doesn't do anything but perpetuate our problems — the same goes for when we blame others for our circumstances.

Always remember that if you want a better life, you must take personal responsibility for the life that you have while working for the life that you want. Because the fact is, no one else is going to do it for you.

The power of choice

Living life by choice and not by chance requires one to take personal responsibility for the decisions they make and the results they get as a consequence of those decisions.

If you want to get on the path towards a better life, you must decide that taking steps down that path is more important than the things that are keeping you from it.

You must no longer allow yourself to be held back by a lack of discipline, a lack of resources, a lack of motivation, or a lack of initiative. And you must no longer allow yourself to be held back by fear. Because — if you have the power to change something that is holding you back, and you don't, that's *a choice*, not a limitation.

If you have the power to seek something that may get you results and you decide not to, that's a choice. And if you focus on what you *can't* do in life rather than on what you *can*, that's also a choice.

Getting on a path towards a better tomorrow means refusing to use what other people do or don't do in your life as an excuse for a lack of progress. It means taking the lead of your life and committing yourself to the actions necessary to get results. And, most importantly, getting on the path towards a better tomorrow means learning to rely on yourself above all else.

Don't let other people — or a lack of action — be an excuse for the reason you aren't living the kind of life you desire.

 Just because you don't know how to do something doesn't mean it has to stay that way. You are in far more control of what you know than the excuses you use that keep you from knowing it.

Who is in charge?

There are many things in this world that you are not responsible for (and have no control over). Your general health, your diet, your education, your inner peace, and your attitude *are not among those things*. These things are a reflection of *choices* you make every day. And these choices are *your* responsibility.

Who is in charge of your life? **You** are.

You, and you alone, possess the key to getting everything you're capable of getting out of life, but in order to get it, you must take personal responsibility for your choices.

Patterns

The recurring themes and patterns in a person's life are far less likely to be the result of random chance than they are to be the result of consistent choices.

If the same kinds of things continue to happen in your life, it's important to understand that something you're doing is conducive to *allowing* those things to happen. As much as we may wish to deflect blame, we are at least partially responsible for the things that show up as patterns in our lives — even if we fail to see how or why.

Those who frequently declare their disapproval for drama, for example, fail to recognize that they are the consistent element in attracting, allowing, or initiating the very drama they say they don't want. The common component of the things that show up as patterns in a person's life is *the person*, not the things.

While we cannot control everything that happens to us in life, we *can* control how we respond to it — including avoiding certain situations we know have a tendency to lead to certain results.

Those with a victim mentality will often blame anyone but themselves for the situations, circumstances, and predicaments they find themselves in, without making a connection between the experiences they have and their role as a common component.

Patterns in a person's life are an indication of consistency on the part of the person experiencing them. By breaking the patterns of our behavior, we also break the patterns that our behavior leads to.

While bad things do happen at random to people, it's important to recognize that what we permit persists. By failing to make the changes necessary to disrupt or deter a series of negative experiences, we are at least partially responsible for creating and participating in the circumstances that allow the negative experiences to happen in the first place.

Taking personal responsibility for one's life means recognizing the ways in which we are responsible for both what we do and the experiences we have as a result.

 Being kind, considerate, generous, warm, tolerant, encouraging, positive, and polite is always a choice.

Change your priorities and you change your life

Rather than take responsibility for their lives and make a change, many choose to complain, blame forces beyond their control, say "that's just the way it is", or convince themselves that there's nothing they can do that they're not already doing.

And yet, these same people will often set up their priorities in a way that limit what they are capable of — and then they willingly *choose* to live that way out of habit or fear that any alternatives will be hard.

In order for a person to get from where they are to somewhere better, they must acknowledge and take personal responsibility for their priorities and the things that they're doing that are keeping them from moving forward.

Crossing paths with idiots

"I get so annoyed when people…"
"If this person [does something I don't like], I'm going to go ballistic!"

Often, when we think things like this, we not only set ourselves up to harbor negativity towards whatever it is that annoys us, we create personal triggers for future negative thoughts, feelings, and actions. And by doing so, we don't set ourselves up to handle situations in a positive or productive manner, we simply perpetuate the current dysfunctional way in which we deal with things.

"I get so annoyed when people…" is the kind of statement that not only creates the *expectation* that we will *feel* annoyed when

something we *expect* to annoy us occurs, we essentially give ourselves *permission* — in advance — to *be* annoyed when it happens.

When we expect to be annoyed, we put ourselves on a crash course to meet our negative expectation. It's a self-fulfilling prophecy. And in the worst cases, we perpetuate the problem by using our annoyance as an excuse to behave badly.

"If customer service doesn't give me the answer I want, I'm going to lose my shit."

But as justified as we may feel when we lose our cool, other people's actions are never an excuse to act badly. Losing one's self-control isn't a sign a strength, it's a sign of weakness. A person is *always* responsible for how they handle themselves, regardless of how angry, upset, or irritated they are.

Overriding automatic pilot

We often deal with situations on automatic pilot and forget that getting annoyed — or at least staying annoyed — is a choice. We don't have to let the bad behavior of others affect us as much as we often do.

Crossing paths with an idiot is not an excuse to also act like an idiot.

An obvious alternative to creating negative expectations is to create positive ones. Rather than give ourselves permission to act or feel badly, we can override our inclination to do so by preparing for a more productive response.

"The next time I encounter something that annoys me, I'm going to handle it in a positive way."

It's much easier to handle the negative situations we encounter in life when we expect — or better yet, train ourselves — to deal with them productively.

"Inner Peace begins the moment you choose not to allow another person or event to control your emotions." — *Unknown*

⚡ It is not uncommon for people to be at least partially responsible for the things in their life that they say they want to avoid. Learn to recognize behaviors that are leading to experiences you don't want to have.

"It makes me mad" vs. "I choose to get angry"

If you're the type of person to say, *"They (or it) made me angry."* consider the statement, *"I chose to get angry."* — because one statement seeks to blame *others* for how *you* chose to deal with something, while the other says *you* take personal responsibility for your actions.

The truth is, no one can *make* you do anything.

The person responsible for how you respond to something that happens to you is always *you*. It *isn't* the person who offended you, annoyed you, or made you angry — it's *you*. It's how you've learned to deal with situations, the permission you give yourself to react in a certain way, and the habit you have as a result.

Some people get angry or upset in some situations. Some don't. Some people yell. Some don't. Some people punch walls. Some don't. Some people get in their car and drive like a crazy person. Some don't. The difference between how one type of person and the other reacts to a situation isn't the *situation* they are responding to as much as *how* they *choose* to respond it.

Everyone has things that annoy or upset them, but *not* everyone allows those things to be a trigger for behaving badly. Some people were fortunate enough to have positive role models that left a lasting impression, others learned from their mistakes, and others made a persistent effort to break their bad habits and build good ones.

The sooner you take personal responsibility for how you respond to certain situations, the sooner you'll able to react to people and situations in a manner reflective of the person you *truly* want to be.

No one has as much control over how you choose to respond to what happens to you in life as you do.

 Behaviors are learned — sometimes unconsciously — and habits are formed as a result of those behaviors, If you don't like how you act in certain situations, create a new habit.

Punctuality

Consistently being on time is the product of proper planning, personal discipline, and a respect for other people's time. Making a *habit* of being late demonstrates *none* of these things and is often a sign of patchy priorities and selfishness.

Habitual lateness says, *"My time is more valuable than yours."*

Learn to be reliable and a person of integrity by adopting the discipline necessary to *be on time*.

Reliability

Being reliable and doing what you say you will do, and when you say you will do it, is one of the most important habits a person can get into.

People who can be consistently counted on to fulfill their personal and professional commitments will earn the respect and trust of others far faster, and more often, than those known to be unreliable.

Refuse to develop a reputation for being unreliable and inconsistent. Stick to your commitments. Be on time. And always do what you say you will do. Even the little things.

"If I were you..."

People will often offer advice to others with the best of intentions. And while some of those people may genuinely care a great deal about you — and may act as if they have your best interest in mind — never forget that no one has a more intimate understanding of your values, priorities, and desires more than *you* do.

Often, when people offer advice, they do so based on what *they* would or would not do, without recognizing the fact that sometimes the best thing for a person to do is *exactly* the thing they themselves would not. *Even if that thing leads to failure.*

Always remember that we learn more from our failures than we do from our successes. And even if one's endeavor ultimately ends in failure, it may be the journey they need to take in order to get them to where they ultimately want to be.

Yes, listen to advice and consider it, but don't let someone else's fears or personal experiences be the defining factor between whether you do whatever it is you truly want to do or not.

Yes, you *may* fail at whatever you attempt to do, but failure is a vital component of success. The lessons you learn from your failures are frequently what you need to ultimately be successful in some area of your life.

If you don't go after what you truly want in life, you'll *never* get it. End of story. And if you *do* go after what you truly want, you will either succeed or you will fail. But if you fail, the knowledge you gain will often be a key component to helping you achieve success somewhere else.

CHAPTER 9

SELF-DISCIPLINE

⚡ Self–discipline is a key to many doors. Not least of which is one that leads to a better, stronger, and healthier version of yourself.

Self-discipline

Your ability to listen to, and take action, based on your inner voice — regardless of how you feel, other influences, or temptations you face — is the key to self-mastery.

When you increase (or decrease) your discipline in *one* area, it increases (or decreases) your discipline in *all* areas that require self-control.

Like a muscle, the more you exercise self-control on a consistent basis, the stronger you get. As your self-control increases, the more you gain the ability to direct your life in a manner that is congruent with the true you. The more congruent your actions are with your thoughts and feelings, the better you feel about yourself and the decisions you make. Every time you feel good about a decision you make, it raises your self-esteem and your self-confidence. You also reinforce in your mind what you are capable of and it makes it less difficult to make similar decisions in life.

Self-discipline and change

One of the more potent approaches to making long-lasting positive changes to one's life is to do so in a manner that doesn't leave one feeling completely overwhelmed by change.

Because of the way willpower works, when a person tries to initiate several challenging changes in their life at once, a failure of willpower at one new change often leads to a chain reaction that disrupts or even halts efforts in all other new changes.

Rather than initiate several major changes in your life at once, consider focusing on just one task, one decision, or one action at a time. By tackling only one major goal at a time, you give yourself the opportunity to develop and maintain the discipline needed to accomplish that goal. And when you're ultimately successful, that success provides you with the confidence and motivation to help you take on and achieve another challenging goal.

Self-discipline is most effectively built by tackling ever-increasingly difficult tasks, *not* by tackling several new tasks at the same time.

 One of the biggest steps to gaining control over one's life is gaining control over one's self.

Fuel your own fire

While inspirational quotes, self-help books, and motivational speakers can be an effective way to temporarily set fire to our desire to achieve, these fires are often quick to burn out because these things live outside of us.

When a person's motivation is dependent on external sources, the moment those sources are absent is the moment that person's motivation begins to fade. This is because motivation is a state of mind. And if a particular state of a person's mind is dependent on the availability of a fuel it doesn't always have control over, it can be difficult to attain the state of mind that runs on that kind of fuel when it isn't available.

This is why it's important to learn how to develop the mental discipline necessary to be the source of one's own motivation. When a person is able to motivate themselves, they create an unlimited source of fuel that can keep their fire lit indefinitely.

This isn't to say it's easy. It's only to say that fueling one's fire from within is something worth aspiring to. In the meantime, use whatever you can whenever you need to motivate yourself, but always keep in mind that once you are able to truly motivate yourself with the power of your own thoughts, you'll never have to be dependent on anything or anyone else to do it.

When you want what you want badly enough, not only will no one be able to motivate you more than you can motivate yourself, no amount of rejection, no amount of criticism, and no one other than you will be able to deter you from what you want to achieve.

Self-control and anger

Displays of patience, tolerance, and emotional stability during conflict are often indicative of self-control, while unbridled displays of anger represent a lack of it. Yet, due to the average person's aversion to conflict, outbursts of anger by others can sometimes be mistaken for displays of strength.

But uncontrolled acts of aggression are often the result of a person's inability to control their anger. And if a person cannot properly manage their emotions, a display of uncontrolled aggression, no matter how intimidating it may seem, isn't proof of power, it's a sign of weakness.

In the hands of someone with mental discipline and emotional stability, an opponent's unrestrained anger and aggression can be — and often is — used against them.

If you truly want to not only *appear* strong, but *be* strong, always remember that being able to control oneself during conflicts is an important part of the process.

"The best fighter is never angry." — Lao Tzu

The self-made prison

Sometimes, and with the best of intentions, we create personal rules for ourselves that we choose to live by. And sometimes these rules end up limiting our ability to fully experience life.

One can get so entrenched in a particular set of rules they create for themselves that they fail to see when those rules stop serving them. People will sometimes choose to suffer the consequences of their rules instead of breaking them in a way that would actually provide a positive life experience. Doing this is like building a cage with an open door, but refusing to ever walk through it.

Never forget that while the rules we create for ourselves are done so with a purpose and with the best of intentions, there will be times that making an exception is actually for one's greater good and not a cop out or a sign of weakness.

You are here to live life. Don't limit yourself from having positive and beneficial experiences because you are not willing to make an exception to a rule that you are responsible for creating in the first place.

Weaknesses

Knowing what your weaknesses are is a major step towards gaining power over various aspects of your life that may often seem beyond your control.

Whether your weaknesses are exploited by others or are simply ways in which you unwittingly sabotage your ambitions, your relationships or yourself, your weaknesses will continue to have power over you until you gain power over them.

Many of a person's weaknesses are disguised as bad habits. They manifest themselves in actions that are often performed without thinking. The good news is that because they're habits, they can, over time, be replaced with better behaviors.

While bad habits can be difficult to break, if you plan on living a long, healthy, and prosperous life, you owe it to yourself to make a conscious effort to improve the things in your life that you have the power to change.

When you make improving yourself in meaningful ways a priority in your life, you not only improve *your* life as a result of those priorities, you begin to make a positive difference in the lives of those around you. Because — *good behavior inspires good behavior.*

What are your weaknesses?

What are the things you do without thinking that are having a negative impact on your life, your health, your career, or your relationships?

If you've never considered this question, you not only leave yourself open to self-defeating behaviors, you leave yourself vulnerable to being exploited by others. Because when people know or anticipate your weaknesses, they can use them against you.

Take a moment to consider anything that causes you to act in a manner that is contrary to the person you want to be and know that the more you are able to gain control over these things, the more control you will gain over yourself, and in turn, your life.

Common self-defeating behaviors:

Quick to anger	Apathy
Easily frustrated	Vanity
Feelings of self-pity	Insecurity
Low self-esteem	Selfishness
Oversensitive	Bigoted views
Lack of self-awareness	Feelings of superiority
Lack of self-discipline	An inflated sense of
Lack of knowledge	importance
Lack of motivation	Poor social skills
Lack of focus	Habitual quitting

The leaky boat

How well a person does in life depends a great deal on how well they can handle and navigate less than desirable circumstances. To illustrate this, I want you to imagine a boat floating on an ocean.

You are the captain of this boat. And the ocean, in this case, represents your life.

With the proper skills, attitude, and approach you can navigate to wherever you wish to go on this ocean. But how quickly and easily you get to your desired destinations depends not only on how efficiently you operate — and how resilient you are to challenges you encounter along the way — it depends on the overall integrity of your vessel.

Now, imagine for a moment that this boat has holes in its hull. And these holes are the source of leaks that cause it to take on water. The holes in this boat represent your weaknesses.

Now, under normal circumstances — and if the holes are small — one can bail out water quickly and easily enough to keep their boat comfortably afloat. But since it takes more time and energy to manage a boat with a leaky hull than it does to manage one *without* a leaky hull, the ideal approach to leaks is to locate and plug as many of them as possible. Because the more leaks that one can plug, the greater the integrity of the vessel and the more efficiently it operates.

In other words, identifying one's weaknesses and then working on ways to overcome those weaknesses not only makes one stronger and more resilient to challenges, it makes one's life more manageable. The less that one is forced to expend energy compensating for their weaknesses, the more efficiently they can set goals, overcome obstacles, and ultimately succeed.

On the flip side, if the leaks in one's boat become too prevalent — perhaps while navigating a stormy sea — one's vessel will take on water faster than one can bail it out. And the energy that *could* be spent moving forward in a storm is, instead, spent dealing with the consequences of a leaky hull.

Now, whether we're talking about leaks in boats or personal weaknesses, not being able to manage them effectively can lead to feelings of being overwhelmed or helpless or depressed. And these feelings can have serious consequences on how well a person is able to do just about *anything*, not just deal with challenges.

The more that a person can identify their weaknesses, triggers, and bad habits, the more they can take steps to reduce the impact that their weaknesses have on their life. And the more that a person reduces the impact of their weaknesses, the more energy they're able to devote to directing their life where they want it to go.

If you can't stamp out your weaknesses, at least find ways to minimize them as much as possible. Because it's far better to deal with something when you *have a choice* than it is to be forced to deal with the consequences of that thing when you don't.

Remove temptations

Willpower is finite and how much anyone has of it at any given time can vary depending on a number of factors.

Recognizing the limits of one's self-control and learning to avoid the things that tempt it can be the determining factor between whether a person achieves what they set out to do or not.

Always make the things that tempt you in your life as inconvenient as possible to access (or non-existent) when a loss of self-control can mean the difference between success and failure.

Acknowledge and move on

No matter how often our minds redirect our attention to problems or self-defeating thoughts, not every problem we have can be solved when it comes to mind. By recognizing this fact, it allows us to acknowledge problems and let them pass rather than give them prolonged attention at times when we are either unable or unwilling to address them.

To repetitively revisit negative and self-defeating thoughts puts us in a state of mental weakness that makes solving problems far more difficult and unlikely than when we attempt to do so from a place of empowerment.

By developing the mental discipline necessary to direct your attention where you want it to go, you gain the ability to take action on things from a mental state able to address issues effectively rather than being forced to whenever they come to mind.

Learn to acknowledge and move on from thoughts that don't serve you.

Decisions, decisions

Making decisions and acting quickly can be beneficial, but always be mindful of times when waiting may be better. People are far more likely to regret decisions they've made when they're tired, unhappy, angry, hungry or otherwise emotional.

Always keep in mind that not everything needs to be decided the moment a choice is presented — and often, waiting can provide additional information, experience, or an emotional state that can help you make better decisions.

Painting the canvas of life

If one's life is a canvas, a person's thoughts are what they paint with and their actions are brush strokes.

It is the skill with which one is able to choose their paint and the manner in which they apply their brush strokes that determines whether they end up with a masterpiece or not.

CHAPTER 10 A

PERSONAL GOALS

"Man is a goal-seeking animal. His life only has meaning if he is reaching out and striving for his goals."

— Aristotle

⚡ Don't sacrifice the kind of life and health you truly desire by catering to your short-term comfort over your long-term goals.

What's your target?

While it is good to be open and flexible in life, having a plan (not to be confused with your life purpose) will provide you with a specific target to aim for.

Knowing where you want to go in life helps you determine what and which kinds of life experiences are relevant and beneficial in getting you from where you are to where you want to be.

When a person doesn't know where they want to go in life, one sign is just as important as any other. But when a person has a direction in mind, it's much easier to differentiate the signs that matter from those that don't.

What can you do? (Not everything)

Contrary to what many may say, clichés suggesting that "you can do *anything* you set your mind to" simply *aren't true*.
It is simply a fact of life that not *everyone* has everything it takes to achieve every lofty goal they set out to accomplish in life.

Some things are physically impossible for *some* people to accomplish, other things rely more on luck than skill, and yet others are so rare in nature that it simply isn't possible for more than one person to do. For example, not everyone who participates in the Olympics wins a gold medal.

No matter what your goals may be, it's important to consider the things that are *within* your control as you attempt to achieve them. If too many aspects of what you wish to accomplish are *beyond* your control, it's possible that you could do everything required to achieve your goal and still not achieve it because the things that were beyond your control never happened.

This *doesn't* mean you *shouldn't* set lofty goals and attempt to achieve them. Nor does it mean that every goal you set has to be realistic according to other people's standards. But it *does* mean that your goals must fall within the realm of what's possible for *you*.

For example: It isn't entirely *realistic* to think you can become an A-list actor, but that *doesn't* mean it's *impossible*. It simply means it is highly *improbable* and you'll be working against tremendous odds to make it happen.

It is one thing to know what you want to do is highly improbable — and *attempting to do it anyway*. It is another thing altogether to sacrifice time, resources, and energy into something that is *actually* impossible.

Whatever it is that you wish to do, no matter how improbable it may be, you have to truly believe it's possible. Otherwise, you are simply relying on luck and wishful thinking to achieve your goals — neither of which are a reliable foundation upon which one's success should rest.

While you may not be able to do the impossible, you as much as anyone have it within you to do the improbable, but you must commit yourself to the task, take consistent steps to achieve it, overcome obstacles along the way, and never give up.

It's your life and your path — keep going

Always remember to keep your eyes on your goals and the steps you can take to achieve them. Focus less on what you don't have or what you can't do or what others are doing.

Yes, it can be difficult not noticing what others are up to or how easy some people seem to have it or how successful they appear. Just know, perception isn't always reality. And if you do notice others, then use what you see as motivation to push forward.

Remember, you're living *your* life and walking *your own path*, not someone else's. Just because someone else is making progress towards their goals is no reason for you to stop making progress towards your own.

Change your strategy if you have to and take time to rest if you must, but don't stop. Every little step you take towards your goals is progress. Keep going.

The time to take action (is now)

Far too many people have far too many reasons for waiting to take steps towards their goals. The consequences of perpetually putting off working towards the things you want to do in life is that you sacrifice any progress you could be making in the meantime.

It is important to remember that even if conditions are not ideal, every little step you take towards a goal — no matter how small — is progress. And from progress comes results.

There is always far more to be gained from taking action and working towards your goals than there is in waiting until conditions are ideal (which they rarely are).

The fact is — while you are still waiting to find an easy way — or a perfect time — someone else is already getting results because they decided making progress is more important than making excuses.

Stop waiting for things to get easier. Stop waiting for the perfect time. Stop focusing on what you can't do and start focusing on what you can.

The time to take action and work toward your goals is *now*.

Enjoy the process

What's important with regard to setting goals is that you not only find enjoyment in the process of achieving them, you don't let your happiness in life be dependent on their fulfillment.

We won't achieve every goal we set out to accomplish in life, but if we enjoy the process — rather than let our happiness be entirely dependent on our success in an endeavor — then the failure to achieve something will never keep us from being happy. Yes, we may be disappointed in our failing, but because we enjoyed the process, we know that we can easily set another goal or simply try again.

Even when we fail, there are inherent benefits in the act of consistently and persistently putting in the effort necessary to achieve a lofty goal, regardless of whether one is *ultimately* able to achieve it or not. For it is from the struggles in life — not the attainment of one's desires — that a person acquires strength. And it is from our mistakes and failures that we learn the most important lessons of our lives.

It may just be that in the effort to chase your lofty goals, you are presented with opportunities that are far more suited to who you are, who you've become, or what you ultimately want to do than the original thing you set out to accomplish.

One of the most rewarding things you can do in the attempt of achieving anything you wish to do is learn to enjoy the process.

Know what you want

While it has been said that discipline is just choosing between what you want *now* and what you want *most*, knowing exactly what you want and *why* you want it can be just as vital to the accomplishment of your goals as the discipline necessary to achieve them.

Without a strong and genuine internal desire to accomplish a very specific goal, it can be difficult to not only do what is necessary to achieve that goal, it can be difficult to simply find the motivation to get started.

Before you start any potentially difficult endeavor, have a *very clear* understanding of *what* you want, *why* you want it, what you are going to *do* to go about getting it, and what you will do if challenges and obstacles arise (this isn't to say you will know *how* to deal with challenges before they arrive, only that you will be mentally prepared to face them).

Knowing exactly *what* you want gives you something to aim for. Knowing *why* you want it provides motivation to help you achieve it. Knowing what you are going to *do* to get it provides you with steps to take. And being *prepared* to face obstacles along the way helps provide you with the kind of attitude needed to overcome them.

 Your world will change dramatically when you stop focusing on what you can't do and start focusing on what you can.

Anticipate potential pitfalls

With every lofty goal you set for yourself, always take the time to identify potential pitfalls along the way and seek ways to resist their negative effects.

Always keep in mind that it's not the challenges we *expect* on a journey that force us to face self-doubt as much as it's those we never see coming. Learn to expect the unexpected and don't be deterred by it.

By learning to expect the unexpected, you can reduce the negative effects that challenges have on your resolve to push forward toward your goals.

Heed your habits

The habits we harbor can have a dramatic effect on the outcome of our endeavors by overriding our desire to achieve our goals and sabotaging our efforts to achieve them.

Despite a desire to make positive changes to our lives, when faced with the discomfort of challenges or change, we often run back to the routines we are most familiar with as a coping mechanism. Even if those routines have proven to not be in our best interest (which is often why we're trying to change them).

On the way to achieving our goals, it's important to not just be *aware* of our tendency to slide back into old habits, it's important to develop the discipline necessary to avoid doing so.

As you proceed down the path towards accomplishment, always keep your long-term goals in mind, always focus on the progress you've made, and always remember why you want to succeed at whatever it is you wish to do.

Patience, persistence, and discipline

Remember to be patient and think long-term on the way to your goals. Resist the urge to seek shortcuts or instant gratification. Know that what you want *most* is often far more important than what you want in a moment of temptation — especially after the temptation for instant gratification passes.

Understand that, whatever your goals may be, even small actions can make a huge difference when repeated with consistency and performed with a persistent focus. By consistently concentrating your efforts and doing what you can with what you have, you can prevail over many of the biggest obstacles standing between you and your goals. But doing this means being patient, thinking long-term, and not suffering unnecessary setbacks due to caving in to instant gratification or trying to do too many things at the same time.

Do it for yourself

Be very careful about attaching aspects of your personal goals to anything you don't have control over — such as other people. Not only can someone else's actions (or lack thereof) sabotage your efforts to achieve, it's possible to invest a great deal of time and energy into working for a result you have no control over.

People are unpredictable. Don't fall into the trap of trying to manipulate others by accomplishing goals and hoping your achievement changes their behavior in a way you want it to.

While things you do may influence or even inspire others, you can never be guaranteed that the results of your actions will cause other people to behave in a particular way. If you're going to do something, do it for the changes it leads to in *you* — and to a larger degree, your life.

CHAPTER 10 B

SETBACKS AND SELF-DOUBT

"Our greatest glory is not in never failing, but in rising up every time we fail." — Ralph Waldo Emerson

The path to success isn't a straight line

Don't stop working towards a goal just because the path to it isn't as direct or as easy as you hoped it would be. It is often the lessons a person learns on their journey that are exactly what they need to complete it.

As a general rule, *there are no shortcuts to success worth taking* because the strength needed to achieve difficult goals is developed from the effort put forth to complete them. The *struggle* to be successful is often a vital component of success itself. So be patient, be consistent, and keep working towards your goals.

And never underestimate the power of small victories and consistency, because with consistency, *small* victories become *big* victories.

Difficult goals & self-doubt

If you create goals with confidence, but sometimes suffer from self-doubt on the journey to achieve them, realize that it's a sign that you're on the *right* track, *not* the wrong one. Because if your aspirations don't push you beyond your comfort zone, you're not getting anywhere close to maximizing your potential.

The most worthwhile and rewarding goals in your life will be mountains, not molehills. And as you work towards achieving them, these goals will not only force you to face challenges you expected when you set them, they'll force you to overcome obstacles you never anticipated when you started.

This is the challenge of worthy goals. They are often more difficult than we imagine for reasons we cannot anticipate. And this disconnect between what we expect and what we actually get is an incubator for self-doubt.

Whenever self-doubt strikes on your journey, remind yourself why you started and focus on your progress and your victories, no matter how small they may be. Focus on the knowledge you've gained and the new insights you can convert into wisdom. And accept setbacks and self-doubt as a natural part of your journey on the way to achieving your goals.

Remember, you didn't pick your goal because you knew it would be easy, you picked it knowing it would be hard but worthwhile.

Unacknowledged progress is still progress

On the way to completing any lofty goal, it's very easy for goal-seekers to trivialize their efforts, disregard their accomplishments, or be blind to any progress they've made. People doing extraordinary things can sometimes be so struck by their struggles that they fail to give themselves credit for what they've done.

Always keep in mind that just because you fail to see the value in what you've done doesn't mean it *isn't* of value — particularly if you receive feedback telling you that it *is*.

Whether it's because of unrealistic expectations, self-doubt, or disappointment, sometimes we're simply in the wrong frame of mind to see the progress we've made, but just because we're unable to *see* our progress doesn't mean it doesn't exist.

Always be mindful of the fact that there is always more involved with your ultimate success than what you can possibly see or be aware of at any given moment — especially when you are feeling discouraged or disappointed.

It is not the results you see from one day to the next that matter as much as the progress you make *over time*. And if you are consistent with your actions, you *will* see progress. And even if you fail to acknowledge the progress you've made, it's *still* progress.

Life is not a competition

Never give up on what *you* desire in life just because someone else appears to have an easier time getting what *they* desire or is making progress more quickly than you are. Remind yourself as necessary that life is not a competition and that some people will always make progress more quickly than others. That's life.

But your life, your circumstances, and your goals are your own. Don't let the simple fact that others are working on and achieving their goals deter you from working on and achieving your own.

Doubters, detractors, and haters

Anyone who ever attempts to achieve lofty goals in life will nearly always have to deal with people who try to deter them from achieving them.

Whether one encounters true haters or simply well-meaning people offering what they consider to be reasonable play-it-safe advice, it may be helpful to know that the most vocal doubters and detractors of other people's dreams are often those who don't have the confidence, attitude, or tenacity necessary to achieve their own.

It's not *achievers* who spend their time trying to talk others out of accomplishing their goals. More often than not, it's those who gave up on going after their own.

People who repeatedly set lofty goals and struggle to achieve them are often the most vocal cheerleaders for others who wish to do the same. Because anyone who has ever struggled to achieve anything great *knows* that the journey to accomplish worthy goals is often fraught with hardship. Achievers know from experience that great tasks often appear improbable — or even impossible — before completion.

Don't waste your time worrying about the doubters who don't believe in what you're working to achieve. And disregard those who find it necessary to point out your mistakes or failures without offering constructive feedback.

Refuse to engage with people who seek to scare you from your chosen path by pointing out all of the things that could go wrong along the way. And resist the urge to repeatedly explain your goals to those who refuse to understand them. You don't need the permission, approval, or understanding of others to achieve great things.

In the course of the journey to reach your goal, always consider the source of advice or criticism. Those who know what it means to set lofty goals and struggle to achieve them are far more likely to offer sage advice than those who don't.

And whenever you find yourself in doubt, consult your inner voice, not your inner demons. Your inner voice knows what you *truly* desire. Your inner demons exist solely to talk you out of it.

> *"Whatever course you decide upon, there is always someone to tell you that you are wrong. There are always difficulties arising which tempt you to believe that your critics are right. To map out a course of action and follow it to an end requires courage." — Ralph Waldo Emerson*

The "what's the point?" wall

In the process of achieving any lofty goal, there will be periods of time in which you feel disappointed, exhausted, overwhelmed, or overcome by self-doubt. At times like this, a dissenting voice in your head will often entice you with the idea that giving up is your best option. When it does, it is important to be mindful of the fact that that voice is often a liar.

This is *not* to say that you should never consider whether it is truly in your best interest to continue on the path you've chosen towards a lofty goal, it is simply to say if you ever choose to quit, you should do so when you are in an emotionally stable state and able to make rational and unbiased decisions.

It's better to take the time to let negative feelings subside than it is to give into them and quit when you still have a chance to finish what you started without having to start all over again at some future time (or worse, never).

Never give the dissenting voice in your head the power to make important decisions when it isn't counterbalanced by the rational part of your brain.

Focus on progress over problems

There will be occasions on which you simply won't have the time, energy, resources, or attitude necessary to break through a wall — or overcome a challenge — on the way to completing your goals. If that is ever the case, always remember that you don't have to overcome every challenge you encounter in the order it is presented to you.

It is frequently far more rewarding to focus on being productive in *some other area* of your life than it is to allow yourself to be overcome by frustration or self-doubt in attempting to solve a problem without the proper tools or mindset needed to solve it. Often, the path to one's goals isn't linear, it's a root with many branches. On many occasions, the answer to problems in one area of your life will come as a result of making progress somewhere else. Refuse to waste time being deterred by something you *can't* do and focus on something else that you *can*. Sometimes the rewards for your efforts on one path will help provide you with what you need to go down another.

Long-term thinking

Many people make the unfortunate mistake of giving up on their goals because they don't achieve them as quickly as they hoped or expected to. Sometimes the most significant thing you can do on the way to reaching your goals is to simply outlast your feelings of failure or disappointment and to keep pushing forward regardless of the time it takes to achieve what you set out to accomplish.

Learning to think long-term can often be the defining factor between success and failure.

CHAPTER 11

LIVING BEYOND COMFORT

"Verily the lust for comfort murders the passion of the soul, and then walks grinning in the funeral."
— *Khalil Gibran*

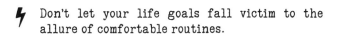 Don't let your life goals fall victim to the allure of comfortable routines.

The impediment of progress

Whether it's a skill we fail to get better at or a period of time in which opportunities appear non-existent, everyone's lives are occasionally punctuated with plateaus upon which little appears to happen.

Whenever one reaches a plateau in life, it's important to remember that *the impediment of progress is comfort*. Too much comfort can cause a lack of ambition, a fear of the unfamiliar, and an aversion to anything that sounds like work.

While establishing routines is often effective in helping people to advance toward their goals, whenever a person grows overly comfortable with a routine — or proficiency in a skill — it means they are no longer pushing the boundary of their comfort zone.

Because one doesn't grow from their comfort zone, a lack of challenges in various parts of a person's life is what impedes their ability to "level up" in those areas. Reaching a plateau in life is simply a sign that in order for things to advance to the next level, either *you* or something you're doing must change. It is the introduction of changes and challenges into one's life and routines that triggers growth.

If you want to continually level up in life, it's important to never grow so comfortable that you stop challenging yourself to make progress. Always remember that true excellence exists beyond the realm of where most people stop trying.

"Good enough" is a graveyard on the path to excellence.

Discomfort and growth

Dealing with discomfort, fear, and situations we don't want to be in — or situations that we are completely unfamiliar with — is an absolutely essential part of growth.

Who we are is a result of everything we've had to overcome in life and the attitude we chose to adopt during — or as a result of — challenges we've faced along the way.

We may not be able to choose or even like the challenges that life puts in our path, but we can always choose our attitude towards them.

You can choose to look at difficulties as disruptive and something to dread or you can look at them as opportunities for growth and self-improvement. Because you can't have growth without some degree of discomfort. Difficulties and discomfort are simply one side of a coin while opportunities for growth are the other.

 You don't get over the fear of doing something by not doing it.

Strength from discomfort

A world that continually caters to making people more and more comfortable creates a world full of people who are less and less capable of coping with — and being open to — even the slightest discomfort or inconvenience.

Not having enough whipped cream on your frozen blended coffee beverage is not a *real* problem. Having to wait in line is not a *real* problem. And being bored is not a *real* problem.

Being on fire is a *real problem*. And not having enough food to eat or a roof over your head, is a *real problem*.

The above inconveniences are simply *symptoms* of a problem. And the problem is that we should all be able to easily and effectively deal with minor inconveniences and discomfort without them turning into some kind of negative "event" in our lives.

The fact is, there will always be inclement weather, flight delays, long lines, loud neighbors, bumps in roads, and rule breakers. It would be impossible to eradicate all of the things that challenge or annoy us in life.

It is far more effective to teach people to be able to deal with the challenges of life than it is to attempt to remove them all.

Yes, making life easier and more comfortable for others is a worthy goal, but we should also work on being stronger and helping others be stronger — not continually catering to a low tolerance for discomfort. The real world doesn't go away just because we dress it up to look like something else. All that does is alienate us from what's real and lessens our ability to effectively deal with the inevitable challenges we all must face in life.

It's not that we should wish to eliminate all challenges from our lives, but instead focus on developing the strength, discipline, and attitude necessary to effectively deal with each and every one that we encounter.

 Courage doesn't come from your comfort zone because courage doesn't exist without fear.

Life isn't always easy

Life isn't always easy — but it helps if you remember that it is by overcoming obstacles that one develops new skills and new ways of handling what the rest of your life has in store for you. If you'd never had a problem in your life, you wouldn't be very able to deal with — well, *life*, would you?

Overcoming overwhelmed

Whenever you feel overwhelmed and doubt your strength, resolve, or ability to survive a hardship — or overcome a challenge in life — always take a moment to remember how many challenges you've *already* faced on your journey and how far you've come.

Remember that stress is caused by trying to have power over things that are beyond your control. And remember to focus on what you *can* do, not on what you *can't*.

And breathe.

Every obstacle we encounter and learn from in life helps provide us with the knowledge and strength necessary to handle whatever comes next. In the same way that we don't build muscles if we don't use them, we don't develop the strength to overcome obstacles while living in our comfort zone. As such, encountering and working through problems is an absolutely *essential* part of life.

Reducing fear

The more we truly understand something that causes us fear, the less power our fear of that thing tends to have over us.

Ignorance breeds fear. Familiarity reduces it.

If you want to reduce the amount of fear in your life, educating and familiarizing yourself with the subject of those fears is far more effective than remaining willfully ignorant.

The unexpected

It isn't what we're *prepared* for that has as significant impact on our growth as what we're forced to face when we're not expecting it.

Adventure starts where *plans end.*

 `We never learn what hidden gems lay along the paths we fear - or are too lazy - to take.`

CHAPTER 12

CONFIDENCE & CRITICISM

⚡ When you truly know who you are – and who you are in the process of becoming – you will no longer live in fear of what people say or think about you.

Keys to self-confidence

One of the keys to self-confidence is recognizing those things that make you feel vulnerable or self-conscious and then accepting them. Because when you accept yourself for who you are — flaws and all — you leave people far less capable of adversely affecting your sense of self-worth.

One of the byproducts of a stable sense of self-worth is self-confidence.

Take the time to get to know yourself. Learn to know the difference between what you can change about yourself and what you can't.

Understand that you are a work-in-progress and that the things about yourself that you have power over — such as your attitude, diet, fitness, habits, and skills — can and will change for the better over time if you work on them. And the things that you have no power over are not worth concerning yourself with for exactly that reason. So it is far more productive to accept them. Albert Einstein once said, *"Once we accept our limits, we go beyond them."* The same could be said of our flaws and imperfections.

Regardless of where you are on your journey, accept yourself as you are at this time. When you finally do, you will likely discover not only how good it feels to be *real*, but that you are now far less vulnerable — or completely impervious — to what other people think or say about you. And with that comes a kind of confidence that can never be taken from you.

Personal power vs. other people's opinions

A person who believes in themselves disconnects from the need for positive feedback or approval from others and doesn't allow themselves to be manipulated by people's opinions into behaving in a way that isn't an authentic expression of who they are or who they want to be.

By disconnecting from the need for approval, one becomes the source of their own strength, self-worth, and encouragement and, as a result, is much better suited to dealing with life's challenges. Because when a person's personal power emanates from within, they create a sort of shield against those who may challenge or criticize them along the way to accomplishing whatever it is they wish to do in life.

While it's important to be receptive to feedback in life, it's equally important to not let the questions, comments, criticism, and doubts of others deter you from expressing your authentic self or going after what you truly desire.

Carefully considering sage advice from experienced individuals is one thing — and it can enhance one's ability to be effective on their journey. Anchoring your effectiveness to the passing opinions of people who will ultimately have very little or nothing to do with your life —or the outcome of your endeavors — is another.

When a person puts too much weight in the opinions of others — particularly negative opinions — they often leave themselves, their effectiveness, and their goals completely vulnerable to people whose *only* significance in their lives is that they made judgements or offered criticism for no other reason than because they *could*. *Not* because they carefully considered what they had to say or how it might affect the person they said it to. *Not* because they had any investment in the outcome. And *not* because they genuinely cared one way or the other. But simply because they took the opportunity to express themselves.

When a person's personal power is anchored to other people's opinions, they leave themselves — and by a larger degree, their life — susceptible to being influenced in undesirable ways.

Always remember that a person's personal power and effectiveness is increased or decreased by what they believe. When a person truly believes in themselves and what they wish to achieve, they become the primary source of their power and in doing so, they maximize their potential to handle whatever life throws their way.

Being liked

While some people are naturally more likable than others, it is a fact of life that no matter how nice, how giving, or how generous you are, not everyone who crosses your path is going to like you. Not being liked by every single person on the planet is *normal*. Some people will just naturally "get you", others won't.

That's life.

It may help to remember that some of the most loved, most admired, and most respected people in history actually made history because they were bold and often thought or acted contrary to popular belief at the time. They had *more* than their fair share of critics, but refused to let that deter them from accomplishing great things.

If you want to self-actualize (reach your fullest potential), then you must learn to accept yourself for who you are and who you want to be and take personal responsibility for your life and how you feel. And along the way to self-actualization, you must be prepared to be unpopular. Don't leave your sense of worth and well-being in the hands of others.

Those who achieve greatness in life don't let others dictate how they feel about themselves — and neither should you. So if you're doing the best you can, and you still have your critics, remember to put your focus on where it belongs — on your greater mission and on the people who want you in their life, not on those who don't.

 Self-confidence is a byproduct of a stable sense of self-worth. A stable sense of self-worth is a byproduct of self-acceptance. If you wish to be more self-confident, learn to accept yourself as you are.

Why likability matters

While one shouldn't change who they are to be liked by everyone, being likable matters because a person's potential is either increased or decreased by how likable they are.

Being able to connect with others is not only an integral part of success, the relationships a person forms in life have a direct impact on their health, wealth, and general level of happiness. Likable people get more positive attention and gain more support, trust, and access to resources than those who are unable to connect with people in a positive way.

While universal appeal is impossible, the more likable a person is considered to be, the greater the effects of that person's likability has on their life.

Key characteristics of likable people include:

- ✓ Authenticity
- ✓ Team players
- ✓ Personal integrity
- ✓ Confidence and humility
- ✓ Compassion and empathy
- ✓ A positive mental attitude
- ✓ A respect for one's self and others
- ✓ Add value to other people's lives
- ✓ The capacity to connect with others in a meaningful way
- ✓ Able to communicate effectively verbally and non-verbally
- ✓ The ability to see things from other people's points of view

Rejection

Rejection is neither an indication of value or talent. Remember that. If you believe in what you have to offer, then don't stop offering it simply because some of those you offer it to reject it. Many people are simply not very good at recognizing talent or value. It doesn't mean you won't eventually find someone that will.

Refuse to let other people — *or the voice in your head* — deter you from the greatness within you.

Dealing with disapproval

Always keep in mind that, in most circumstances, another person's thoughts or opinions will generally have absolutely no impact on your life unless you choose to let them.

So long as you spend your time being the best person that you can be, there's no need to concern yourself with those who may disapprove of how you live your life.

There are *billions* of people in the world and every single one of them has different thoughts and opinions. It makes no sense to let a single person's opinion disrupt your life in any significant way.

Haters

It's difficult to do anything in life without eventually running into someone who not only decides that they don't like something you've done, they don't like the person who did it — *you*. And rather than simply live in peace with their opinion, they feel the need to express it — repeatedly — to anyone and everyone who will listen.

At times like this it's important to remember that the people who are so inclined to spew insults *at* you or make offensive remarks *about* you to others are rarely the kind of people who will be swayed by defensive arguments or an explanation of your actions — no matter how logical.

As wrong as you may consider a hater to be — no amount of time spent trying to convince them that they are mistaken will change their beliefs — and it certainly won't make them *like* you. In fact, engaging haters directly often makes matters worse because they feed off the attention they receive as a result of their negative behavior.

While you can't control haters, you *can* control how you *react* to them. And one of the most effective ways to deal with people who seek to assault you with negativity is to simply ignore them. Because explaining yourself to someone who is going out of their way to criticize or make offensive remarks about you will rarely make them stop — and it isn't going to make them *like* you more. It's only going to give them what they want: *attention*.

Learning to not have to explain one's self is one of life's rewards. Learning to not get emotionally invested in what people think of you one way or the other is another. Refuse to give power to those who seek control over your sense of self-worth and emotions.

Perception of self

It isn't uncommon for people to have a very low estimation of themselves, their looks, or their accomplishments while simultaneously being someone that other people admire and are attracted to.

Whatever you consider your flaws, faults, and imperfections to be, know that they are nowhere near as clear to other people as they are to you. Always keep in mind that the people in your life don't see you in the exact same way that you see yourself. Resist the urge to magnify your mistakes, failures, and flaws because it's not only an inaccurate way to look at yourself, no one cares about these things as much as you do.

The more that you accept yourself for who you are, while actively working towards being the person you want to be, the less time you'll waste on being overly critical of yourself and the more confident you'll become.

(And as your confidence increases, you may come to see that everyone has flaws and imperfections and no one cares about yours as much as you do.)

You are not a bicycle (and why that matters)

If a stranger came up to you on the street and called you a bicycle, would it ruin your day? What if a *friend* called you a bicycle? Would it upset you?

Would the fact that someone *called* you a bicycle *actually make you a bicycle*? Of course not. So, if someone called you a bicycle, would you feel the need to go to great lengths to defend yourself by explaining to that person — and others — why you are, in fact, not a bicycle? Probably not.

The fact that someone calls you something doesn't make you that thing. And if that thing is really off-base, it's almost ridiculous to spend time trying to convince someone that you are not what they think you are.

Now realize this can be applied to *any* word, not just bicycle. Remember this the next time someone accuses you of being something you know you are not. Because if you're *not* a bicycle, *you're not a bicycle*.

 Insecurity is a spotlight. The more insecure you are about something the more visible it becomes to others. Conversely, the more comfortable you are with something the less people tend to notice it (or care).

You are who you choose to be.

Every day that passes becomes another page in the story of your life. A story that no one has as much control over as you do — but only if you refuse to let other people write your story for you.

It's important to understand that anything that anyone observes about you is filtered through the lens of their life experiences and how they're feeling at the time. What a person perceives to be "true" about you is only an *interpretation*. No two individuals interpret an experience in exactly the same way. Any number of people can watch an event take place and none of them will share exactly the same story with exactly the same details about what they saw or felt. The fact that someone forms an opinion about you doesn't make it a universal truth, it simply makes it a truth based on what *they* perceived, how *they* felt, and how *they* chose to interpret it.

It should go without saying, but you are not other people's opinions of you unless you choose to accept them. You don't have to let someone else's opinion or interpretation of an experience become your own. You are who you *choose* to be.

"That doesn't count"

People will sometimes try to trivialize your accomplishments. They'll suggest that something you did — or are in the process of doing — "doesn't count" because it doesn't conform to their standards or expectations.

Never let someone else's personal standards or self-importance interfere with your self-esteem or sense of accomplishment. Because your efforts and your achievements in life — no matter how small — count.

While we may occasionally share similar paths of travel with people, the route each of us takes through life is uniquely our own. No two individuals are on exactly the same journey.

Set high standards, but resist the urge to measure your accomplishments by other people's ideals. It isn't up to others to decide whether your accomplishments count, it's up to *you*.

Social proof vs. social media

Always remember that social media responses are not an accurate representation of people's actual interest in your offerings. Users of social media platforms are always working against mechanisms that are intentionally kept a mystery.

Be very careful about using the response to something you or someone else posts as an indicator of its actual value. Lots of quality content goes unnoticed. And lots of crap gets promoted.

Social media systems can easily be manipulated to make one thing appear more valued or popular than another.

Every platform has algorithms that are designed for the host's benefit, not your own. And as long as there is a financial barrier between who can afford to pay for views and who cannot, it will never be a fair system based on the quality of the content.

People can pay for all the things that can make them appear valued, popular, desirable, and successful. People can pay for views, pay for likes, pay for followers, and pay for engagement. And all these things become part of a psychological phenomenon called social proof. And social proof can easily be leveraged to influence people to act and behave in ways that they wouldn't if they knew the reality of a situation vs. what marketers and others want them to perceive to be true.

Social proof can also deter people from pursuing a chosen path because they get discouraged when they compare the results they're getting with the results that someone else appears to be getting. It may simply be that someone is paying for those results. And even if they're not, your life and your path are your own. Just because someone else is making progress towards their goals is no reason for you to stop making progress towards your own."

Personal preferences

When someone judges you harshly for what you appreciate in life, realize that it says more about *them* than it says about *you*. Your preferences are just that, *your preferences*. Just because someone else doesn't like what you like, doesn't make what you like any less worthy of your affection.

Whether it's music, movies, books, TV, fashion, art, animals, people, even social media statuses — whatever it may be — you don't need anyone's approval to genuinely like what you like.

Being yourself means being unapologetically affectionate about the things you like, *regardless* of what others may think. Remember, you're not here to live your life according to other people's preferences and opinions. You're here to live your life according to *your own*.

Judgers

Always remember that people who judge you do so based on their own personal biases and within the context of their own life experiences. People don't know why you actually do the things that you do. They can only guess. And people are not only inherently bad at guessing why people do what they do, the less context they have, the less accurate they will be.

People judge you looking through the lens of their own life experience. Which is just one of many reasons why it makes no sense to let the conclusions that other people come to impact you in any way other than how you *choose*. And choosing to let it ruin your day should never be one of those options.

Be your own champion

You won't always get the support you want in life. You and your ideas will sometimes be criticized, mocked, or rejected. And the goals you set for yourself will occasionally be seen as silly, impractical, or unreasonable to others.

Refuse to let criticism or a lack of support keep you from going after what you truly want and believe you can achieve in life. Don't leave it up to others to determine whether your goals are worth aspiring to.

By always focusing on the progress you're making on your journey — even when you feel alone in the process — your life will become a far more accurate reflection of your potential than it will if you let a lack of support deter you from getting to where you want to go.

The fact is, there will be times in your life when you will just have to suck it up and be your own champion when no one else will.

Thieves of self-esteem

Always keep in mind that — although it's nice — you don't need people to believe in you, support what you've done, or rally behind what you want to do. When you truly believe in yourself, no one can rob you of that belief.

The fact is, no matter how good your intentions or how much value you provide to the world, there will always be those who will doubt you, criticize you, and attempt to tear you down.

When you no longer allow people who criticize you to affect your sense of self-worth, you remove their power over you.

Advice from those who mean well (or don't)

Be mindful of the fact that people often provide advice based on their own priorities, *not yours*. It can be difficult for someone to provide advice (or encouragement) that conflicts with what they consider important in life or to provide advice that goes against their own personal values.

For example, if a person considers money to be the most important thing, then the advice they provide will often make money a priority. If a person considers comfort to be the most important thing in life, they will likely suggest solutions that provide comfort. If a person is adventurous, then they will provide advice that is congruent with an adventurous lifestyle. And if a person is a people-pleaser or simply wants your business, affection, or attention, they will often tell you whatever it is you want to hear.

Always consider the values and priorities of the people who provide advice. And if those people are making money to dispense it, be mindful of the people who pay them and consider their motives and any potential conflicts of interest that may be involved.

Sadly, sometimes the people who have information to share don't have *your* best interest in mind, they have *their own*.

It's ok not to know

Although there are people in the world that will inevitably try to make you feel foolish for not knowing something, it is simply a fact of life that *no one knows everything* — even things that are considered common knowledge, common experiences, or common sense. You should never feel ashamed for not knowing something. It is a sign of *confidence* to openly admit a gap in your knowledge. And a sign of intelligence to express an interest in learning what you don't know.

Do note, however, there may be times when it is in your best interest to keep your ignorance to yourself — but these usually revolve around situations that have less to do with knowledge and more to do with experience. For example, if someone offers you an amazing opportunity that would be in your best interest to take advantage of, you don't have to eagerly admit why you're lack of experience is a reason you shouldn't be considered. So long as you are not trying to oversell yourself, you experience, or your abilities, if the person offering you an amazing experience didn't think you were a good fit for it, they wouldn't have offered it to you.

"You're doing it wrong."

People have a habit of telling others that they're doing something the wrong way because another way (most likely their way) is considered better.

Always remember, it's not *wrong* if you get the results you want doing it. While it is *true* that one way may be more efficient than another, a person who is very good at doing something one way may not be very good at doing it another way — even if that way is considered better.

Keep an open mind and explore and learn as many ways as possible to make yourself more efficient, but don't abandon something that works for you simply because someone says you're doing it wrong.

Universal appeal is impossible

If one is to fulfill their potential in life, it's important to recognize that universal appeal is impossible. Even the best and brightest people, products, and ideas have critics.

Every time you deviate from acting authentically out of fear of what others may think or say, you allow your fear to affect your life in a negative way and you create limits where none should exist.

Refuse to let the fear of criticism stand between you and the life you desire.

> *"There is only one way to avoid criticism: do nothing, say nothing, and be nothing." — Aristotle*

Ignored vs. unnoticed

The difference between being ignored and simply going unnoticed is huge — and yet people frequently mistake the two. Never forget that the lack of a response to something isn't always an accurate reflection of what someone thinks. More often than not, the lack of a response to something is simply the result of inopportune timing.

People can't react to what they aren't aware of. Don't take it personally if it isn't personal.

Boundaries

Always remember that we teach the people in our lives how to treat us by how we act and what we're willing to allow. As such, it's important to set *your own* personal boundaries and not let others do it for you.

It is an exercise in futility to complain about how you are treated while at the same time allowing yourself to be treated that way. If you don't set your boundaries, be prepared for other people to set them for you.

CHAPTER 13

SELF-TALK

The voice in your head

The person whose voice in their head is confident & encouraging will always have an advantage over the person whose voice is constantly putting them down and filling them with fear and thoughts of failure.

Every person has the ability to be the single most supportive person in their lives or their own worst enemy. Learning to recognize when the voice in your head isn't helping and developing the ability to direct your mind to more empowering thoughts is one of the most valuable and life-changing skills you can learn.

How to find your inner voice in difficult times

How to find your inner voice in difficult times: When facing a challenge, ask yourself: *"What would a stronger, more confident, and even better version of myself do in this situation?"*

When you truly give it thought and get an answer, that's your inner voice talking — and it's generally a good idea to listen to it.

Skip and volume control

When you don't like a song in your playlist or grow tired of one, what do you do? Do you play it even louder? Do you put it on repeat?

No. You skip the song and play something you like better. Because *you* control your playlist.

So why then would you play the same old tired negative thoughts when they pop into your head over and over again?

You control *your thoughts.* Learn to hit skip.

Whenever you catch yourself thinking undesirable thoughts that do nothing but make you feel bad, realize that you can *choose* to think something else. But you must also understand that until you have mental discipline, your mind will always seek to find ways back to whatever thoughts trouble you when you're feeling down. This is because your mind habitually follows the thought patterns it's most familiar with.

The first step to training yourself to think more empowering thoughts is to simply learn to catch yourself whenever your thoughts are leading you to places you don't want to be. Once you're aware of your negative self-talk, you can choose to deliberately and repeatedly direct your attention to something else for as long as is necessary to overcome the onslaught of thoughts attacking your well-being.

As you learn to catch your negative thoughts and direct your attention to more desirable things, you'll not only begin to develop the mental discipline needed to catch your negative thoughts earlier and more often, you'll be able to replace your negative thoughts with more empowering ones. As with most things, this process gets easier with repetition — particularly as your new thought patterns overwrite old ones — so don't lose hope.

One doesn't gain the ability to avoid negative thought patterns overnight, but if you're patient and give yourself time to learn new, more positive, more productive, and more empowering ways of thinking, you will be rewarded in ways that could completely change your life.

The power of self-talk

The way in which we speak to ourselves can be a powerful tool when we use it with intention and a source of strife when we don't. This is because the manner in which we talk to ourselves has a direct impact on our subconscious mind which, in turn, can have an impact on how we feel.

A person's subconscious mind is like a dumb, but diligent robot. One of the ways it receives instructions involves listening to what we say when we talk to ourselves and then responding accordingly.

Questions

Whenever a person asks themselves a question, they give their subconscious mind instructions to seek an answer. And this is great — except one's subconscious mind has a habit of answering questions according to how the questions were formed and not necessarily how a person wants them to be answered.

This becomes more evident when you consider questions formed in the negative versus questions formed in the positive. When a person asks themselves a question in the form of a negative, such as —

- Why am I single?
- Why can't I stay in a long-term relationship?
- Why don't people think I'm funny?
- Why don't more people like me?

— one's subconscious mind will answer, "You can't because...."

Contrast this with when a person asks themselves a question in the form of a positive —

- *How* can I attract the love of my life?
- *How* can I stay in a long-term relationship?
- *What can I do* to make more people think I'm funny?
- *What can I do* to be more likable?

— and you begin to see how the way in which we talk to ourselves has a great deal of influence over the type of answers and information our subconscious mind responds with.

Negative questions often yield negative answers. And these answers don't *solve* problems so much as perpetuate them. Positive questions, on the other hand, may not yield immediate solutions, but they are far more likely to put one on a path towards getting productive answers than negative questions will.

Always pay attention to the instructions you give your subconscious mind when you ask yourself questions.

Challenges & focus

Questions aren't the only way we talk to our subconscious mind. We do it all the time whether our self-talk involves questions or not — so it's important to recognize how and when we speak to ourselves in a way that it isn't beneficial to our well-being.

For example, in the middle of performing a difficult task we may focus on the *difficulty* of the task and how *little* we enjoy it. Our self-talk will likely reflect this with statements like, "This sucks." or "I hate this." which not only amplifies how we feel about the task, it can actually make it seem *harder*.

On the other hand, self-talk statements like, "This isn't so bad.", "I can do this.", "I'm getting better.", "I'm making progress.", or "I'm learning something." energize and empower us and can make challenges easier to bear.

Problem-solving

Even how we think about problems that we don't have a solution to can have a significant impact on whether we find one or not. When we think about problems as if answers exist, our subconscious mind is free to look for solutions. When we think about problems as if they are impossible to solve, our subconscious mind is stuck with the belief that none exist — so it doesn't bother looking.

It is in this way that our perceived limits can become our reality even when we are capable of achieving far more than we believe. Always remember that when a person approaches a problem as if a solution exists, it is far more conducive to finding a solution than when a person looks at a problem as if they are powerless to address it.

Beating yourself up & tearing yourself down

If you wouldn't tolerate a friend belittling your accomplishments, rubbing your mistakes in your face, or trying to put you down, why would you accept that kind of behavior from *yourself*? It should be obvious, but there is no upside to making one's self feel miserable.

Even if you've made mistakes, are not exactly where you want to be in life, or are simply unsatisfied with your current situation or circumstances, beating yourself up over the fact that things aren't as you wish them to be only serves to make matters worse. Rather than help, this kind of negative thinking puts the *one* person most capable of fighting for your well-being at a disadvantage. It turns *you* into your own enemy.

If you have a tendency to beat yourself up and tear yourself down, it's time to find a more productive means to cope. While you may not be able to immediately change the situation you find yourself in, you *can* change your attitude and how you choose to deal with difficult times.

Always remember to focus *not* on your problems or how badly you can make yourself feel, but instead, direct your attention to solutions and actions you can take to change things for the better. Even if the most immediate solution is to stop beating yourself up — because *that's a problem you can solve*.

You, more than anyone, have the ability to be the hero of your life and the champion of your well-being, but in order to play that role in your life, you must stop beating yourself up and tearing yourself down. Don't give power to your unfriendly thoughts.

Embracing imperfection

The person who screws up and learns from the experience has much more to offer than the person who *appears* perfect because they never risk making a mistake or being seen as anything other than flawless.

One gains far more from their struggles in life than they do from their successes. People who suffer one failure after another — only to ultimately succeed — have a much broader and more detailed understanding of experiences than those who get lucky or cheat their way to success.

In fact, as long as they put in serious effort, even people who never achieve a goal they set out to accomplish often have more wisdom to offer about the experience of attempting to achieve that goal than those who were able to attain it easily or without effort.

If you have a habit of being hard on yourself for making mistakes or failing to achieve goals, it's time to stop and recognize the value of being imperfect. It's time to forgive yourself and others of past mistakes and, instead, put your focus on where it is of most value, what was learned from them.

Aiming for excellence in life isn't about striving for perfection, it's about striving for progress regardless of the mistakes one makes along the way.

Filling in the blanks

- They didn't call me back...
- They didn't reply to my text...
- They didn't like my post...
- That person is staring at me...

It must be because _____

When we fail to get feedback from an event, we often fill in the missing information in a way that becomes our own made-up version of the truth. We then refer to this fictitious filler as if it's the *reality* of the situation, rather than what it really is, a *fabrication*.

Always resist the urge to rely on information that hasn't been confirmed in some way. Because believing something negative that isn't true, can not only have a significant impact on how you respond to a given situation, it can also have an adverse effect on your work, your relationships, and your sense of self-worth.

Don't fill in the blanks for things you don't know the true answers to with negative stories you tell yourself are true.

"I can't do that"

If you've never practiced to the point of making progress in something, don't let your present lack of skills at that thing be an indicator of your inability to do it. While it is true some people are more naturally talented at some things than others, most people who are good enough at something to be recognized for it have put in countless hours practicing that thing.

Be very wary of convincing yourself that you can't do something when you've never actually made *doing* that thing a priority. When a person tells themselves they can't do something, they give little incentive to prove themselves wrong. Refuse to let a lack of effort or the failure to improve at something be the source of your limitations.

The chances are, it's not that you can't do something, it's that you never tried long enough to make progress at it.

> *"Whether you think you can or whether you think you can't, you're right."* — Henry Ford

Overcoming embarrassment

Screwing up or embarrassing one's self in front of others can feel humiliating, but the humiliation one feels is typically triggered by what one *imagines* other people will think and what the consequences will be.

Mistake makers often have a habit of imagining worst-case scenarios when the worst-case is far more likely to be the exception, not the norm. Rarely are one's flaws or embarrassing moments as significant as they can sometimes seem to be. Embarrassing experiences rarely receive as much scrutiny from, or are reflected upon, more than they are by the person who experienced them.

Never forget that making mistakes is how we learn. And having flaws is part of the human experience. No one is perfect.

One of the keys to overcoming embarrassing experiences is to simply move on with intention. Don't perpetuate undesirable feelings by repeatedly reliving, re-imagining, or reminding yourself of things that you'd be better off forgetting.

What other people are thinking

People are always far more likely to overestimate their ability to correctly guess what other people are thinking than they actually are. One of the reasons behind this is that our brain makes up stories in an effort to make sense of what we perceive or to fill in the narrative of our life, but the stories that our brain tells us are never challenged or corrected. And because the stories are never proven to be false, our brain carries on assuming that it's right.

This makes about as much sense as someone coming across a random house with a purple door and telling themselves a story about why the owners chose that color and assuming that their explanation is true.

The fact is, you will never know exactly what another person is thinking unless you ask them. And the truth is, people think about us and our actions far less than we often give them credit for.

And whether someone is thinking about or judging you or not, unless they confront you to express how they feel, what they think will have no impact your life unless you choose to let it.

Always remember that *actual* feedback is far more reliable than guessing what other people are thinking.

CHAPTER 14

AUTHENTICITY & BEING YOURSELF

⚡ Every time you change something unique about yourself in order to be just like someone else, a piece of the best part of you dies.

Know thyself

Nearly everything that gives us power in life comes from having a deep understanding of ourselves. The greater one gets to know themselves, their beliefs, their values, and what they want out of life, the more control they gain over their thoughts, feelings and actions — and the less vulnerable they are to the opinions of others.

By knowing one's self deeply and accepting one's self completely, one creates a solid foundation of identity upon which an authentic and meaningful life is built. When a person has only a superficial understanding of themselves, they become vulnerable to being defined by others and less confident and capable of defining themselves.

If you wish to improve yourself, your life, and your relationship with the world, take the time to truly understand yourself, your influences, and how the person you are came to be.

To thine own self be true

It's not until we take the time to question who we are, what we know, and *how* we know what we know that we begin to truly find our true selves. And it isn't until we've distinguished ourselves from our influences that our genuine self is revealed.

Many people spend so much of their lives living under the influence of their friends, family, advertising, and societal pressures, that they fail to recognize when their views are no longer — or never were — an accurate reflection of their actual beliefs and values. Instead, their views are a result of their relationships and other people's expectations.

Not only do we grow accustomed to behaving a certain way with certain people, the people we interact with learn to *expect* us to act this way. And often out of fear of criticism or rejection, we choose to continually cater to expectations rather than act and communicate as we *truly* desire. To act in a manner that is contrary to one's true values and beliefs is to surrender one's personal power, integrity, and freedom to other people.

By constraining our behavior to other people's expectations, we create our own "behavior box", the boundaries of which represent our expected behavior or our respective roles within family and friendships.

The consequences of continually catering to other people's expectations can affect everything in our lives, from the types of jobs we hold, to what we buy with our money, to the people we have relationships with, and how happy and fulfilled we are as a result. This is why if one wants to truly live an authentic and fulfilling life, it's important to not only know thyself, but *"To thine own self be true."* (Shakespeare)

If you want to live an authentic life, it's vital to not only have a fundamental understanding of your true beliefs and values, you must live your life in a way that is congruent with both.

Don't sacrifice your personal power — and to a larger degree, your life — by continually living within the constraints of other people's expectations.

> *"He who knows others is wise; he who knows himself is enlightened." — Lao Tzu*

The unique you is beautiful

Your quirks. Your interest in unusual things. The small things that bring you joy. The odd things you do because they feel right to you. The unique things that you find funny — or fascinating — these are the things about you that make you truly unique and different from others — and they are among, if not the most beautiful things about you.

It can take courage to exert your individuality, but the alternative — to conform — is to become less of an individual. While the comfort of conformity can be a good thing, it represents the ordinary, the status quo, and is, ultimately, the enemy of creativity and self-expression.

Being able to establish rapport and live in harmony with others is vital to one's well-being and an important part of life, but to actively change yourself to be just like the crowd is to surrender one of the greatest gifts any of us are given in life, the ability to be and express our true selves.

The freedom to be

- Are we free if we live our lives in a way that regularly requires the approval of others to feel accepted?
- Are we free if we frequently force ourselves to live within the confines of other people's expectations?
- Are we free if we consistently dilute our true selves to please others?
- Are we free if our emotions are easily altered by what other people say or do?

No.

When we give other people power over our thoughts, feelings, and emotions, we become a servant to circumstances. We essentially let people dictate what we think, how we feel, and in some cases, how we act.

If you wish to be the master of your destiny, you must first reclaim the freedom to be your true self by defining your own identity and wrestle back control of your thoughts, feelings, and sense of self-worth from those you have inadvertently given power over you.

Remaining true to one's self means not allowing others to manipulate your behavior in a way that isn't congruent with how you wish to be. And one of the benefits of simply being yourself is that you never have to worry about being consistent with how you act because how you act is a *true* reflection of who you are.

Give yourself the freedom to be as you *truly* are.

Fear of self-expression

If you do the best you can to be a decent human being, show tolerance and kindness to others and still live in fear of what people think of you, your possessions, your opinions, or your beliefs, and then alter your behavior to be "approved" by as many people as possible, that *isn't* freedom, it's a form of self-imposed slavery.

One becomes a slave to conformity every time they decide that living within the confines of other people's expectations is a more attractive alternative to living with the freedom to truly be themselves.

Don't live your life wearing a disguise.

It's better to be your genuine self and have fewer of the right kinds of people in your life than it is to surround yourself with those who only accept you as long as you conform to their idea of who you should be.

When you refuse to be anything but your genuine self, you give those who are most compatible with who you are a chance to find you.

Don't live your life wearing a disguise.

Who we are today

Who we are today is a result of all the decisions we've ever made in life. Whatever we wish to be in the future depends on our present actions. To become who you wish to be, simply determine how that person would act and then, little by little, act like that person.

You are who you choose to be.

Acting with authenticity

When a person maintains their integrity and acts with authenticity, their behavior becomes consistently congruent with their beliefs, values, and identity.

By remaining genuine and living and acting in accordance with your true beliefs, the people you attract into your life get to know the *true you*, not some distorted or diluted version of yourself. As a result, there isn't any need to feel as if you must act a particular way in order to maintain a person's friendship or approval.

Of course, not everyone you cross paths with in life will like you, but those who do will like and respect you for who you *truly* are and not as someone you pretend to be.

Integrity and independent thinking

Gathering data to make an informed opinion is one thing. Simply waiting to agree with the crowd is something else entirely.

Being yourself and maintaining your integrity means standing up for what you believe to be right and true whether it's in the company of a crowd or not.

It's OK to be weird

In case no one told you, it's OK to be weird — and the best people usually are. But if one is to get away with being odd — *without becoming an outcast* — it's vital to be aware of some things.

First, it's important to consider the consequences that come with behaving in a way that is inconsistent with social norms. Society is often a hypocrite. On one hand, "being yourself" is encouraged — and there are countless movies with this message — yet the consequences of eccentric behavior will inevitably attract people who automatically judge and look down upon those who deviate from cultural customs and social norms.

A strong sense of identity and being comfortable with one's self is an important prerequisite to acting in unconventional ways without letting those who will judge you for it have a negative impact on your sense of self-worth. If one is already battling a low self-esteem, it's crucial to find a balance between being one's true self and acting in a way that doesn't attract an overwhelming amount of negative attention.

Second, even if you don't wish to conform to the crowd, it's important to conduct yourself in a way that is compatible with the culture in which you find yourself. Those who behave in an offensive fashion will often find themselves at odds with others. Rather than be appreciated for one's uniqueness, one can eventually be ostracized for it. And no matter how much one appreciates solitude, numerous studies find that a key ingredient of happiness is a sense of connection to others. If your behavior is constantly causing friction or leaving you at odds with people, it may be time to reconsider your actions.

Third, it's important to recognize that there's a distinct difference between acting in *authentically* odd or unconventional ways and being weird for the sole purpose of getting attention. One is genuine behavior and the other is a fabricated performance.

And finally, being weird isn't a free pass to disregard other people's comfort or to disrespect individuals, customs, or the environment. Doing so can obviously lead to undesirable consequences. Being yourself is not an excuse for negative behavior.

It's ok to be weird, but if you're going to express yourself in a manner that attracts attention, it's important to not only be confident in yourself and comfortable with the attention you receive, it's important to conduct yourself in a manner that isn't entirely incompatible with others or the environment you find yourself in.

> *"Eccentricity has always abounded when and where strength of character had abounded; and the amount of eccentricity in a society has generally been proportional to the amount of genius, mental vigor, and courage which it contained."* — John Stuart Mill

The courage to be imperfect

The less that one has to pretend to be someone or something they're not, the more power they gain from remaining true to themselves. The most effective and respected people in the world are not those who pretend they have no flaws. They are people who have the courage to admit their mistakes and imperfections and have the desire to overcome them.

Many people mistakenly believe that they will be liked less for not being perfect, but the truth is that people are much more likely to respect and admire those who express themselves authentically than those who they suspect are pretending to something they're not. When one refuses to hide who they are behind a facade, they no longer have to live with the fear of being discovered as "false" or less than perfect.

Have the courage to be authentic. The courage to take responsibility for who you are and how you act. And the courage to be imperfect.

"Real men..."

Seen in a meme: "Real men..." [do, say...]

No. Regardless of a person's gender, *real people* do what they do *not* because it conforms to someone else's standards of what "real people" do, but because it's congruent with how *they* want to be.

Real people don't confine themselves to other people's expectations. They're not content with being labeled. They have no desire to fit within a box. And they don't cave-in to peer pressure or act with the intention of pleasing everyone.

Real people like what they like, do what they do, and act how they act because real people are more concerned about living with authenticity than they are with whether or not other people approve of their decisions or how they live their life.

The problem with the expression "be yourself"

The problem with the expression "be yourself" is that many people don't actually know who they are.

Part of the problem is that many live their lives completely oblivious to the consequences of their actions. People who lack self-awareness also lack the ability to accurately evaluate themselves. As a result, they have a distorted sense of self.

Another part of the problem is that as we go about our daily lives, we have a habit of judging ourselves by our *intentions* rather than *our actions*. Often, and with very little thought, we reflexively excuse ourselves from actions that may result in negative consequences for others.

For example, when we cut someone off in traffic, we either recognize it as an honest mistake or we justify our action for a specific reason. That reason may be as simple as we're running late and trying to get somewhere in a hurry.

When we feel justified for doing what we're doing, we often disregard the potentially negative effects our actions may have had on others — so much so that we often don't even register the incidents in our minds. So even if we cut someone off while driving, we don't see ourselves as the type of person that cuts people off while driving.

In order to "be yourself", one must know who they are. And in order for a person to know who they are, they must be able to recognize not just the qualities about themselves they're content with, but also the things about themselves they may wish to change for the better.

By developing a sense of self-awareness that allows a person to see how their actions affect or inconvenience others, they give themselves the perspective necessary to see aspects of themselves they wouldn't otherwise be aware of. The more a person is able to see themselves for who they truly are — without blind spots — the more they're able to truly "be themselves" — or better, the person they aspire to be.

Where "being yourself" fails

If you're kind, compassionate, and authentic, if you aim to make a positive difference with what you have to offer, and if you continually strive to better yourself, then by all means, "be yourself".

But if you're someone who goes through life making things more difficult, painful, or inconvenient for others, then perhaps it's better you don't just "be yourself". Because "being yourself" is never an excuse to treat other people poorly.

Perhaps it's better if you aim to be the kind of person you and others can be proud of, rather than just accept who you are with no intention of changing. Or as Joss Whedon put it, *"Be yourself, unless you suck."*

Forging one's character

Because our character is not a static thing, but an ever-evolving entity that we synthesize through intention, action, attitude, and experience, we are who we choose to be. Yet there will be times in life when how we act isn't congruent with the person we see ourselves as.

At times like these it's important to consider ways in which we might have acted better. By doing so, we provide ourselves with positive alternatives from which to draw from should we ever find ourselves in similar situations. If we don't, we leave ourselves prone to reacting in the same undesirable ways.

The more we mentally rehearse positive responses to negative experiences, the more we give ourselves the tools needed to bring who we are in line with who we want to be. And by doing so, we take an active role in our own development.

Dr. Jekyll and Mr. Hyde

The person we *like* to see ourselves as and the person we are when we are tested are often two completely different people. The more that these two people are congruent with one another — to the point of being one — the better we tend to feel about ourselves when we are challenged.

CHAPTER 15

KINDNESS

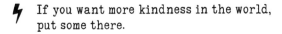

⚡ If you want more kindness in the world,
put some there.

Be kind without expectation

Being kind without expectation is the truest kind of kindness.

When one learns to be kind selflessly and without expectation, they discover that the reward for an act of kindness is simply to have done it.

The dark side of kindness

There is an unfortunate dark side to kindness. And it is that some people will make the pretense of being kind as a way to get your guard down. Or, some people will appear in need of something as a way to use the empathetic nature of others against them. In both cases, the ultimate goal of these individuals is to take advantage of or harm you in some way.

While it is important to understand that the vast majority of people in the world are not out to hurt or take advantage of you, the fact is, *some* are. So it's important to be careful. Particularly when dealing with strangers in unfamiliar territory.

This doesn't mean you shouldn't be kind. And it doesn't mean you shouldn't accept the kindness of others. But it does mean you should learn to recognize signs that things are not as they seem. And to avoid situations that may put you in jeopardy.

Don't immediately give your trust to or make yourself vulnerable to someone simply because it appears as if they want to be helpful or they seem to be in need. Especially if what they're doing or how they are presenting themselves seems out of the ordinary or unnatural in some way. This could be a sign that you are being manipulated towards some undesirable endgame. In cases like this, you should extricate yourself from the situation as quickly as you can without any need to feel guilty about how the other person may feel.

While it is entirely possible to misread someone with good intentions, a kind person with *truly* good intentions would want you to feel safe and comfortable in their presence. And they would rather have you dismiss them and leave than make you feel like you are in danger or being manipulated or set up in some way.

If you want kindness, be kind

If you want kindness, be kind. If you want friends, be friendly. If you want help, be helpful. If you want love, be loving. If you want respect, respect yourself and others.

One will most often get more of the things that matter in life by *giving them first* than they will by desperately trying to get them or asking for them.

If you want to be treated well by those you cross paths with in life, make it your mission to leave people feeling better, not worse, for having come in contact with you.

A single act of kindness

Every act of kindness contains within it the power to change not just one life, but *many*. Not only is the positive energy of one's act of altruism often reflected by the recipient, it has the potential to touch countless lives by creating a chain reaction of goodwill.

Never underestimate the power of a single act of kindness to make a significant difference in someone's life. Your act may just be the added lift that someone needs to go from falling to flying.

Be kind in your own way

While traditional acts of altruism can be extremely beneficial and the world can always use more people who do them, there's nothing wrong with finding your own unique or unconventional ways to make a positive difference. Because, whether an act of kindness is common or not, it's *still* valuable.

People who enjoy donating to charities, volunteering for causes, or joining groups can do that — and the world can always use more people to do these things — but the manner in which someone adds value to other people's lives shouldn't be judged, it should simply be appreciated.

Always remember that one doesn't have to conform to conventional kinds of kindness to add value to other people's lives. What you have to offer as a result of simply being yourself provides you with the potential to impact others in a way that *only you* can.

The strength in kindness

People sometimes mistakenly believe that being kind, compassionate, or attentive to other people's needs is a sign of weakness. Nothing could be further from the truth. Being kind in an unfair world full of unkind people is an act of courage and shows strength of character, not weakness.

Kindness, when given selflessly and without expectation, is often a sign of a compassionate mind and a strong moral compass and is a demonstration of one's ability to deal with life's challenges without becoming bitter or apathetic to the needs of others.

Those who withhold kindness out of fear of being judged by others demonstrate weakness — not strength — by allowing other people to control their actions. While not every act of altruism that one performs in life will be appreciated or interpreted as it was intended, those who refuse to initiate kindness out of fear of rejection — or being judged — only serve to make matters worse by setting a poor example for others to follow.

Every time a person refuses to let an unkind world rob them of their desire to be kind, they demonstrate strength, not weakness.

On kindness & disrespect

You can be a kind person and still be the kind of person who yells profanity at the car that cuts you off in traffic. Being kind and not tolerating bullshit are not mutually exclusive. Being a kind person doesn't mean you can't verbalize your disapproval for disrespect.

Crossing paths with idiots is never an excuse to act badly and you should always strive to set a good example, but it doesn't mean you have to stay silent or put up with abuse.

Sometimes the biggest favor you can do someone is to stay calm and speak the truth. And sometimes that truth is, "You're being an asshole and here's why..." At other times it may mean not giving your time and attention to someone who doesn't respect it.

You don't have to be perfect. You don't have to be a Zen Master. And you certainly don't have to tolerate bullshit. Just lead with kindness and always do your best. Even when others are not at their own.

Sincere appreciation & authentic encouragement

Whenever it seems appropriate, always take the time to notice specific things that people do well and tell those people what you've noticed. While people don't always know how to accept compliments, kind words — when spoken with sincerity — are always appreciated even if that person doesn't know how to express it.

Always remember that the time it takes to provide kind words, sincere appreciation, and authentic encouragement is often far eclipsed by the amount of time your words linger in the mind of the person you direct them to. And sometimes, what you say can have such a dramatic impact on a person that it changes their life.

Appreciation and gift-giving

While there is certainly something to be said about being appreciated — and showing appreciation — on holidays, one could make an argument that the sincerest times to show appreciation are those times when a person you care about was simply on your mind and you thought enough of them to take the time to say so.

Always keep in mind that nearly *anytime* is a good time to show appreciation, express thanks, or give gifts — and some of the *best* times are *not* on culturally convenient and highly commercialized dates, but simply when you thought enough of a person to show them that you cared.

Take the time to express it

- *"You know what I really like about you..."*
- *"I love it when you..."*
- *"I really respect you for..."*
- *"I really appreciate it when you..."*
- *"I admire you for..."*
- *"One of my favorite memories of you is..."*

Whether it's through their actions, words, or works of art, if someone touches you in a meaningful way, always make a conscious effort to express thanks or send a kind word to those who do.

Often, the gratitude and appreciation we show others becomes a source of motivation that allows those who touch and inspire us to continue doing what they do.

By taking the time to accentuate the positive in others, you may just have as positive effect on someone else as they have on you.

Is there someone in your life that you could show appreciation to right now? *Take the time to express it.*

Is there anything I can do to help?

If it's truly your desire to make a positive difference in the world, never underestimate the effectiveness of offering assistance instead of waiting to be asked. Regardless of whether or not someone takes you up on your offer, proactively asking if you can help is not only an effective way to show people that you care, it's also a great way to form friendships and improve relationships.

While people you cross paths with may occasionally question your motives or decline your offers of kindness (sometimes rudely), one should never feel bad for attempting to help or add value to other people's lives.

Always remember that those who react rudely to kind gestures are often the same cynical people that are most in need of experiencing authentic attempts at altruism, whether they accept them or not. The more that cynics see genuine gestures of kindness, the less cynical they become.

Never let the fear of having your offer of kindness rejected deter you from offering it. If you wish to be an effective force for good in the world, it is far more effective to lead by example than it is to do nothing and simply *hope* for the change you wish to see.

"Is there anything I can do to help?" is a magical question. Use it often to show you care.

 A single act of kindness may seem like such a small thing, but so is the ember that starts a wildfire.

Empathy, selflessness & guilt

People in need can get so caught up in their own problems that they fail to see the strain it puts on others. It's one thing to be temporarily inconvenienced by someone else's needs; It is another thing entirely to allow yourself to be overwhelmed and collaterally damaged by someone else's issues.

As much as you may care for others and as selfless and helpful as you wish to be, there will be times when your needs are more important than someone else's. Always remember that you are not responsible for solving *every* person's problems. Nor will you be able to.

Don't let your desire to be kind and help others be taken advantage of in ways that become an overwhelming burden on your life.

Do what you can when you can, but always be mindful that people will sometimes try to set you on fire in order to keep themselves warm.

 Silent appreciation is easily confused with silence.

Experience is the best teacher

It's important to understand that while learning from others is effective, *experience is often the best teacher*. People have a natural tendency to want to protect others from failure or discomfort without understanding that failure and discomfort *may* be exactly what a person needs to grow.

Before you discourage someone from doing something you wouldn't do, consider whether it might be an experience they need to have. People who live sheltered lives tend to be less capable of dealing with life when the shelter they're used to isn't available.

While you may not feel comfortable encouraging someone to do something you personally wouldn't do, sometimes the *kindest* thing you can do is to *not* protect someone from something *you* fear.

CHAPTER 16

TOLERANCE

Ster·e·o·type
1. a widely held but fixed and oversimplified image or idea of a particular type of person or thing.

The world is a dog park

People who don't mingle with other people outside of their social, ethnic, religious, economic, political, or peer groups are like dogs that grow up without ever having been socialized with other dogs (they tend to be skittish around the unfamiliar and react to other dogs with hesitation, suspicion, and barking).

Socializing dogs is recommended for good reasons. Not least of which is that they exist more harmoniously with other dogs.

This doesn't just apply to dogs. The world is a dog park.

With respect, tolerance, and an open mind

As the media and politicians continue to polarize people, it's important to remember that one doesn't have to agree with another person's particular point of view or share their politics to get along.

People sometimes forget that many of the best relationships are often composed of people who are not mirror images of each other, but instead fit together like pieces of a puzzle. It is not what we have in common with each other that helps us grow as much as what we don't.

It has been said that people become the average of the five people they interact with the most. What kind of picture does it paint if you share exactly the same likes, dislikes, and view of the world as everyone else in your circle?

People who only interact with and surround themselves with other people who agree with them and share their points of view tend to end up with a very narrow and distorted view of the world.

To think you have to agree with everything about a person is to deny yourself of some of the best friendships the world has to offer. And to automatically dismiss someone because they are different than you does the same.

To simply take offense at something without giving it any thought is to deny yourself an opportunity for growth — even if that growth simply means reaffirming what you already believe.

Always keep in mind that the attitude one harbors when they interact with other people can have a dramatic impact on the outcome of the interaction. Those who treat others like a potential friend are far more likely to find a friend than those who assume anyone with an opposing view or an alternative lifestyle is an enemy.

With respect, tolerance, and an open-mind, one creates a potential path for peace, harmony, and friendships that would be unlikely to occur without them. Refuse to dismiss people, their opinions, or their lifestyles simply because they are different than what you are used to.

One of the most valuable gifts one person can give another is an expanded point of view because being able to see things from a different perspective is like being given a key to a world you wouldn't otherwise know existed.

Stereotypes

The fact is, not everyone in the world likes you. But the weird thing is, a number of the people who don't like you don't even know you exist.

Whether it's because of your profession, the color of your skin, your cultural background, your religion (or lack thereof), your economic bracket, sexual preference, tattoos, geographical location, or something else entirely, you are disliked by people who don't even know you simply because you fall within a stereotype. And while there's nothing you can do about these people, there is something you can do about yourself. And that is to refuse to play a part in stereotyping others.

Refuse to oversimplify a group of people. Because the fact is, every person on the planet draws upon a unique history of life experiences that shape who they are, how they see the world, and how they act. And no matter how on point you perceive your perspective to be, no two people are exactly alike.

Resist disrespecting and speaking badly about others just because family, friends, the media, or society considers it acceptable to paint an entire race, culture, or group of people in a negative light. Whatever your lifestyle preferences may be, respect people enough to give others a chance to show who they are by *how they act*.

A point about safety:

This is not to say throw caution to the wind when you are in unfamiliar territory. In which case you should be cautious, remain aware of your environment, and understand and respect cultural differences. This is simply to say that if you don't like being stereotyped, don't stereotype others or use stereotypes as a justification to have negative discussions about groups of people.

Breaking barriers

When a person resists reading, watching, or doing anything that challenges their views, they inhibit their growth by limiting what they are capable of learning or experiencing.

When a person surrounds themselves only with people that think, look, and act exactly like they do, the world in which they live becomes a misrepresentation of reality.

When a person lives in such a way that they intentionally inconvenience or condemn those who simply think or act differently than they do, they do little more than exemplify ignorance and intolerance and stunt their own growth.

If you want to maximize your potential and live life to the fullest, resist building barriers between yourself and others simply because they choose to live their lives differently than you do.

"It is the mark of an educated mind to be able to entertain a thought without accepting it." — Aristotle

Comparison creates conflict

All one has to do is open a magazine, turn on a TV, or browse the Internet to see that we're constantly bombarded with marketing messages that tell us that if we want to be happy, feel powerful, or be successful, we need to fit in.

According to pop culture, you've got to:

- ✓ wear the right clothes
- ✓ root for the right sports team
- ✓ drink the right liquids
- ✓ drive the right car
- ✓ listen to the right music
- ✓ attend the right school
- ✓ buy the right ring
- ✓ and make the right amount of money.

— and if you don't, you or your life are lacking in some way.

And, as much as these things are an artificial construct of advertising, many people believe them. Not only believe them, they embrace this view as a lifestyle. And by embracing this lifestyle, they become part of an ever-expanding group of people who are often not only the first to notice those who don't conform to their standards, they're the quickest to conclude that those who don't like, have, or do the same things that they do are inferior in some way.

Even when we *know* the standards by which we live our lives are a contrived construct of clever and manipulative advertising, we still fall victim to using these standards to compare our lives to others because how we judge others is a reflection of how we judge ourselves.

By making a deliberate effort to fit in as much as possible, one must not only constantly direct their attention to ways in which they can and do fit in, they must direct their attention to ways in which others could fit in, but don't.

This not only creates an unhealthy habit of constantly comparing one's self to others, it creates the inclination to judge people and it perpetuates the illusion that those who don't live their lives by similar standards are, in some way, the enemy. Rather than facilitate friendships, this "us versus them" attitude often creates conflict where none need exist.

"I could never see myself being friends with someone who roots for [national sports team]."

Do you actually believe the world would be a better place if we all bought or liked or found pleasure in the same things? If a person is a good person, contributes to society when and where they can, and is a positive force in the world, absolutely none of this superficial stuff matters.

"Dude, come on. That's a girly drink."

Would you really deny a perfectly good friendship because someone likes or dislikes something you don't? Especially if they were willing to find common ground?

"OMG. Look at their hair."

Is it really a bad thing that someone has a strong enough sense of self that it allows them to express who they are in a way that isn't the same as everyone else?

Isn't it hypocritical to encourage people to "be themselves", but then criticize them harshly when they do?

"What a bunch of geeks."

Do you really believe that those who find certain things appealing are weird because *you* don't share their enthusiasm for those things?

By all means, fit in as much or as little as you are comfortable with, but resist the urge to judge those who choose to express themselves — or find meaning in their lives — differently than you do.

Remember, people who see the world in the same way that we do have far less to teach us about the world than those who don't. But in order to learn what those people have to teach us, it's necessary to keep an open mind about the ways they choose to live their lives differently than we do.

The mock of shame

We live in a culture that suggests that "thinking differently" and standing out from the crowd is something to be celebrated. While, at the same time, poking fun of anything or anyone that deviates from the norm is *not* just acceptable in most circles, it's commonly used as a conversation starter.

Perhaps it's because anything that stands out from the ordinary not only attracts attention, it's more interesting to talk about for *precisely* the reasons it stands out. And yet, people's observations of such things are often unflattering or catty.

"Oh my god. Look at that person's..."
"Look at the weird way they..."
"I wouldn't be caught dead in that..."

The fact that our critical remarks are not the sort of things we would feel comfortable sharing with the person being spoken about is a strong sign that they're being said at that person's expense.

If you *truly* admire independent thinkers and those who are brave enough to express their individuality, refuse to use these people as a target for critical comments or participate in conversations with people who do.

If you *truly* appreciate uniqueness in others, learn to express it in a positive way. Don't be a person that says they believe that people should be themselves, but then pokes fun of people for doing so.

Remember, it takes courage to be one's true self and stand out from a crowd — and as long as someone isn't harming or disrespecting themselves or others in the process, displays of individuality should be applauded, not mocked.

If you wouldn't like it done or said about you, don't do or say it about other people.

The world's problems

The world's problems will not be solved by building walls, discriminating against anyone who isn't like "us", or harming innocent people. Hate, violence, shutting people out, and turning a blind eye to the needs of others never solved anything for long. In fact, these strategies are far more effective at perpetuating problems than anything else.

The world's problems will not be solved without taking steps to work together for the common good of the inhabitants of this planet. And one of these steps is deciding that tolerating our differences and making peace makes a lot more sense than making war.

If you want to make an impact at the global level, start first at the local one. Every time you show tolerance and act with kindness towards those who are different than you, you set an example for others to follow. And the more you set a positive example for others to follow, the more you influence people into influencing others in a positive way.

Just because you wouldn't...

Preferences are not one-size-fits-all. Not everyone likes the same things or has the same priorities. What's best for you and your life isn't universal. Let people live their lives according to how they choose to live and resist the urge to be judgmental about how they do it.

Just because *you* wouldn't doesn't mean *they* shouldn't. As long as people are not harming themselves or others, concern yourself less with how others choose to live their lives and more with how you can make *your* life the best it can be for *you*.

CHAPTER 17

LEADERSHIP, INFLUENCE & CHARACTER

Be an encourager

It is far more effective to be a person who encourages others than it is to spend one's time finding faults, criticizing, or judging people. Not only will you feel better about yourself as a result of being a force for good, you'll be making a positive difference in people's lives.

Refuse to put people down. Refuse to judge those who aren't exactly like you. Refuse to do to others what you wouldn't like done to you.

Remember that everyone lives their lives in a way that reflects what they've learned from life experience. Not everyone thinks the same things. Not everyone knows what you know. Not everyone has the same level of awareness.

Help people live their lives in a positive way by encouraging more of what you'd like to see in the world. Lift people up. Raise people's spirits. Make friends, not enemies.

Help educate people by being a good example. Be kind. Be encouraging. Be honest. Be tolerant. *Provide the inspiration that others can use to provide the inspiration that others can use.*

Give kindness and do good because you can. Because the world needs more people who do. And there's no better person to do it than you.

Integrity

Integrity is doing the right thing for the right reasons. It's acting with sincerity, honesty, and honor. It's remaining true to one's self and values — even in the face of adversity or temptation.

Integrity does not involve feeding people's egos in an attempt to manipulate them into getting something you want. Integrity is not being nice with the expectation of reward. Integrity is not preying on people's weaknesses to meet your own needs. Integrity is not making promises you cannot keep. Integrity is not withholding key information until you have won someone over by fueling their desires. Integrity is not waiting until they've signed the dotted line to reveal the fine print or legally manipulative part of the contract.

What those things encompass can be described quite simply as inauthentic, offensive, and manipulative.

In a word: **bullshit**.

Talk is cheap

People are far more likely to reveal their genuine selves by what they do and how they treat other people, than they are by what they say.

Talk is cheap. You show who you truly are by what you consistently do, how you treat people, and when your actions are congruent with your words.

Integrity isn't only for when life is easy

What you do and how you act when you are challenged and put to the test says a lot more about you and your true character than what you say or do when life is easy.

It is precisely the moments when one faces temptation or their values are challenged that integrity matters most.

Having integrity means refusing to take advantage of another person's misfortune for one's personal benefit. It means doing the right thing, even when it's difficult.

Influence by example

People are more likely to be influenced by the attitude of others — and the examples they set — than they are by being criticized or having others impose their beliefs on them.

There's enough judgement in the world. Enough name calling. Enough bullying. Enough "this vs. that" and "us vs. them". Enough imposing of beliefs. People rarely change for the better by being bullied, criticized, or being told that they're wrong.

Want change? Keep an open mind, find common ground, and influence by example. If the beliefs you live by add value to the world, the life you live will speak for itself far more powerfully than force or criticism ever will.

Diminishing the effectiveness of negativity

In a world of negativity, every positive act you perform, no matter how small, not only helps to set a good example, it helps to diminish the effectiveness of those who spew hate and negativity.

If you want to do some good then literally do some good. Make a positive difference in someone's life. Do the things you wish more people would do.

What you do for people and the moments and memories you help create can literally change a person's life (including your own).

It's OK to be concerned, angry, and upset about the state of things. It's OK to speak out against hate, intolerance, and injustice. It's OK to stand up for what you believe is morally right. Just be sure that when you do, you do it in a way that has a positive impact and doesn't just add to the negative energy that you oppose. Convert your positive or negative energy into positive *action*. Lead by example by performing actions that you can be *proud* of no matter how you are feeling.

Make sure children and adults alike can see that there is far more to the world than the things that get shown in the news. That there is far more good in the world than hate. And far more people wishing to create something beautiful than those who wish to destroy it.

Some people may be beyond your reach, but there are still countless individuals of all ages and all walks of life in the world that could use the guidance of your good example.

Don't ever let your disapproval for anyone or anything turn you into someone you don't want to be.

A good example

If the world would not be a better place if everyone on the planet followed your example, it might be a good idea to periodically stop and consider ways in which you could change that.

Be a good example of what it means to be a good example.

> *"May you live your life as if the maxim of your actions were to become universal law." — Immanuel Kant*

"Why bother?"

People often make the argument that things aren't worth the effort because nothing will change. But nothing (much) tends to change without effort.

Always remember that it's often a lot of little things that build upon one another that make change possible.

Recognition

Yes, you may sometimes feel like putting in the effort to make a positive difference isn't necessarily worth it. And not everyone cares about the things you care about. And sometimes you will feel like you are the only one that something actually matters to. But you're not.

Never let a lack of recognition of your efforts to make a positive difference get in the way of doing what you feel is right. Because sometimes, the most effective thing you can do is to simply set a good example.

The people who make a positive difference in the world are the ones who keep trying to. Not for fame. Or recognition. Or personal benefit. But because it's the right thing to do.

*"You may never know what results come of your actions,
but if you do nothing, there will be no results."*
— *Mahatma Gandhi*

If you like it, encourage it

The world in which we live is not some static thing. It changes. But change starts with the individual. You. Me. And the people we cross paths with.

If you want to see more of something in your life, start by doing the things you want to see more of — even when you think no one is watching.

You may never know *who* you influence by your actions, but if you always strive to set a good example, you'll never have to worry about *how*.

If you like it, encourage it. If you admire it, say so. If you appreciate it, express it.

- ✓ *Promote good ideas.*
- ✓ *Discuss solutions.*
- ✓ *Talk about what you love.*
- ✓ *Share your enthusiasm.*
- ✓ *Readily admit your mistakes.*
- ✓ *Try new things.*
- ✓ *Encourage tolerance.*
- ✓ *Keep an open mind.*
- ✓ *Stop bad habits and start good ones.*

The right thing to do

It should go without saying, but if it doesn't feel like the right thing to do, don't do it. And if you've inadvertently found yourself having done something that doesn't sit well with you, have the courage to do what you can to make it right.

Influence

You may never know who your actions, words, or creations inspire, but those who appreciate the things you offer to the world are out there, even if they are not always visible to you. For every person who takes the time to acknowledge the value in what you're doing or what you have to offer, there will always be others who won't.

Always remember that the lack of acknowledgment for a deed well done does not make that deed any less valuable or significant. The power of a person's influence nearly always appears much smaller than it actually is.

Lanes merge ahead

- *"Yes, I see the "lanes merge ahead" sign, but I'm really in a hurry today. Besides, I see those other jerks do this all the time."*
- *"I know the light is turning red, but I have important things to do."*
- *"I can't find a trash can and I'm really tired of carrying this bottle, so I'm just going to drop it. Besides, there's another bottle on the grass over there."*
- *"I don't want to have to walk across the parking lot to throw my fast food trash away, so I'm just going to leave it next to my car. People get paid to clean this stuff up, right? I'm not littering, I'm giving someone a job."*
- *"I'm not walking another 40 feet to put this shopping cart in a rack. I'm just going to leave it in this parking space. Look at all the other carts in the parking lot. I'm sure someone will take care of it."*
- *"This thing I found doesn't belong to me, but it's kind of nice and I don't want some thief to take it. So I'm going to."*

When you do things that you don't like others to do — or wouldn't want someone to do to you — you set an example for even more people to follow. Always do the things you want to see more of in the world, not less.

Leadership & power

Some people in positions of power who claim to be leaders want you to feel like they're important. They'll talk about their accolades, achievements, and education. They'll claim seniority. They'll drop names and try to associate themselves with important people. They'll do just about anything but truly inspire you.

True leaders don't waste time trying to convince others of their importance because they know that their leadership skills are demonstrated by *how they act* and how they make others feel, not by how highly they speak of themselves.

True leaders are far more likely to make *others* feel important than they are to spend time trying to convince people of their importance.

Always remember that true power doesn't demand action, it *inspires* it. And true leaders don't demand respect, they *earn* it. A true leader is someone that people believe in and want to emulate, follow, or help without being required to.

Always be the best version of yourself

Refuse to let the decline of inspiring leadership, integrity, personal responsibility, and rational thinking deter you from setting the best example you can for others to follow.

Don't lower your standards to confront other people on their level. Always be the best version of yourself that you can be.

CHAPTER 18

THE PATH LESS TRAVELED

⚡ The love you put into what you do always finds its way back to you.

The path less traveled

Some people choose to drift through life. They follow the path of least resistance and simply go wherever it leads. Others take a more active role in directing themselves where they want to go in life, but even then, most who *do* follow pre-existing paths. These paths may not be easy, but those who take them benefit not only from well-defined markers along the way, but from numerous resources available to aid them on their journey.

And then there's the path less traveled — a deliberate departure from the crowd and a journey into the uncommon and unfamiliar. There is a reason most people don't take it, not least of which is because to do so can be both a huge risk and an immense challenge. More so than following conventional routes.

Embarking on the path less traveled is a risk because without clear markers indicating that one is taking the right steps towards their destination, there's no guarantee that one will ultimately end up where they wanted to go when they started. This is further complicated by the fact that because the path less traveled is a journey of discovery as much as anything else.

What a person learns about themselves on the path less traveled can cause them to change their priorities. And when a person's priorities change, where they want to go on their journey can change as well. And so, a person can easily end up in an entirely different place than the one they expected to go when they started.

A significant challenge in taking the path less traveled is, that because it is unique to each person who takes it, one's journey is far less likely to be identified with or understood by others than more common and conventional routes. And just as being disconnected from others can lead to feelings of loneliness and isolation, so too can choosing a path that leads one away from the comfort of a crowd.

But the fact is, one can also feel lonely in a crowd. And often, those who ultimately choose to take the path less traveled do so because they feel disconnected from the desires of the crowd and where it's going. And as long as one travels with the crowd, they will forever be under its influence and limited by its constraints.

> *"The one who follows the crowd will usually go no further than the crowd. Those who walk alone are likely to find themselves in places no one has ever been."*
> — *Francis Phillip Wernig*

The most difficult challenges that one faces on the path less traveled will likely *not* be the challenges that they anticipate having as much as the ones that they *don't*. A new breed of problems will arise that will often make one feel as if they are unprepared. But this venture beyond one's comfort zone is what leads to the most meaningful discoveries and personal growth.

It's not so much what happens to you in life that matters as much as how you choose to learn from and respond to what happens. Because you can't control everything that happens, but you *can* control how you respond to it.

Choosing the path less traveled is not only about discovering one's way towards a desired destination, it's about discovering one's *self* as well. Every challenge that pushes a person beyond their comfort zone leads to personal growth.

There is a reason so much ancient wisdom revolves around knowing thyself. The better a person knows themselves, the more that they're able to bring the person they are in line with the person they want to be.

It is very difficult to truly know one's self if all a person has ever done is what they've seen others do. When a person spends all of their time under the influence of the crowd — family, friends, mass-marketing, and the media — they may ultimately be defined by these things rather than be a true reflection of themselves.

Breaking away from the crowd can provide insight that allows one to determine who they are. And if they don't like that person, a chance to reinvent or redefine themselves and their role in the world.

Always remember that it is very difficult to grow stronger without resistance — and one faces very little resistance in the comfort of a crowd.

Everyone else knows better (but not really)

Making the decision to take the path less traveled may be one of the best decisions you ever make, but if you choose to take an unconventional path in life, it will not come without complications or consequences.

For one thing, the moment you act on your decision to buck the status quo is the moment you not only leave yourself vulnerable to battling your own self-doubt, it's the moment you'll have to face unsolicited advice and criticism from those who question your choices, your goals, or your methods.

Most people live in very conventional ways following very conventional sets of standards and traditions. Anything that deviates from the ordinary automatically attracts attention — not all of which will be complimentary or constructive.

While some may offer you practical advice, be careful how much weight you give to the opinions of those who haven't done anything similar to what you're attempting to do. People with little experience — and no investment in the outcome of your decisions — are often very vocal and overconfident in the advice that they dispense.

Some may even try to talk you out of whatever it is you desire to do because it doesn't make sense to them or it is simply something *they* wouldn't do. Always remember that the path less traveled is *the path less traveled for a reason.*

Most people do not "think differently" — and among those that occasionally do, few have the courage necessary to break from the constraints of conformity and take steps into uncharted territory. It *isn't* common or easy to do — but then, nothing exceptional ever is.

With your self-doubt on one shoulder and the well-meaning advice of others on your other, it may, at times, appear as if everyone knows better than you do. At times like this, you must learn to listen to your inner-voice and remind yourself of the reasons you chose the take the path you did in the first place.

Always remember that whether you ultimately succeed at what it is you set out to do or not, you'll not only learn invaluable lessons from the experience, you'll never have to live with the regret of wondering how your life would be different if only you'd had the courage to leave the comfort of the crowd and go after what you truly wanted by taking the path less traveled.

> "If a man does not keep pace with his companions, perhaps it is because he hears a different drummer. Let his step to the music which he hears, however measured or far away." — Henry David Thoreau

Not everyone will understand your journey

Always keep in mind that the only person that is *truly* aware of your emotions, your intentions, or your interpretation of experiences — which is all they can be — is *you*.

As much as others may at times identify with you or your actions, it is impossible to go through life without occasionally being misunderstood. While you *can* control what you say and how you act, you *cannot* control how others choose to interpret these things. And it may sometimes seem that no matter how much you try to explain yourself to others, they just don't "get it".

This should be *expected*.

Not everyone will understand your journey. That's fine. It's not *their* journey to make sense of. It's *yours*.

When one deliberately chooses an uncommon route through life, it will by its very nature be less understood by those following more conventional paths. And it'll occasionally trigger comments like, "Why would anyone want to do that?", "What's the point?", and "You're just looking for attention." and so on.

It may help to remember that you don't have to explain yourself or justify your actions to others *unless you want to*. The need to explain one's self is often prompted by fear and a desire to control the outcome of a conversation — for both validation and approval.

It should go without saying, but just because someone doesn't agree with something you've done — or want to do — in life doesn't mean it's wrong. Abandoning the comfort of the crowd and taking the path less traveled is one of the bravest, most challenging, and personally rewarding things a person can do.

Pursuing the path less traveled is not about impressing people or earning approval. It's not about recognition, accolades, or money. It's about authenticity and living life in congruence with one's true desires and values.

If you're truly going after your heart's desires and you truly believe in yourself and what you're trying to accomplish, then you're not doing it for others or what they think about it — you're doing it for you.

Where you go, what you do, and where you end up on your journey isn't for anyone else to decide but you. Just because someone doesn't understand your journey doesn't mean you're heading in the wrong direction.

Arguments against taking the path less traveled

Without looking closely, people often interpret Robert Frost's poem, The Road Not Taken, as a celebration or endorsement of taking the road less traveled. After all, Frost clearly states in the most frequently quoted excerpt from his poem, that taking the road less traveled "made all the difference". But *what kind* of difference it made is open to interpretation. And, upon closer inspection, one could easily make the argument (and many do) that Frost's poem is the *opposite* of a celebration.

While I *am* an open advocate of taking trips beyond comfort, staying true to one's self despite societal pressures, and occasionally straying from the status quo, I do not believe *extended* journeys along the path less traveled are in *everyone's* best interest. So, with that in mind, here are my arguments against taking the path less traveled...

Because taking the path less traveled means deviating from existing standards and breaking away from conformity, one doesn't always know what kind of results they'll get from the actions they take on their journey, or if those results are typical, or what exactly needs to be done to change them. This can lead to feelings of self-doubt. Particularly when numerous attempts at something lead to numerous failures.

It's easy to commit to doing something difficult when life is predictable. It is much less easy to stay committed to that thing when life is not.

Anything that people do that is considered out-of-the-ordinary attracts attention. And people are far more likely to criticize and ridicule *anything* that attempts to stray from an existing standard — including people.

If you choose to take the path less traveled, there will be those who will tear into you, your ideas, your methods, or your productions as if they are a personal insult to that person's existence. Without a strong sense of self, this attention can be painful and demoralizing.

Although there may exist a group that supports you, the more exposure you get, the more criticism you will invite. While your support group may also grow, it is very likely that there will always exist a vocal group of people who hate whatever it is you're doing (but then, *that's life*).

You won't necessarily get the support you want or expect. In fact, those who are close to you may oppose your plans and ideas. This can lead to friction in your relationships and the loss of people in your life.

It can take *years* to see the kind of success and results you want. Nor is there *ever* any guarantee that you will succeed or end up wherever it is you wish to go. Your journey may take not just a little longer than you expect, but *much* longer. And you may repeatedly find yourself questioning whether it is in your best interest to quit or continue without ever being entirely confident in whatever you decide at that time.

Depending on how you interpret your experiences and what you ultimately expect to get out of your journey, it is entirely possible that you may feel that the years of your life that you spent along the path less traveled could have been better spent doing something else.

When things don't go as you expect them to, you will have to decide whether the experiences you have and the lessons you learn from the mistakes you make along your journey are worth the time and resources that you're trading for them.

If all you seek is success, achievement, and a sense of comfort at the end, then the path less traveled may not fulfill your needs. You will have to learn to judge success by factors other than money, accolades, trophies or any of the typical signs that people use to recognize success.

While there will always be those fortunate few who get lucky and succeed quickly — or whose journey is exactly as they hoped it would be — for most, the journey won't just be hard, it will likely be much harder than they imagine for reasons they cannot foresee.

It's important to recognize that real-life is not like it is in the movies. For example, not everyone bordering on bankruptcy suddenly bounces back to become enormously successful. Nor does everyone who takes a gamble and risks everything see the benefit of their bet. Some people take losses that they never recover from.

The reason we always see and hear stories of successful people who risked everything to succeed is precisely because *those* stories are considered the only stories worth telling. Failure and quitting isn't noteworthy unless it was either preceded by or is followed by a significant success of some kind. History doesn't tell the tales of the masses who tried, failed, and never went anywhere. It's too depressing.

Not everyone has the mental strength, discipline, determination, and resilience necessary to take the path less traveled. Not everyone can deal with the consequences of their decision to chart a course into unknown territory. And not everyone can turn whatever they discover on their journey into something of value to themselves or others. If you believe *you* can, then the path less traveled may be for you. But the decision to take it should never be made without immense consideration given to the potential consequences.

People's lives can be forever changed by taking the path less traveled — and often are — but not always in the way they hoped when they started.

Dealing with negative feedback

What can sometimes start as a simple quest for gathering feedback from others can sometimes lead to a battle of differing opinions.

Learn to listen to feedback with an open mind, but not take it personally when someone doesn't "get" or agree with you or your decisions. Realize that when all is said and done, you can choose not to let the feedback you've received from others have an impact on your decision-making process or your journey.

Also realize that *you* are in control of your emotions. You don't have to go into a defensive emotional state when someone is critical of you or something you've done. Remember that this heightened emotional state is most often motivated by one's insecurities and a need to be accepted.

What others think of you, your ideas, your decisions, or your journey isn't nearly as important as what *you* think of these things. Your value doesn't reside in others or what they think of you — it resides in you. Don't leave your sense of worth and well-being in the hands of others. The more confident you are in yourself, the less concerned you will be about what others think of you (for good or ill) — and counter-intuitively, the more people will tend to respect you for it.

"Inner Peace begins the moment you choose not to allow another person or event to control your emotions."
— *Unknown*

The struggle to achieve

Anyone who has ever struggled to achieve something great knows that the journey to accomplish worthy goals is often fraught with hardship. They know that great tasks may sometimes appear improbable — or even impossible — before they are ultimately completed. They know that there is far more value in attempting great things — and learning from the experience — than there is in never trying.

Listening to sage advice from experienced individuals who wish to help you is one thing, entertaining criticism and fear mongering from people who have little understanding of what you want to do is another.

Refuse to engage with those whose sole goal is to try to scare you from going after what you want in life by pointing out all of the things that *could* go wrong or how *weird* what you want to do is. Know that, more often than not, the people who try to deter others from going after their dreams are those who fail to have what it takes to go after their own.

If you truly believe in what you're trying to accomplish in life, don't be overly concerned with those who don't. Anyone can take the easy path, follow the crowd, or do nothing. Refuse to entertain criticism from those who do.

Find your title or make one

There exists within each of us the potential to do and excel at things that not only have the power to transform our lives, but the lives of others. And as we share our gifts with the world, they become the building blocks of our legacy.

If you haven't found your passions or purpose yet, don't lose hope.

It's important to understand that not everything that everyone is most suited to do in their lives has a pre-existing job title. Sometimes the ideal job for a person is the one they have to *create*.

If the ideal job for you and what you have to offer doesn't exist, create it.

Extraordinary things

If you want extraordinary things in your life, you either have to do uncommon things to make those things possible or you have to have the courage to let unusual and uncommon things into your life when they present themselves to you.

No, not every uncommon experience, opportunity, or person you encounter in your life will lead to extraordinary things, but the alternative is to maintain the status quo and simply hope that by continuing to do and accept the same things in your life as you always have, you will somehow get extraordinary results. To do this is to gamble with your life.

If you wish to attract extraordinary things into your life, you can start by increasing your tolerance for things that are different from what you are accustomed to, consciously pushing yourself beyond your comfort zone, and continually aiming for excellence in all areas of your life.

Extraordinary people

Extraordinary people are, by their very definition, *not* normal. They play the game of life in unconventional ways. They take risks. They challenge the status quo. They push their boundaries to see how far they can go.

Follow your passion (or don't!)

Some suggest that "follow your passion" is bad advice, while others advocate it as the answer to leading a fulfilling life. It's important to recognize that there is rarely a single bit of advice — or a single approach to life — that works best for all people.

Because everyone operates according to a very unique combination of values, priorities, and beliefs derived directly from personal experience — what's in the best interest of one person isn't necessarily in the best interest of another.

The problem with "Follow your passion"

The problem with the expression "follow your passion" is *not* that it's *bad* advice, it's that it offers no indication of *how, when, or why* one should follow their passion nor mentions any of the potential pitfalls of doing so.

The question of whether following your passion is good advice for *you* or not depends entirely on the type of person you are and what you desire in life. For some, pursuing one's passion may be the answer to all that they seek in life. But for others, the answer lies elsewhere.

Why passion is important

The importance of one or more passions in one's life is that passions generate a potentially endless amount of enthusiasm. Passions very often become priorities and priorities are what people voluntarily invest their time in.

The time that one spends doing something they love is exactly what allows them to become better at it. The better one becomes at a thing, the more they tend to enjoy it. And the more a person enjoys it, the more enthusiasm they have for it. It is in this way that having a passion for something creates a positive cycle of energy that feeds itself.

What "Follow your passion" means (and doesn't)

"Follow your passion" means to simply do that thing you are passionate about because it brings you joy. *Period*.

"Follow your passion" does *not* mean that one *must* make a career of it — or even attempt to make money from it. In fact, turning one's passion into a business can not only reduce the amount of joy one feels from doing it, it automatically associates their passion with things required to maintain it as a business. It's one thing to pursue one's passion out of desire and do it for the joy it brings, it's another to have to do it out of necessity to make money.

A pitfall of following one's passion

A pitfall of following one's passion is that not everything that someone loves to do is something that others are willing to pay money for.

Before you make the decision to pursue your passion, it's important to determine whether there exists a *proven* manner in which you can earn an income doing it. Because unless your passion involves doing something that someone else is willing to pay for, you can pursue it nonstop and never do enough to generate a sustainable income, let alone a viable career.

Like doesn't mean love

Not everyone has a passion to pursue. While potential passions often leave hints to their existence, they are not always obvious. Sometimes people stumble upon their passion by accident.

While there may be things you *like* to do, there's a big difference between enjoying something because it's *fun* and being *so enthralled* by something that hours pass like minutes and doing anything else feels like a distraction.

Just because you *like* doing something doesn't mean it's a passion — but that doesn't mean you should ignore it either. The things people like to do can lead to fulfilling careers.

Passion doesn't mean proficient

While having a passion for something often leads to proficiency in that thing, it doesn't always. And even when one is proficient in something it isn't a guarantee that they'll be able to do it at a level that others are consistently willing to pay for.

Before you decide to turn their passion into a business, it's important to be brutally honest about the value of and demand for what you have to offer.

Location matters

When one has honed their skills enough to finally be able to pursue their passion at a professional level, *where* they do it and *who* their competitors are matters.

Being good at something isn't always enough to be successful at it, let alone at the rate needed to be competitive. In fact, around 80 percent of first-time business owners shut down within the first eighteen months due to lack of funds.

If you're going to pursue your passion and succeed, it's important that you do so in a location that doesn't work against you.

Don't quit your day job (too soon)

Even if the job you have isn't related to the job you want, it should be viewed as a resource, not a mistake. Because the fact is, if the job you have helps provide you with the means to get to the job you want, it's an asset.

While quitting your job to jump for glory may sound grand, the moment you abandon your source of income to pursue your passion is the moment that you must rely on the income from your passion to survive. There is a big difference between doing what you love for fun and doing it because you absolutely have to.

The alternative

The alternative to following your passion and doing what you love is to find ways to *love what you do*.

But what if you fail?

It's simply a fact that not everyone achieves everything they set out to accomplish in life. Sometimes the timing is bad.

Sometimes the resources one needs are unavailable. Sometimes opportunities simply pass — or better opportunities present themselves. Any number of things can lead to failure.

Regardless of how many times you fail, do yourself a favor by refusing to think of yourself as a failure. Because you are *not* a failure; You are *a successful person* dealing with and overcoming challenges on *a journey*.

Because life is a journey, it isn't logical to think of ourselves as being in one place — such as the place where we failed — when every moment that passes puts distance between where that failure occurred and where we currently are. Where we've been doesn't dictate where we're going. So it makes no sense to think of yourself as a failure when your failures are *not* your final destination.

There's *no* shame in going after what you want and *no* shame — *if you truly put in the effort* — in failing to achieve it. By treating mistakes and failures as learning experiences, they simply become the solid foundation upon which success is built.

Life, lemons, and lemonade

With the right *attitude*, even if you *fail* to meet the lofty goal you set for yourself, you *will* see the value in — and reap *rewards* from — your efforts. This can include new skills and insights that you can not only apply to future endeavors, you can use what you learn teach others — even if it involves sharing what *not* to do. Failure is a huge part of success.

One doesn't have to be at the top of the mountain they strive to reach in order to share meaningful information about their journey to get there. Everyone has something to offer others along the way to their destination whether they ultimately reach it or not.

The nature of one's failure is often *far* less significant than the knowledge derived from one's experience at failing and the value that comes from applying what they learn from failure in a positive way to their life (and others).

"I told you so"-ers

The world is full of people who will respect and support your journey down the path less traveled — and who will continue to support you even if you fail to get to where you want to be.

But there also exist a small minority of people who, if you fail, will be relieved that you do. Because, in a way, your failure reassures those who habitually play-it-safe that attempting to do anything but follow the status quo will be a waste of their efforts and resources.

People always look for evidence to prove themselves right. So when a person fails to achieve something they didn't have the courage to try, it reaffirms their belief that even if they had the courage to go after what they wanted, it isn't worth the risk.

Don't concern yourself with those people. Some people are so engrained in the system in which they live that they cannot only not imagine themselves living outside of the box, they don't actually see the box in which they live.

Advice & intuition

While it is good to listen to and consider feedback, sometimes the best thing a person can do is *ignore* it — especially the more unique or unusual the thing a person plans to do is.

If everyone listened to everyone who ever said that something shouldn't, wouldn't, or couldn't be done, nothing would ever get done.

Although well-meaning, people have a natural tendency to offer advice with the intention of keeping the people they are giving it to as safe and as comfortable as possible. But this is often in direct conflict with one's goals because the path less traveled is inherently unknown and risk-prone.

Also keep in mind that the less that people are able to understand your situation, circumstances, or desires, the less that what they'll have to share with you will be relevant or applicable to you. Instead, they will likely be offering fear and disapproval in the place of worthwhile feedback and encouragement.

The most valuable advice you will likely get will come from those who have also gone after something they've wanted despite the challenges and risks involved. And it isn't just those who have succeeded who will feedback worth listening to, it will also be those who failed. Because failure frequently provides far more feedback than success does.

Learning to listen to your intuition and going against the force of feedback and advice you receive is often a necessity when it comes to going after anything laying along the path less traveled.

Decisions & goals

Be careful when it comes to making decisions around people you know or suspect won't approve of your choices or be supportive of your goals. While it can be argued that if someone can talk you out of something you want to do, then you don't want it badly enough, many things are often worth the effort of attempting and the experience one gets as a result. And sometimes you don't know how badly you truly want something until you put in the effort to try.

People who aren't going anywhere in their lives will often hold others back in theirs. Always consider the feedback you get in the context of the person who is providing it and their motivation for doing so.

CHAPTER 19 A

SUCCESS & FAILURE

The road to success

There are loads of people who make a living off of telling others that the road to their lofty goal — whatever it may be —is *simple.* And all you have to do is follow the steps outlined in their books, videos, or seminars, and you'll be bound for glory in no time.

While the advice that a person offers *may* be solid, sensible, and momentarily motivating, anyone who tells you that the road to success is *simple* is inexperienced, selling something, or both.

In reality, the road to success is *rarely* simple *or* easy. And for the rare few that it *is*, they're the *exceptions, not the norm*. They're often people who just happened to be in the right place at the right time, with the right resources or connections.

For the vast majority of people, navigating the road towards lofty goals is *not* just difficult, it is one of the *most* difficult things they'll ever attempt — because success is often *not* just as hard as someone imagines it to be, it is often *harder* and for reasons they couldn't anticipate.

Those who buy into the belief that the road towards their goal is simple are far more likely to abandon that goal when obstacles arise. *Knowing* that achieving lofty goals is not just hard, but harder than one imagines is beneficial because it helps one develop the mindset necessary to deal with obstacles along the way — and even failure.

As one prepares themselves for achievement, it is important to not buy wholeheartedly into marketing that suggests that something is simple, quick, or easy, but instead, harbor the belief that *if* it turns out to be more difficult than they expect it to be, they'll rise to the challenge instead of being deterred by it.

So I'm not going to tell you that the road to your goals is easy. I'm going to tell you that if your goal is lofty, you will sometimes doubt your ability to achieve it.

And if you fail, you will struggle with the decision to try again. And if you fail *repeatedly*, you may feel foolish — or believe that others *think* you are.

You may be subject to ridicule by those who don't share your values or see things the same way. They may tell you to stop what you're doing, that you'll never succeed, or that your goal is inferior to what others are doing. They may even be people you're close to.

If you're going to reach your goal, you must believe so much in what you wish to do that you're willing to battle whatever demons cross your path along the way.

You must learn to live within a world of uncertainty. You must be ready for the unexpected — the things you'll never see coming. And if you fail, you must learn to fail forward by using what you learn from failure as fuel to *try* again.

Dealing with failure

No one gets through life without occasionally faltering or falling short of their goals or expectations. Learning to deal with failure in a productive way is vital to the art of achievement.

One way to cope with failure is to remind yourself that you are *on an ongoing journey* — and that failure is simply something you occasionally encounter on that journey. It isn't a place you're stuck in or something you can pick up and take with you. It is simply something you *learn* valuable things from in a way that makes it an *essential* part of success.

It is a fact that not every path one goes down in life leads a person to where they wanted to go. Just because you end up somewhere you don't want to be doesn't mean you can't take another path to get there eventually.

Like everything we experience in life, we can choose to dwell on things that block us, bind us, or rob us of power *or* we can make an effort to learn what we can from an experience — especially failures — and *move on*.

Always remember, that when it comes to success, it is often not so much a matter of where we are at any given moment that's as important as where we're *consistently heading*. And because it is not a matter of *if* we will ever fail, but *when,* the way we deal with failure can make a huge difference in how quickly and efficiently we eventually get what we strive for.

When you learn to see your life as an ongoing journey, it allows you to recognize failures for what they are, simply things to acknowledge and learn from as you pass them by on the way to where you want to be.

> *"Success is not to be measured by the position someone has reached in life, but the obstacles he has overcome while trying to succeed." — Booker T. Washington*

Failures and setbacks

In order to succeed at any goal worth achieving, one must not only be prepared to face fear, challenges, hardships, and failure, one must be willing to overcome each of these things repeatedly.

It isn't enough to simply try and fail and try again. One must build the tenacity necessary to keep trying long after one's expectations of success have been challenged beyond imagining.

From the limited perspective one has at the onset of any journey, the pathway to one's ultimate destination is often far less clear than it's imagined to be — with a potential "plot twist" lying in wait at every turn.

As such, it's important to remember that failures and setbacks are as much a part of the process of success as small victories are along the way. The road to success is often revealed most by the lessons learned from *failed* attempts to navigate it without a map.

Every failure in life provides valuable experience that, in turn, can provide illumination on one's journey. But to reap the most from that experience, it's important to not allow our failures to discourage us from pushing forward towards our goals.

As the Chinese proverb goes, *"The temptation to quit will be greatest just before you are about to succeed."*

In other words, never underestimate the power of persistence.

Success is not a standard

Define success on your own terms. Refuse to rely on other people's standards as a measure for what it means to be successful. Not everyone measures wealth with money, success with status, or accomplishment with accolades.

Success is not a standard, it's a reflection of what an individual believes to be of value. Whether a person is ultimately considered successful on their journey isn't for anyone to decide but the person taking it.

Embracing failure

People often desire to downplay their failures as if they're something to be embarrassed about, but failure is, in fact, an extremely important component of success.

Remember, it isn't necessarily the person who accomplishes something in a short time or a single attempt that has it mastered. The person whose failures force them to attempt something multiple times — before ultimately succeeding — has a much more extensive set of meaningful experiences from which to obtain data.

Remember, there's a big difference between having a superficial understanding of something and actually being able to explain it in intricate details. It is far more valuable to know *not* just that something works, but *why* it works when it *does* and why it doesn't work when it doesn't.

Failures provide feedback. It is the process of acquiring knowledge and the act of having meaningful experiences related to that knowledge — including what we learn from our failures — that provides insight.

Those who are unable to show or admit their failures may actually have far less to offer than those who do. Because failure is a building block of success, not something to avoid or be embarrassed by.

Learn to embrace failure as a necessary component of success. Allow yourself to fail because failure isn't the end, quitting is.

An opportunity in every experience

It is a fact of life that sometimes we get what we strive for, and sometimes we don't. But a lack of success in an endeavor should never be considered a true failure as long something is learned from the experience. Hint: something is *always* learned from the experience.

There is an opportunity in every experience — even failure — to make yourself better and turn it into something of value.

Wanting success doesn't ensure it

Intense desire can provide the motivation to act, but without action, desire — like wishful thinking — does very little.

One can want to succeed as badly as they want to breathe, but without being both willing *and* able to take the steps — and make the sacrifices necessary — to meet their goal, one won't survive the road to success long enough to arrive at their desired destination.

The desire to breathe doesn't keep people from drowning. Taking the steps necessary to get oxygen and having the skills to stay afloat does. And this starts with learning how to swim.

An intense desire to be successful does not ensure success. One must be willing and able to learn and commit to the actions necessary to achieve it.

The most successful people in the world

Even the most successful people in history have had their confidence rocked, their good ideas ridiculed, and the door of opportunity slammed in their face.

Even the most successful, most intelligent, most attractive, and most beloved people in the world have felt tired, lonely, scared, ugly, stupid, and alone.

Even the most successful people in the world have been knocked down, suffered serious setbacks, and failed at things they set out to do. Not once, but repeatedly.

But being knocked down is *not* the same thing as being defeated. And the missteps one makes are as much a part of the journey to success as every step that draws one nearer to their goal.

What made many of the most successful people in the world successful is that no matter what happened or how to felt about it, they chose to keep moving forward.

They persisted. And you can, too.

Comparison is the thief of joy

There will always be someone better at something than you are.

A wise person once said, "Comparison is the thief of joy." Don't let the success of others discourage you from your own endeavors or make you bitter. If someone has done or is doing something you would like to do, let it inspire you and be an indicator that you, too, can achieve great things.

One's greatness is defined by the value they add to the world throughout their lives — and that value is created through a combination of talents, skills, and actions that are totally unique to every person on the planet.

Know that whatever it is you wish to accomplish, no two people, businesses, or ventures are exactly the same. No matter what it is that you desire to do, you can't help but bring a unique perspective to your endeavors and a unique combination of talents and skills.

So even if the field is crowded, understand that you can succeed, too, but in order to do so, it is essential that you put in the effort and take action to achieve your goals. Getting discouraged at others' accomplishments and giving up because you feel you can't compete gets you nowhere. Constantly comparing yourself to others is waste of energy.

Always remember that we all have the potential for greatness, but one doesn't become great by comparing themselves to others or conforming their lives to someone else's concept of what it means to be successful.

The illusion of success & mastery

Appearances are important, but those who go to great lengths to try to convince others of their value often do so out of insecurity. This includes exaggerating one's qualifications, excessive self-promotion, and flaunting one's accomplishments.

People who are very good at what they do often have a quiet confidence that makes going to great lengths to appear knowledgeable or successful unnecessary.

Beware judging other people's success and expertise based on what you *see*. Looks can be deceiving. Not everyone who appears successful or claims to be an expert actually is — and not everyone who doesn't is not. This should be obvious, and yet people often use the appearance of success as an important criterion to judge whether someone is successful or not.

Always keep in mind that not every type of success can be represented visually and not everything of value can be measured. Being good at something and appearing successful involves far more than wearing a fancy suit and flashy marketing.

Success is fickle (don't quit)

Whether it's art, writing, music, photography, or some other endeavor, you may *already* have the skills necessary to be a success at what you desire to do in life, but for whatever reason, it still escapes you. And if you believe this is the case, you're *not* alone.

Success is fickle. It comes more easily for some than others. And often, it has more to do with being in the right place at the right time to connect with the right people than it does with simply being skilled at something.

If you are confident in your abilities and can picture a way in which you can be compensated for your craft, don't give up just because you haven't yet been recognized for it.

There are *a lot* of people in the world and *a lot* of noise. It's likely not so much that your skills are being *ignored* as it is that they're going unnoticed amongst a cacophony of people screaming for attention.

Many of the most successful people in the world struggled for years before being recognized for what they had to offer. It has been said that it takes ten years to become an "overnight success".

You may *already* be skilled at your craft, but use the time between now and the day you are finally recognized for your offerings to hone your skills. Rather than let the passage of time discourage you, use it to increase your strengths knowing that when the spotlight is finally on you, you will be ready.

For some, success comes *too* easy or *too* soon and rather than be ready for it, they unravel under the pressure. But not you, because you acquired the strength, attitude and experience necessary to handle it from the journey to achieve it.

Beware building on expectations

While positive expectations can be a good thing, and it's good to plan, be very careful solidifying future plans on the expectation that things will go as well or better than you expect them to. Always keep your expectations as realistic as possible and create contingency plans in the event that things do not pan out as planned.

For example, if you make future plans around the expectation of making a certain amount of money within a certain period of time, and it doesn't happen — and you don't have a contingency plan — your life will be far more disrupted than if you'd considered what you would do if your expectations weren't met.

Being successful means being able to plan for and push forward after unexpected and undesirable things happen.

Anticipate failure

Always be mindful of ways in which you have suffered from self-defeat in the past and take steps to avoid them.

Always set yourself up in a way that makes the things that you want to accomplish as convenient to do as possible. Conversely, if there are specific things in your environment or routine that lesson your resolve or cause failure, remove or make those things as inconvenient as possible to access. By looking at past points of failure, you set yourself up to avoid making the same or similar mistakes.

CHAPTER 19 B

ACCOMPLISHMENT AND "STUFF"

Success isn't just about accomplishment

Success isn't just about accomplishment. It's also about how the things you do in your life motivate and inspire others to do something motivating and inspiring in theirs.

It's about helping people you come in contact with. It's about making other people's lives better for having been a part of it. It's about making a positive difference, no matter how small.

Success has a lot more to do with what isn't immediately visible than it does with trophies, awards, wealth, or material things.

Stay pure

Many people who see just a little bit of success or popularity have their values corrupted by it and lose track of what's important. Rather than focus on the quality of what they have to offer, they focus on what they want to get.

What started as a genuine love for what they were doing turns into a love for money, popularity and feeling important.

A little monetary success often creates the desire for more monetary success. And a little popularity often creates the desire for more popularity. Rather than focus on the things that made the money or the popularity they attained possible, people focus on the money and the popularity itself.

They also focus on making themselves seemed important. Rather than let others be the ones who talk about how great they are, they do it themselves. (And if they're writers, they might do it in the third person so you can't tell the difference.)

Some people who have attained a certain level of importance in the world will then let that importance get to their head. They will then try to Market themselves based on their importance. Rather than their ideas and what they have to offer.

Someone who is acting authentically will never lose sight of the bigger picture and who they are. These are the people who continue to act like real human beings long after they've attained success. These are the people that don't pretend to be perfect. The people who remain approachable and in tuned with other people's needs.

Always remember that when you strip away marketing. And you strip away a person's previous accomplishments. What you are left with is a human being. And how that human being chooses to ack, regardless of - or because of - their success or popularity, says a lot about the kind of person they are.

The impact of possessions

Be very careful about falling into the trap of thinking that happiness lies in having "stuff". Every possession that a person acquires is yet another thing they must be responsible for.

Pets require supervision, dwellings require upkeep, and vehicles require maintenance. And even small things that don't require regular attending to still require space to store them.

While the degree to which a possession impacts a person's life depends on the possession, all possessions begin to exert some degree of influence over their owners almost immediately. As small as the influence of one's possessions may be individually, the combined impact of many things can have a major effect on one's life.

The more stuff a person acquires, the more space, time, and attention they have to devote to it. It is in this way that the more stuff a person owns, the more what they own ends up owning them.

A consequence of acquiring more and more stuff is the less attention each item receives, the less use one gets out of it, and by that nature, the less value it adds to the keeper's life. So it's important to be mindful of acquiring possessions for reasons other than the value that one anticipates getting out of them. Remember, it's not the *having* of something that's powerful, it's what you choose to *do* with it.

Always keep in mind that the less you own and need to be responsible for, the more you're not only able to act without being constrained by your possessions, the more you're able to appreciate and make use of the possessions you already have.

The cost of ownership

When your possessions disallow you from doing something you want to do the cost of ownership is your freedom.

It's beneficial to periodically take a step back and consider whether something you own is really adding the kind of value to your life that makes it worth keeping. Or whether it's something you could sell or donate to someone who would value it more — and more importantly, get more use out of it.

It's not a coincidence that the happiest people on the planet live with less. Don't let a modern materialistic society convince you that you need things that you don't actually use. You may just find yourself happier without another mass-produced piece of plastic.

Be careful where you place your values and what you collect in life. Don't let the things you own end up owning you.

If you don't use it, lose it.

Use it or lose it

When one learns to let go of the non-essentials that contribute very little value to their life, they create more space for things of higher value. And sometimes what one values most from the removal of something from their life is the time and space that's created by its absence.

Many people surround themselves with things that may, at one time, have been useful, but no longer serve the purpose for which they were acquired. They hold onto this "stuff" with the hope that it may one day once again be useful, but for most things, that day rarely comes. (Think of fitness equipment gathering dust. Bottles. Old clothes.)

Others remain habitually obligated to ongoing activities or functions that they'd no longer commit their time, energy, or resources to if they were to start over. In both cases, people's lives are adversely affected by a commitment to things they no longer value.

As one only has one life to live, it's important to not waste it caught up in things that no longer matter — or in the acquisition and subsequent storage of items that add little to no value to their life.

Isn't it time you take inventory of the things you truly value in your life and to let go of those things that are simply taking up your time or space and no longer serve you?

Dramatic life changes can occur when one makes a conscious and deliberate effort to surround themselves with only those things that they truly value in life instead of being weighed down and exhausted by things that they don't.

It's not about how much the things that one has are worth, it's about how much one values the things that they have. *Use it or lose it.*

The real measure of one's value

The truth — for many of us — is that we rarely make *full* use of what we already have. Much of what we own sits in closets, attics, garages, and storage units where it is not only rarely thought of, it's nearly never used. And while it makes very little sense to hold onto things that don't add value to our lives, we not only do, we continue to collect things that will likely end up in a box or gathering dust.

Refuse to be fooled by a consumer driven society that more stuff equals more happiness — because the opposite has been shown to be closer to the truth.

Judging one's life by the material things they own leads one on a never-ending quest for *more* — because when a person anchors their sense of worth to tangible objects they will never be totally content with what they have.

When two people have nothing, it's the person who still has something to offer others that's the most valuable.

It isn't what people *gain* in their lives that makes them *truly* valuable, it's the value they *add* to other people's lives that does.

Mementos

If the only reason you keep some things around (or in storage) is because they are a reminder of something, recognize that a picture or a video can be just as effective without taking up unnecessary space or costing us money to keep.

Things have as much meaning and sentimental value as we choose to give them. And some of those things are more of a burden than an asset to your life.

Take inventory of the things that aren't providing as much real-world value to your life as you have tricked yourself into believing. Consider whether taking a photo or a video would be nearly or just as beneficial to you as the actual item.

What it means to be truly wealthy

True wealth isn't measured by the value of the things a person has, it's measured by how valuable a person is *without* them. It's accumulated through the positive impact one has on the world. It is the kindness and positive energy traded between people.

If you want to know what it feels like to be truly wealthy, never underestimate the time spent doing things that have a positive impact on others.

> *"Money never made a man happy yet, nor will it. There is nothing in its nature to produce happiness. The more a man has, the more he wants. Instead of its filling a vacuum, it makes one." — Benjamin Franklin*

CHAPTER 20 A

HAPPINESS

⚡ Surrounding yourself with as much brilliance, wit, good humor, inspiration, creativity, genius, and positivity as you can is like taking vitamins for your life.

Happiness is not a destination

Happiness is *not* a destination, it's a byproduct of enjoying the journey. If you're simply passing time or rushing through life waiting to be happy or hoping to reach some magical milestone in which happiness is bestowed upon you, you are missing the point of life.

One doesn't attract happiness into their life by longing for the life they want while ignoring the life they have. One attracts happiness into their life by seeing, appreciating, and learning from the moments that pass and using what they learn in the present to help attract what they want in the future.

A state of happiness

People sometimes believe that one's life must be free of problems in order to be happy, but this isn't true. One can be happy whether they get something they want — or not. Whether they achieve a goal — or not. And whether they are currently facing challenges — or not.

Lasting happiness comes not from what is happening externally in one's life, but from what is happening within. A person's happiness is influenced by the quality of their thoughts and the manner in which they acknowledge and interpret life experiences as they happen.

One is far more likely to attain a state of happiness by adopting an attitude that allows them to see the value in all life experiences, whatever they may be.

By reducing one's resistance to what *is* — and by accepting the current moment without judgement — one is far freer to transition from one experience to the next without getting mentally, physically, or emotionally hung up on things they have no control over. It is often these "hang ups" that inhibit one's ability to attain a state of happiness.

The more one is able to accept experiences as they happen without trying to change the moments after they've passed, the more one is able to put their energy into shaping the future in ways they desire.

Happiness is not a choice

Seen in a meme: "Happiness is a choice."

No. Happiness is *not* a choice. *Attitude* is a choice. Happiness involves more than putting on a fake smile, acting cheerful, and pretending everything is OK. Sometimes things are *not* OK. And that's OK. That's life.

Stop for a moment and imagine that you're grieving over having just lost a loved one. Now imagine someone comes up to you and says, "Happiness is a choice." Would you believe it? Would you be able to let go of your grief, shrug your shoulders and say, "Ok, I'll be happy now" and *actually be happy*?

Would you tell a suicidal person that "happiness is a choice" and expect this superficial catchphrase to solve the problem? What about people suffering from depression or those who have experienced a psychological trauma? Of course not.

Even if attaining a state of happiness was as simple as making a choice, telling someone who isn't happy that "happiness is a choice" is as about as helpful as teaching someone how to fish by telling them that "there are fish in the sea". It *isn't* helpful.

Happiness is a byproduct of enjoying the journey of life, not a byproduct of willpower.

You teach people to achieve happiness by providing them with the tools necessary to deal with life's challenges in a positive and productive way. You teach people to achieve happiness by showing them ways to navigate their mental and physical world in such a way that they can enjoy their journey. And one of the most effective ways to enjoy one's journey is to adopt a healthy attitude that allows one to appreciate life experiences regardless of one's circumstances.

Suggesting that being anything but happy all the time isn't a healthy way to view life. Making people feel bad about feeling bad isn't terribly effective at making people happy either. The fact is, there is nothing inherently wrong with being unhappy.

Unhappiness and feelings of discontent are an important part of one's emotional alert system. Feelings like these are often a symptom of a greater issue and a sign that something in our life needs to change. Unhappiness with one's situation is often a prerequisite for progress. By putting on a fake smile and ignoring our discontent, we perpetuate our unhappiness by denying ourselves the ability to right what may be wrong in our life.

> *"Healthy discontent is the prelude to progress."*
> — *Mahatma Gandhi*

We may not like everything that happens to us in life and we may not always be happy as a result of what happens, but we can always choose our attitude when dealing with it.

While happiness is not a choice, attitude is. A healthy attitude when dealing with one's issues in life is far more likely to attract genuine happiness than one will by putting on a fake smile and pretending one's discontent doesn't exist.

The danger in believing "Happiness is a choice"

No matter how happy one may act, pretending to be happy doesn't equal happiness. Habitually convincing yourself that you're happy when you're not is potentially dangerous — and here's why:

When a person who is not happy convinces themselves that they are, they remove the incentive needed to make the changes that are necessary to put them on a path to being genuinely happy. This only serves to perpetuate the problem because pretending to be happy doesn't rid a person of any underlying dissatisfaction in their life — it simply covers it up.

It's far more productive to be unhappy and honest with one's self than it is to cover up the symptoms of unhappiness by pretending they don't exist. It is from pretending to be happy that people often fool themselves into settling for careers or relationships that do little more than cause them to drift further from the things that they truly care about.

And the further one drifts from the things that bring them genuine joy, the further they drift from the most potent sources of happiness that exist for them.

Attitude & happiness

The simple decision to be happy isn't as much of a precursor to happiness as a healthy attitude is. A healthy attitude is what enables a person to truly appreciate their journey regardless of their circumstances or the obstacles they encounter along the way.

It is a healthy attitude that allows a person to recognize and be grateful for what they have, to view mistakes as little more than learning experiences, and to see strangers as friends they simply haven't met yet.

It is a healthy attitude that allows a person to survive negative experiences in positive ways, to see the world as a playground instead of a cage, and to recognize the value in all life experiences, not just the "good" ones.

The more one is able to adopt an attitude that allows them to see the value in not just the highlights of their life, but the complete journey, the less one's happiness is interrupted by events that might otherwise rob them of it.

It's OK not to be happy

While being happy is something to celebrate, there are some who promote happiness as if any other option isn't acceptable. As if, if you aren't happy, there's something wrong with you. And that simply isn't true. The ability to feel a full range of emotions and different states of being is an important part of the human experience.

It's ok not to be happy. And in many cases, a large part of personal growth is dependent on recognizing when one is not happy and then actively working through it. Feelings other than happiness are what lead to changes that trigger our transition from one level of awareness to the next.

While not being in a constant state of happiness is not unhealthy, it's important to channel one's mental energy in a positive way and not simply dwell on feelings of discontent, but instead use them as motivation to make productive changes in one's life.

A key to lasting happiness

A key to lasting happiness, inner peace, and a stress-free life is refusing to allow other people to gain control over your emotions. Because if it's something you can't control, it isn't something you should ever anchor your emotional state to.

Anytime a person's emotional state is dependent on or anchored to something beyond their control, a person's emotional state becomes a slave to circumstances. In order for happiness, inner peace, and a stress-free life to last, it must be initiated and maintained from the inside out, not the outside in.

A sense of purpose

Having a sense of purpose in one's life is often enough to generate enthusiasm for living and creates the motivation needed to keep one actively moving forward even when obstacles arise.

Never underestimate the value of setting desirable, achievable goals and pursuing those goals with a sense of purpose.

If you want to be happy

Imagine how hard it would be for someone to be happy if they spent a great deal of their time dwelling on problems, shortcomings, mistakes, criticism, negative events, and the absence of what they desire. And yet people do this and wonder why happiness escapes them. It certainly isn't because they don't know what they feel bad about, it's because of how often they focus on and remind themselves of it.

While it's ok to identify problems, make mistakes, acknowledge criticism, and not be pleased with any of these things, it's important to not let what we consider to be negative experiences hold us back in life or lock us into cycles of self-pity. By holding onto and focusing on what we don't want, we only make it more difficult to distance ourselves from it.

Acknowledging and working through negative experiences is often an integral part of getting us from where we are to where we want to be in life. But occasionally people focus more on what they don't want in their lives than taking action to attract what they do.

If you wish to make it easier for happiness to find you, it's important to visit the problems and negative events in your life as a short-term guest and not a long-term resident. Negative emotions and feelings of discontent are far more useful as motivation to initiate positive changes in our lives than they are as sources of self-doubt and pity.

The more you release yourself from the negatives in your life and let go of the things that are holding you back from being happy, the more you free yourself to adopt a lifestyle that creates an environment that allows for, nurtures, and sustains happiness.

If you want to be happy, don't make a _habit_ of doing what is typically associated with what unhappy people do.

Things that unhappy people do more of:

- ✗ Focus on faults, failures and shortcomings (imagined or not).
- ✗ Focus on feeling miserable.
- ✗ Focus on dreading the future.
- ✗ Consume junk food with reckless abandon and then feel miserable because of it.
- ✗ Isolate themselves from others.
- ✗ Focus on what they've lost or lack in life.
- ✗ Constantly compare themselves to those who are more fortunate than they are.

✗ Unable to accept themselves for who they are.

✗ Unable to see their value as a person.

✗ Lack any sense of purpose.

✗ Pessimistic. Always assume the worst.

✗ Cynical of others' motives without justification.

✗ Make excuses or blame others for bad behavior.

✗ Act rudely or without regard to others.

✗ Refuse trying new things and resist adapting to new situations or environments.

✗ Let what other people say or think impact their sense of self-worth.

Things that *happy* people do *more* of:

✓ Focus on making the most of what they have.

✓ Focus on what they're grateful for, not on what they lack.

✓ Focus on building and furthering relationships.

✓ Focus on accepting themselves for the work-in-progress that they are.

✓ Focus on the now — this moment — and make it the best it can be. Let the future take care of itself.

✓ Focus on improvement, not perfection.

✓ Focus on truly knowing who they are, what their values are, what they stand for, and the type of person they ultimately want to be.

✓ Focus **not** on their mistakes, but on the lessons they learn from them.

✓ Have a purpose. Stand for something. Find something to be passionate about.

✓ Focus on **not** letting people control their feelings or emotions.

✓ Focus on taking responsibility for their life and not blaming others for their well-being.

✓ Don't live in fear other people's thoughts or opinions.

✓ Focus on solutions, not problems.

✓ Do more of the things that make them happy.

✓ Show compassion and value the wellbeing of others.

✓ Act with generosity and maintain an abundance mindset.

✓ Try new things. Learn new skills. Adapt. Say yes to opportunities.

CHAPTER 20 B

UNHAPPINESS

 Depression is a very serious & complex condition. *The contents of this book are not intended to treat depression nor should this information be used as a replacement for professional help. Your life is important to me. Please seek professional help if you need it.*

Please note: *I do not use the words "unhappiness" and "depression" as interchangeable terms. While I can see how unhappiness and depression can be related, they are not the same.*

Note: *The emphasis on distracting one's self from their undesirable thoughts in the lessons in this book are a part of the strategy that has proven to be effective for some people (including me). It is not my intention to suggest that distracting one's self from self-defeating thoughts is easy, a long-term solution, or a cure for any ailment.*

Battles in the dark

No matter how dark things may seem at times, always remember that the demons in your head will do their best to convince you that your worst and most pain-inducing thoughts are the result of rational thinking. They'll use whatever tactics they can to convince you to recalibrate *your entire life* in a way that makes your current situation and feelings seem *normal*.

Your demons will try to deceive you into believing that all the good you've ever experienced and all the positive memories you have are just an exception, or worse, based on falsehoods. They will try to convince you that your *other* life, the one in which you feel better than you do now, is *the lie* and that your current situation is the reality.

Your demons will not only highlight how alone you feel in the world, they'll do their best to convince you that there's no one you can talk to. And that no one cares.

Your demons know your vulnerabilities and will do *everything* they can to exploit them. They will say things like, "There's no point in talking to anyone because no one will understand what you're going through."

They'll lie and suggest that even if you *did* talk to someone:

- They won't be able to "fix" you or your problems (so there's no point)
- They will just feel sorry for you
- They will think you're making a big deal out of nothing or just want attention
- Or they'll suggest that how you're feeling will just freak people out and make things a bigger deal than you would ever want them to be

The demons will use as many unscrupulous tactics that they can to bring you as low as possible. They may suggest that there's no way forward from your current situation or circumstances or feelings.

They may try to convince you that the people that you're closest to in life are not really your friends and that they just put up with you because "you're there". They may suggest that everyone thinks you're stupid or someone to feel sorry for. And if they are particularly brutal, they will try to strike you down with one of the most hurtful lies ever, that it doesn't matter if you're here so it doesn't matter if you're not. They might even suggest that the world would be a *better* place if you weren't in it.

And as I write this on my laptop, while sitting on a stool at a bar in a coffee shop, I have to stop to wipe tears from my eyes. Because I know from experience how painful these thoughts can be and I wouldn't wish them on anyone.

So I need to break away from my "author voice" and speak to you directly as one human being to another. I need you to know that the worst thoughts you have are not true. And that you. are. not. alone.

While it is true that no one may ever know *exactly* how you feel or understand *exactly* what you are going through, *that doesn't matter!* There *are* people in the world who can relate to you, your experiences, and what you are going through in ways that can still be helpful.

And no matter what the demons say, people *do* care. Even people who are not a visible part of your life. Even complete strangers. Because, I can tell you that *I* care. I care about you and your life. I care about your existence. I want you to be here. And I want you to carry on living. And I'm not the only one who does.

The world is full of people who want to help ease the pain and suffering of others. Who want to show people that no matter how dark things may seem at times, there is a way forward and that life can get better.

Just because your demons make you feel weak, doesn't mean that *you* are. In fact, fighting one's demons may just be the most difficult battle anyone ever faces in their life. And if you can hold on long enough to win it, you will see how strong you really are and how much your life can truly change for the better.

So please, don't listen to your demons. Refuse to listen to their lies. Know that no matter how dark things may seem at times, there is a way forward into the light. And that you have within you the power, strength, and resolve to get there.

And that's the truth.

You have the right

You have as much of a right to be here as anyone else. Never let anyone else try to convince you otherwise. And don't ever let anyone — including the voice in your head — make you feel like it would be better if you didn't exist.

It's your life and you have the right to live it. You are not here to live for the approval of other people. And you are never under any obligation to oblige the negative thoughts associated with whatever is making you miserable.

⚡ Life is hard. And it isn't fair. And it really hurts like hell sometimes. But if you focus on what is within your power to change for the better, you can. And you will.

"Don't think about it." Yeah, right.

It's one thing for someone to suggest that simply distracting one's self from their worst thoughts can be an effective way to overcome them, it's another thing entirely to try to do it — especially at a time when a person feels like they need to.

The fact is, a person's mind is likely the most arduous opponent they will ever be forced to face in their life. Our thoughts can be very difficult to escape from and our brain knows all of our tricks. We habitually fall into patterns of thought that are very difficult to break out of. And efforts to redirect our thinking frequently end in failure.

Often, people who we consider to have little understanding of how we feel or what we're going through, say, "Don't think about it." as if it's easy or a cure for whatever it is that ails us.

Redirecting one's thoughts is neither easy or a cure for anything. It can, however, be an effective strategy to reduce the amount of time we spend feeling miserable or thinking undesirable thoughts. But it takes a tremendous amount of mental discipline and *many* attempts to make it work with any consistency.

One thing that can assist us is in this process is how we choose to talk to ourselves and the kinds of questions we ask ourselves when we're feeling bad. Here are some examples:

If I focus on the worst of this situation and all of the things that I *don't* want or *don't* want to happen, will it improve my situation or make me feel better? No. Then this probably isn't a good thing to do.

Have I experienced difficult times before? Yes. Have I survived them? Yes. And the chances are good I will survive this one as well.

Does beating myself up or focusing on how things *could* have gone if I made different decisions going to help? No.

Is this simply a life experience that some people are forced to go through (despite no interest in or intention of doing so)? Yes.

Can I do anything positive and productive about [whatever it is] now? If I can, I should do that thing. If I can't, then is there any point in continuing to focus on how bad it makes me feel? No. Particularly because the worse I feel about something and the more emotional I get, the less likely I am to make rational decisions.

I may not be able to solve my problems right now, but are there any positive or productive things I can do to make this situation *easier* for myself so I don't continue to feel miserable?

Is focusing on the things that make me feel the worst the best possible thing to do at this time? No. Is it possible for me to skip ahead, focus on something else, and bypass feeling as awful as my brain wants me to? What are some ways I can do that?

*The questions above are reflective of a line of thinking that helped me through a hard time. **Your results may vary.***

In all of this, it's important to be more persistent in your attempts to get out of your train of thought than your brain is in trying to remind you of all the things you wish to avoid thinking about.

But if one is already feeling miserable, even the effort of distracting one's self can be a welcome distraction from what would otherwise be an unhindered string of tired, old, repetitive, abusive thoughts. And with practice, one can, at least, shorten the amount of time that one spends feeling miserable or letting their mind run rampant with thoughts that don't do anyone any good.

Don't you ever give up

You may be hurting. And feeling powerless. And feeling tired. You may be surrounded by people and still feeling alone in the world. But you will get through this. And you will be stronger because of it.

There are kind people in the world that you don't even know, who would do anything in their power to help lift you up, if they could. But in order for it to really make a difference, you're the one who has to do it. You have something inside of you that is stronger than anything holding you down. You have to find the strength to focus on what really matters to you. Your loves. Your joys. The things that make you laugh and smile and make you want to share it with the world.

You may not always feel like it, but you make a bigger difference in the world than you can possibly imagine. Your smile alone can change someone's day for the better. And that single day can lead to any number of good things in the future. The ripple effect of a *single* act of kindness can change an *entire* life.

You may sometimes feel like the whole world is against you — perhaps even now — but it just isn't true. There are countless compassionate people who don't know you, but still care greatly about you and your well-being. If you've ever been smiled at or treated kindly by a complete stranger, then you've experienced just a tiny glimpse of this. It may sometimes feel like no one cares, but they do. I promise you — they do.

So please, let go of your negative thoughts and focus on what is within your power to change for the better. It is through the steady process of taking positive action that you will get through this difficult time. Maybe not today. Maybe not tomorrow. But keep trying and you will.

Rid your mind of the notion that giving up is an option and find the courage to keep trying. It may not be easy, but it will be worth it.

 Depression deceives people into believing that their worst thoughts are rational.

Downward spirals

Whether the problems are your own or those presented to you by the news or social media, one of the most deceptively easy ways to begin feeling bad is to start focusing on problems without considering solutions and, ultimately, taking action. The chances of miraculously solving problems by doing nothing other than focusing on how bad they are and how bad they make you feel are next to none.

Not only is casually or subconsciously focusing on problems one of the quickest ways to feel uneasy and overwhelmed, many times you won't even realize *why* you suddenly feel miserable, only that you do. This is why it's important to be aware of how one's focus and attention affects one's mental energy.

The more a person focuses on problems or self-defeating thoughts without doing anything about them, the more likely they are to slip into a state of mental weakness.

Because our feelings affect our interpretation of what we see, problems not only appear more frequently when we're down, we see them as more severe than we do when we're feeling good. It is in this way of focusing on a series of small or seemingly insignificant problems — or repetitious negative thoughts — that one can slowly slide into a negative mental state in which problems appear more frequently and more significant. This then leads people to focus more and more on an ever-increasing series of problems or negative thoughts that cause them to feel increasingly worse. Until eventually, they find themselves sucked into a negative downward spiral from which there appears to be no way to escape.

One way to slow or even reverse one's descent into feelings of increasing unease is to deliberately redirect one's focus. It's important to recognize that problems are far less likely to be solved from a state of mental weakness than they are from a state of empowerment. So when a person finds themselves feeling worse and worse as a result of focusing on negative thoughts, purposefully abandoning those thoughts and redirecting themselves to better ones can allow them to re-attain their state of emotional equilibrium. It isn't at all easy. And it takes many attempts, but trying to do something to help one's self with the possibility of success is a far more productive alternative to feeling miserable and doing nothing.

We are helped by helping

Happiness is more likely to manifest itself in one's life as a result of making a positive difference in *other* people's lives than it is by solely seeking to benefit one's own. One of the most positive ways to distract yourself from your own negative thinking is to focus your energy and attention on helping someone else.

Don't dwell on what isn't going well

Sometimes work sucks or our relationships suck and we find ourselves feeling down as a result of thinking about all of the things that aren't as we wish them to be in our lives.

At times like this it's important to remember that whatever one focuses on grows stronger. This can be to one's *benefit* or one's detriment depending on *where* one places their attention.

If you truly desire a positive change in your life, then focus on what actions you'll take to change things for the better — don't dwell on what isn't going well.

 If you treat your mind like a trash can, don't be surprised when you reach for a thought and all you get is garbage.

When the state of the world gets you down

When the state of the world gets you down, remember to focus on what is within your power to change. Don't forget that you are in control of where you place your attention and what actions you take as a result.

There is always something you can do to improve *yourself* or the life of *someone else*. And if you can't figure out how to do the former, then focus on the latter. Because when we help make a positive difference in other people's lives, we also make a positive difference in our own.

In a world where bad examples are prevalent, let how you live your life be a good one.

CHAPTER 21

WELLNESS

⚡ Never underestimate the value of good health. Your health impacts every moment of your life.

Self-deception

If you're lying to yourself or intentionally avoiding the truth about some aspect of your life, it's likely not a matter of *if* you will regret it, but *when*.

If you have a problem in your life — and you *know* it — consider this a sign that it's time to *face reality and fix it*. And if you could use some help to do it, *get some*. Even seemingly small issues can turn into *huge* problems when left unchecked.

You and your life are far too important to keep putting off until later what you can do *today*. When you respect yourself enough to let go of the lies and embrace the truth about your life or situation, you put yourself back on a path that no longer needs lies to make life bearable.

Effort required

If you frequently find yourself feeling bad, unhealthy, unfulfilled, or unsatisfied, recognize that these are all signs telling you that something needs to change. And while we instinctually know this, our habits of thought will sometimes work against us by continually talking us out of doing things that we know would be good for us.

Your brain will sometimes suggest that the changes you are thinking about initiating will do you no good or that they are not worth the effort or discomfort you anticipate.

It's important to always be mindful of the fact that the more that you do nothing, the more that nothing will change. And the more that nothing changes, the worse you may feel.

Refuse to continually put off doing things that have the potential to make you feel better and change your life in a positive way. Don't listen to the part of your brain that says making changes isn't worth it. Because if you are miserable, attempts to make things better are always worth it. Even if you fail, they provide valuable information that can then help push you forward.

Do more of what makes you healthy

Seen in a meme: "Do more of what makes you happy."

Not everything that makes a person "happy" makes a person *healthy*. Too much of a good thing can have *negative* consequences.

Because at least to some degree of happiness stems from feeling good about one's self, it stands to reason that the better one feels about themselves, their decisions, their life, and their health, the greater their sense of well-being.

Happiness is more likely to manifest itself in one's life as a result of seeking a *healthy **mind**, a healthy **body**, and a healthy **spirit*** than it is by seeking the instant gratification of doing only more of what makes them happy.

Do more of what makes you ***healthy*** and happiness will follow.

 Healthy habits harbor happiness. Unhealthy habits hinder happiness. Choose your habits wisely.

The power of consistency

Because small actions when repeated often enough can lead to significant results, anything you do with consistency over prolonged periods of time can have a major impact on your life. This is one of the ways in which seemingly insignificant bad habits can have devastating consequences over time. The power of consistency is a very simple, yet often overlooked and under-appreciated concept.

You don't have to be the best, the brightest, the fastest, or the most talented to reap the rewards of consistency, you just have to be consistent. This means continually taking steps towards your goals despite challenges, hardships, and the unexpected. It means not allowing anything to deter you from making progress over time.

There is an immense amount of power in being consistent — especially if you're deliberate with what you do and how you spend your time. Whether you wish to be successful in a manner that is meaningful to you, or you simply want to better yourself in some way, first determine exactly what it is you wish to do and then commit to taking steps towards what you want.

No one can make you get fit

No one can make you get fit. And no one and nothing can stop you from getting fit if you truly want to. Your fitness is *your choice.*

The most powerful foe you will ever face on the road to improving your health is yourself.

 Create an environment in yourself and your life where good things feel welcome, and good things will come.

Improve your fitness, improve your life

The discipline you learn from getting fit is discipline you take everywhere. The strength you acquire from physical fitness is strength you carry everywhere. When you improve your fitness, you improve *your life.*

Do your future-self a favor every day

No matter what kind of day you're having and no matter what is going on in your life, do *at least one thing every day* that gets you at least one step closer to your goals. No excuses.

No one has as much of a stake in your well-being, your goals, and the rest of your life than *you* do. Do your future-self a favor *every day.*

Invest in bettering yourself and the future you. Let your future self look back on the changes you make today and be thankful you made them.

Healthy is a lifestyle

People often put a great deal of effort into getting into shape only to fall out of it after they achieve their goal. This is because they abandon the things they did that got them results.

It's important to understand that being healthy requires more than short-term changes to one's life that are abandoned after one reaches their goal. Getting what you desire in life is as much about the process of *getting* it as it is about creating the circumstances and environment in your life to *keep* it.

Unless your life is set up in a way to keep and maintain what you get, you won't be able to hold onto it for very long. This is why it's important to build good habits that *support* your efforts in *not only* getting what you want, but also in creating an environment that allows you to keep it.

Think of it this way: Anyone with enough money can buy a pony, but just because one can *have* a pony doesn't mean anything about their life is set up in a way to accommodate one.

Always keep in mind that in order for a person to attain the kind of life and health they desire, one must not only take steps to *get* it, one must *also* be able to accommodate it after they do.

Under the influence

Be very careful about growing dependent upon "recreational substances" that alter your mood and attitude. The more you seek substances as a means to escape life, the more difficult it may become to separate who you *truly* are, the thoughts you have, and the decisions you make from the chemicals you're under the influence of.

It is not uncommon for people to look back and regret how much time they spent escaping from life instead of actually living it with intention. Recreational substances can create the illusion that everything is copacetic in a person's world, while in reality, their life drifts further and further from the places they truly want to go.

The secret of the Fountain of Youth

The secret of the fountain of youth is not in anything that can be bought. The secret of the fountain of youth is *a healthy attitude towards aging.*

It is a healthy attitude towards aging that allows a person to concern themselves less with the lines on their face and more with adopting a mindset that allows them to age with grace.

The energy one has, the enthusiasm they carry, and the playfulness of their spirit often does far more to make one appear youthful and full of life than perpetually applying chemicals to one's face in order to reduce the signs of aging.

Wrinkles are superficial. If you wish to combat the effects of aging, start from the inside out by making your physical and mental well-being a priority in your life.

Besides obvious things like being active and following a healthy diet, reducing stress on both your body and your mind is one of the most effective ways to minimize the effect that aging has on your body.

Develop positive relationships

Whether it involves family, friends, coworkers, or complete strangers, feeling a sense of connection with others is vital to one's emotional well-being. Research shows that developing and maintaining positive relationships can not only boost one's immune system and help one deal with stress, it can actually increase one's life expectancy. Those who fail to develop strong social relationships are far more susceptible to stress, depression, and a lowered immune system.

CHAPTER 22

INTERACTING WITH OTHERS

⚡ Not everyone with a problem needs you to solve it. Sometimes all a person needs is to feel like they've been heard. Listening without judging can be more effective than injecting your opinions or trying to solve a problem that doesn't have an easy answer.

The value in difficult people

"He that wrestles with us strengthens our nerves, and sharpens our skill. Our antagonist is our helper."
— Edmund Burke

In the same way that the hardest lessons we learn in life are often the most valuable, so, too, are the difficult people we meet along the way. Even the unfriendliest and most challenging person we cross paths with has something of value to teach us about ourselves. Sometimes we need to learn patience. Sometimes it's self-discipline. And sometimes it's to not let other people have so much control over our thoughts, feelings, and emotions.

Whatever it may be, the people we find particularly challenging are valuable because they can instantly highlight weaknesses in our self-control. They can trigger us to think, act, or behave in such a way that isn't congruent with the type of person we want to be.

But every experience we have in life — whether we choose to label it as "good" or "bad" — is an opportunity for growth. And every encounter we have with difficult people provides us with an opportunity to identify the things we need to work on in order to close the gaps between the person we are and the person we want to be.

One of the keys to surviving experiences with difficult people — without being brought to the brink of behaving badly — is to see their behavior as an example of how you *don't* want to be.

With practice, we can choose to refuse to let others cause us to act in ways that are in direct conflict with the person we picture ourselves as. Rather than relinquish our power to other people by allowing their bad behavior to be a trigger for our own, we can act from a position of strength, not weakness, by remaining true to our ideal self. And we can create the frame-of-mind necessary to do this by choosing to see the *value* in the difficult people we encounter in life by actively using our experiences with them in such a way that we become *not* bitter, but *better*.

Dealing with mean people

One of the reasons that being mean to mean people isn't terribly effective is that people learn most through the observation of others or through personal experience. Giving someone a taste of their own medicine is very unlikely to teach them anything new or show them that there's a better way.

By being mean to a mean person, you're simply showing that person a behavior they're *already* familiar with. All your negative actions do is demonstrate that *you* can stoop to *their* level. And now instead of just *one* person acting badly, there are *two*. And rather than *solve* the problem, it makes things worse. Two people acting badly does not solve the problem of one person acting badly.

If you want to teach someone a "lesson", *be a role model and set a good example*. Don't let the bad behavior of others be an excuse to also act badly. You'll know you're on the right track when, if everyone imitated your actions, the world would be a nicer place.

> **Remember:** *We judge ourselves by our intentions and others by their actions. Other people don't know what you're thinking. They don't hear your internal dialogue. They can only guess what you're thinking by interpreting how you act and carry yourself.*

One less idiot

Idiot (noun): 1. a foolish person

I'm an optimist. I like to see the best in people. I believe human beings are inherently good. I believe people are capable of achieving far more than they believe. I encourage tolerance, kindness, and open minds.

That said, knowing this one simple fact may prove beneficial in getting through life: Idiots are everywhere (and sometimes we are those idiots). That probably won't change. But what *can* change is who we are and how we act when we cross paths with idiots. Because, sadly, we often let other idiots turn us into idiots without thinking.

The more we resist the urge to let others control our emotions and our actions in a negative way, the less likely we are to let idiots turn us into idiots and the happier and more in control of our lives we will be.

Our attitude and how we handle ourselves is always our responsibility. Always remember that although we may not know exactly what to do when we cross paths with idiots, we can *always* choose how we act. And by choosing not to let an idiot turn us into an idiot, that's one less idiot there will be in the world.

Negative expectations

When it comes to interacting with others, *expectations matter*. How we approach and communicate with people has a huge impact on how they respond. By simply *expecting* someone to be hostile towards us, we add to the probability that our expectation will become a reality.

Body language and non-verbal communication speak volumes even when *we* don't. If you wish to maximize your ability to connect with and interact with people in a positive way, be sure not to sabotage your efforts with negative expectations.

This doesn't just apply to encounters with people, it also applies to life. Negative expectations often lead to negative experiences. By learning to always see the possibility of positive outcomes — even in difficult situations — one makes the positive far more possible than they ever will with negative expectations.

Your network

The person with a broad personal network of people they can turn to for advice, services, friendship, and more will always have an advantage over the person that doesn't. As they say,

"It's not always *what* you know, but *who* you know that matters".

Recognize the value in developing relationships with all kinds of people from all walks of life — from personal to professional. Get to know your neighbors, local shop owners and service providers, and others you cross paths with. It is often as simple as asking questions and expressing genuine interest in people.

Not everyone you meet will work their way into your lives in a truly meaningful way, but it doesn't hurt to *know* people. The more people you have in your personal network, the more likely you or they will eventually be an asset to you or someone else you can connect them to.

Always keep in mind that the person who develops meaningful and mutually beneficial relationships with others will be presented with far more opportunities as a result of those relationships than the person who goes it alone.

The good, the bad, and the rude

It should go without saying, but not every act of rudeness is intentional. In fact, many are not. This is an important thing to remember because how we react to perceived misbehavior or bad manners often has a significant impact on the outcome of an encounter.

When you treat someone you perceive to be rude with rudeness, it doesn't give the person you are reacting to the impression that *they* are being rude, it gives them the impression that *you are.*

You don't have to allow yourself to be treated poorly or abused, but there is a better way to deal with perceived offenses than with rudeness or hostility. Remaining calm in an encounter not only assists you in thinking clearly and maintaining a level head, it allows you to avoid saying or doing anything that you may later regret or that can be used against you.

By refusing to sacrifice your self-control in response to perceived offenses, you maintain your personal power, increase the likelihood of a positive resolution, and avoid having to take responsibility for making a situation worse.

Always remember that we don't all perceive the world the same way. We don't all use the same words or type of language when we communicate. Words are not always used in ways that relate to their conventional definitions. We don't all value the same things equally or have the same priorities. And we especially don't have the same level of awareness.

Don't attribute to intentional rudeness to what can easily be explained by a lack of self-awareness or poor social skills. And don't respond to perceived offenses in a way that will make you as guilty of bad behavior as the person you're reacting to.

Clarity

Clarification is often the difference between wasting time, effort, and money or not. Refuse to let a lack of clarity or someone's poor communication skills keep you from getting the information you need to make proper decisions and take appropriate actions. It is not your responsibility to read people's minds or guess what they are trying to say. Always ask for clarity when it's necessary.

Relationships & teamwork

From acquaintances to best friends to married couples, all great friendships involve teamwork. Teamwork sits alongside trust, communication, and tolerance as a building block of the best relationships.

Teamwork is *not* "What can I *get* out of this relationship?", it's "What can I *bring* to this relationship to make it better?"

It's the combined commitment to overcome obstacles. It's support. It's encouragement. It's working together. It's rising to the challenge of bettering yourself for the benefit of the whole.

Teamwork is providing the support and encouragement necessary to help others better themselves and succeed in their endeavors.

Whether it's providing a kind word, sincere appreciation, a listening ear, or something else entirely, never stop trying to add value to your relationships. Never underestimate the power of *teamwork*. And never stop asking, *"What can I do to make this relationship better?"*

Relationships 101

Many people make the mistake of no longer putting effort into doing the things that created the conditions for falling in love with their partner possible. If you don't want to look back and wonder how you lost what you had, never stop doing the kinds of things that made you and your partner fall in love with each other in the first place.

Relations & relationships

Many of the strongest and most rewarding relationships are formed by people who don't agree on everything. With a respectful attitude and an open mind, people with conflicting views can help each other grow and learn by assisting one another in seeing the world from a different perspective. An expanded point of view is a good thing.

No matter how much the media wants to pit one group against the other, nothing is ever as black and white as it's made out to be. The fact is, we're all human, we all share this planet, and on many levels, we're on the *same* side.

One will always find that making peace with people is far more rewarding — and leads to far greater things — than waging battles with anyone who holds an opposing view.

Living in harmony

Being able to live in harmony with other humans is largely dependent on being able to effectively communicate with those who choose to live their lives differently than you do. Always remember that spewing negativity and hate never leads to less hate and negativity.

The justification of everything

Regardless of whether the outcome of an action is considered "good" or "bad", everyone does things for reasons they consider *reasonable* at the time. Knowing this is an important key to understanding people.

- *I steal because I'm poor.*
- *I poach endangered animals because I'm trying to feed my family.*
- *I flipped that guy the finger because he cut me off in traffic.*
- *I beat my dog because he crapped on the carpet again.*
- *I'm a drug addict because it helps me cope with life.*
- *I hate on a particular group because their beliefs are against my religion.*
- *I hit my girlfriend because she was pissing me off.*
- *I treat men poorly because a man was abusive to me.*
- *I litter because I know it always gets picked up.*
- *I run red lights when I'm in a hurry.*
- *I'm demanding of wait staff because it is their job to serve me and I expect good service.*
- *I work for a company that causes harm because I need the job.*
- *I double park because I don't want my doors to get dented.*
- *I shot an unarmed kid because I felt threatened.*
- *I text when I drive because I'm careful, unlike everyone else.*

Whether it's "right" or "wrong", everyone feels *justified* for doing what they do.

---

*Having made this point, I want to make it clear that the ends don't always justify the means. Having a reason for bad or immoral behavior doesn't excuse it. But if you want to find common ground or communicate effectively with people, it's important to understand that everyone has what **they** feel are legitimate reasons for what they choose to do. Although sometimes those reasons stem from ignorance or a lack of self-awareness.*

Dealing with drama

People like to declare that they don't like drama without recognizing that the drama in a person's life is often in direct proportion to their involvement with that drama.

Just because you have an invitation to drama doesn't mean you have to attend. Never add fuel to a fire if you don't want to deal with the consequences. Drama may enter your life unexpectedly, but it won't live there if you don't let it.

And saying you don't like drama isn't necessary because *no one likes* drama. Even the people who always find themselves in it. Saying you don't like drama is often an admission of how much drama there is in your life.

Wait. Don't settle.

It's important at the beginning of any relationship not to confuse short-term attraction and desire with long-term chemistry and compatibility.

Many people live with the hope of meeting someone special to share their lives with, but then settle for far less than what they *truly* seek. They fall for the false first impression. They fall for the physical and superficial. And they grow comfortable with the convenience of being with someone — even when that someone isn't ideally suited to who they are or where they want to go in life. Or worse, they let their fear of being single override their desire to leave what turns out to be an unhealthy and dysfunctional relationship.

It's important to not want something to succeed so badly that you sacrifice who you are or what you truly want out of life in the process of trying to make it happen.

For relationships to last, it is essential that couples are able to truly connect with one another on multiple levels and demonstrate that their core values are compatible enough to allow them to stay together long after the honeymoon phase has passed.

Anyone can chase you, put their best foot forward, and adopt an attractive demeanor. Anyone can act agreeable, put in a little effort from time to time, and make you their flavor of the week. But if you're looking for a serious, sincere, and meaningful relationship that lasts, always remember that it isn't just *anyone* that you seek.

- Wait for the person who accepts you for who you are without seeking to change you into someone they want you to be.
- Wait for the person who can appreciate your quirks without simply seeing them as something they have to tolerate.
- Wait for the person who sees in you the potential for true friendship and not just a warm body or a matter of convenience.
- Wait for the person who values you and your relationship enough to actually communicate their feelings.
- Wait for the person who will let you grow as an individual without insisting that you never change.
- Wait for the person who trusts you enough to not try to control or manipulate you.
- Wait for the person who doesn't simply see you as an option, but as a priority in their life.
- Wait for the person who isn't just nice when they want something — or who shows you appreciation only when it's convenient.
- Wait for someone with integrity and whose words are reinforced by their actions.
- Wait for the person who wants to be the best person they can be for themselves, for others, and for you. Not just for a night, a day, a week, or a year, but always.

Wait. Don't settle.

The other one

Always keep in mind that while it *is* important to find someone who works *with* the person you are as well as the person you want to be, it's also important to not get so caught up in the idea of not settling that you seek something that isn't attainable. While people who are perfect *for you* do exist, if you are looking for a perfect person, that person will remain elusive, because *perfect people do not exist.*

Anyone that presents themselves as perfect or who initially appears perfect will never stay that way. Everyone has a history. Everyone has made mistakes. And everyone has thoughts, opinions, beliefs, and experiences that will not match your own.

In your desire to find someone to spend your life with, it is important to remain open to people who you haven't always considered to be your type. Because if you haven't found someone yet, part of the problem may be that you haven't been looking in the right places or considering people who could actually be perfect for you if you only gave them the opportunity to show it (and yourself the chance to see it).

Also, keep in mind that rarely are the things that we repeatedly experience in life the result of random chance. The patterns in our lives are often the result of things *we* do that make *those* things possible.

If you have repeatedly found yourself in dysfunctional relationships for example, it is often a sign that something you are doing is attracting into your life or being attracted to the kinds of people and situations that make these relationships possible.

While physical chemistry is important, always be mindful of the fact that how a person looks on the outside will *always* change. As much as you may be attracted to the physical aspects of a person when you meet them, understand that the physical characteristics of a person will change dramatically over time. And if you are not deeply connected to *who* the person is, *how* they act, their values, their beliefs, and how they make you feel, then it isn't likely that how a person looks will be enough to keep you together as their appearance changes.

While it isn't necessary to find someone who is walking the exact same path as you are in life (and to do so would be extremely unlikely), it *is* important to find someone who is heading in the same general direction. Because, as close as you may seem at the time you meet, the more you progress along your paths in life, the more that the distance between those paths will cause issues. It is these differences in direction that cause people to be unhappy when they are in one place, but wish they were in another.

While people will occasionally come along that make us consider changing our direction in life in order to accommodate their desires, and because we allow ourselves to believe that their path could be as enticing as our own, if their path requires us to change our core values or our major life goals, we will forever find ourselves conflicted between how things are and how we would like them to be.

Ultimately, if you're looking for someone to spend your life with, it is essential to be compatible with your mate in such a way that your lives can grow together rather than grow apart.

Always make a point to discuss the things that are of most value to you in a relationship and most valuable to your future. While you should never look for a perfect person, you should also never settle for someone who will force you to compromise your core values or your major life goals.

Accept people

Accept and love people for who they are. Never enter into a romantic relationship expecting or wanting someone to change. If you can't like, live with, or love someone as they are, then any relationship you enter into with that person will likely lead to issues.

Only the changes that people make of their own accord are the ones that reflect what that person wants. You can influence someone to develop better habits, for example, but actively pressuring a person to change some aspect of who they are so that it meets your standards or approval *may* lead to changes, but this often means that a person is pretending to be someone they wouldn't naturally be.

It is far better to be with someone who is being true to themselves than it is to be with someone who is only *pretending* to be the kind of person you want them to be.

Extreme isolation

While it can be very good to occasionally get away and distance yourself from people as a way to reset, rebalance, or get to know yourself better, refuse to be allured into thinking that isolating yourself for longer and longer periods of time will lead to feeling better. Because, as comforting as it may initially seem, extreme isolation can lead to *more* discomfort and *more* pain than whatever it is that made you desire isolation in the first place. This is because human beings are social creatures.

The human brain is a wonderful thing, but it is not without its faults. One of its faults is that it continually tells us stories to help us make sense of what we perceive in the world. Our brain is forever writing the narrative of our life, and often, when it doesn't know the actual reason for something, it will simply fabricate an explanation that seems to make sense. And we reflexively believe this explanation because no evidence exists to prove that what our brain is telling us is false.

When a person spends an excessive amount of time alone, their brain continues to narrate the story of their life and fill in the gaps about why other people did what they did (or do what they do), but without any verification that the stories our brain is telling us are actually true. And the longer we go without a significant connection to other people, the more of this made up information we may believe that has no basis in reality.

Accentuate the positive

Every day you have the power to bring out the best in people simply by sincerely highlighting those things you appreciate about them.

When you focus on the things you enjoy most about people, you not only encourage more of the types of behaviors you like to see in others, your focus on the positive makes it even more likely you'll find it.

CHAPTER 23

COMMUNICATION

⚡ Don't mistake someone's willingness to show vulnerability as weakness. It takes a great deal of courage to show vulnerability. And that takes strength.

If you want to be heard

Ranting, raving, and shouting at people may allow you to get something off your chest, and like-minded people may cheer you as you do, but if what you say falls on deaf ears, it won't make a difference.

In order for a complaint or criticism to make a significant difference, it needs to be communicated in a way that allows the person or people who need to hear it to remain open to hearing it.

If all you do is shout at or insult your opposition, your opposition isn't going to listen. Getting people to consider what you have to say, particularly if it challenges them, means communicating in a way that keeps them *open* and receptive to what you have to say, even if they don't agree.

Until you can communicate your thoughts and ideas in a way that people are open to considering them, you can talk, shout, rant, or complain until you're blue in the face, but you won't be heard by those who actually need to hear it.

Sincerity

There is a big difference between saying or doing something kind because you feel it is expected of you out of politeness, and saying or doing something kind because you *truly* mean it.

When your true intention is kindness, don't just go through the motions without communicating in a way that reflects your sincerity. Know that people can not only *hear* the difference when you speak with or without sincerity, they can *feel* it.

If you wish to give your acts of kindness the power they deserve, take the time to express yourself like you mean what you say. Speak clearly and sincerely and use your eyes, your body language, and your actions to convey your message.

You might be surprised at how much of a difference it makes when it's completely obvious to others that you mean what you say. When you convey your message sincerely, it feels better for everyone because it *is* better for everyone.

Sincerity is *huge*.

Magic words

"Please", "Thank you", and "You're welcome" are magic words, but they lose much of their power when expressed as reflexive gestures as opposed to when they are communicated with intention and sincerity.

If you're going to take the time to express things like, "Please", "Thank you", and "You're welcome — and you truly mean what you say — don't just say the words without putting some thought and feeling behind them, or acknowledging the person you're saying them to in a meaningful way.

"Yup" does *not* hold anywhere near as much power as "*You're welcome.*" does.

Caring, appreciation, and gratitude

Always remember to reinforce your positive thoughts and feelings with *actions* because until you convert a thought into an action, it's just potential energy.

Kind words, when spoken sincerely, *are* wonderful, but they become even *more* powerful when you reinforce the truth in what you say with actions that are congruent with your words.

If you care about, appreciate, or are grateful for something or someone in your life, be sure your actions consistently communicate these sentiments.

The perfect person, candidate, cause, or product

From personal relationships to business to politics, the person who isn't afraid to be themselves, make mistakes, and even challenge you, is generally acting with far more authenticity and integrity than the person attempting to do, say, and convey all the right things in order to win your affection, support or business.

Beware of those afraid to show their human side or the work or the thought process that led to whatever they're saying or selling.

Beware of those who repeatedly deflect personal responsibility or blame others for their own mistakes, failures, and shortcomings. And beware of those who repeatedly change their message in order to make themselves, or what they have to offer appear more valuable.

Don't fall victim to those seemingly perfect people or products that cater to your ego, or sense of self-worth, in order to profit from your patronage. No one in this world is perfect. There are only people who pretend to be.

Saying what needs to be said

There's a reason why coaches don't always speak at the same volume with the same tone of voice. Having the greatest positive impact and having the greatest number of friends are often at odds with each other.

Often, what people *think* they want and what they *actually* need are not one and the same. Sometimes the words people need to hear, in order to make the greatest positive difference in their lives, are not soft and gentle, but instead, communicated in a way that hit them like a kick in the ass.

If you speak bluntly at times, you won't please everyone, but your message will be far more effective than if you always try to.

It is far more respectful to your audience to say what needs to be said than it is to always water down what you want to communicate to the point that it is no longer effective.

The best coaches, the best bosses, the best CEOs in the world don't do their jobs effectively by always telling people what they want to hear. They do their best jobs by making the greatest positive impact, by saying what needs to be said.

Matters of miscommunication

The same page

Many miscommunications are perpetuated by people who fail to check that they are either being understood correctly or correctly understanding someone. One effective means of reducing misunderstandings is to repeat back to the person what you think they said.

"If I'm understanding you correctly, what you're saying is..." It is in this way that you can make sure you're on the same page as the person you're speaking with.

Active listening

While it's important to be able to express yourself clearly, it's equally, if not more important to be able to *listen* effectively.

Many misunderstandings occur because, rather than listen closely when others are speaking, people use the time to plan what they're going to say next. They listen with the intent to reply, rather than listen with the intent to understand. By listening carefully when others are speaking, we are not only likely to learn more, we're better able to make meaningful contributions to conversations.

Interrupting

Unless it is for the purpose of clarification, interrupting someone to steer a conversation in a different direction is not only an indication that you aren't listening closely, it's a sign that you think what you have to say is more important than what the speaker is saying.

While interrupting someone can be acceptable in fun and playful conversations between friends, it can be disrespectful and offensive in any exchange meant to be taken seriously.

Always use caution before interrupting someone and, by all means, learn to recognize when you have a habit of doing so.

Your voice is always a choice

It's important to be mindful of the fact that we are not only responsible for *what* we say when we speak, we are also responsible for *how* we say it.

The volume at which a person says things and the tone in which they say them are always controlled by the person speaking.

Your voice is always a choice.

An honest enemy is better than a false friend

An honest enemy is better than a false friend. When in doubt, pay more attention to what people do and less to what they say. Actions not only speak louder than words, they are more difficult to fake.

> *"Lieber ein ehrlicher Feind, als ein falscher Freund"*
> *"Better an honest enemy than a false friend"*
> — *German Proverb*

Liar liar

If you have a problem with "Tell the truth, even if it hurts", then know that what you're essentially saying is that it's *okay* for people to lie to *you*, as long as the lie appeals to your ego and sense of self-worth.

If you want to build a relationship based on false beliefs and miscommunication, then lying to a person because it makes them feel better — or makes you feel better about yourself — is an excellent way to accomplish this.

Not only is this *not* an open or honest way to communicate, it's one of the reasons why so many friendships and marriages fail. Because rather than *truly* address and resolve issues, friends or couples choose to cover them up with "little white lies."

Note that the definition of a liar doesn't say anything about the size of the lie or whether it makes someone feel better. Lying to people to comfort them caters to their weaknesses rather than helping them develop their strengths.

Often, the answer to improving relationships is not to pretend to be interested in or supportive of something, or to say things that one doesn't mean, it's to simply be truly honest, open, and sincere. By knowing that you can always expect the truth from someone, regardless of what it's about, you develop a kind of genuine trust that can't be built any other way.

Airing of grievances

If a disproportionate number of the conversations you have with people involve complaining or highlighting things you don't like, it might be wise to consider either accepting the things you can't change, changing the things you can, or both.

Whatever the case, unless you are explicitly invited to express your ongoing dissatisfaction with people, places, or events in your life and have a goal of working through and solving your problems, there's a very good chance no one actually enjoys listening to you complain.

While venting is often associated with a release of frustration, it is also known to perpetuate problems because it temporarily fools people into feeling as if they've reduced or resolved an issue in their life when all they've really done is complain about it.

Always keep in mind that complaining about how life isn't treating you fairly doesn't make life treat you any more fairly. Complaining about how something isn't going your way, doesn't make it suddenly go your way. And complaining about how difficult something is doesn't make it any easier.

The solution to one's problems is not to be problem-focused, but *solution-oriented*. This means not just identifying problems, but taking an active role in trying to solve them.

When a person makes it clear they want to *solve* an issue and not just complain about it, they don't just invite solutions to the problem, they create an opportunity for others to help solve them. And helping to solve problems is something most people are far more interested in doing than simply listening to someone complain.

Always remember that pointing out problems doesn't fix problems as much as working towards solutions does.

How to tell when someone just wants to fight

How to tell when someone just wants to fight:

- Rather than talk about the issue, they talk about *you*.
- Rather than actively moving towards a peaceful resolution, they turn *you* into the opposition.
- Rather than making it an "us vs. the problem", it becomes "me vs. you."
- Rather than taking what you say at face value, they choose to twist or misinterpret what you say to meet their own narrative.
- They may accuse you of being defensive when you are simply stating facts or your opinion.
- They may tell you what you think, put words in your mouth, or provide their own justification for your actions.
- They may tell you what good things they used to think about you before telling you they don't feel that way anymore.
- They may tell you how much you disappoint them.
- They may try to bully you into apologizing and saying you're sorry.
- They may recruit others to do all of the above.
- And as you communicate, things get progressively worse, despite your efforts at working towards peace.

If someone uses the above techniques in a "conversation", that's not called being open-minded or "working things out". That's called trying to "win" through submission. And the fact is, no matter what the outcome is, there are *no winners*.

Distortion (of truth)

If you lie — or simply present an *exaggeration* as the "truth" — to make a point or to "win" an argument, it not only invalidates your argument, it destroys your credibility.

Friends and enemies

Working through a problem with a third party is one thing. Speaking badly about another person simply because you don't like them is something else entirely.

If you wouldn't say it to the person you're speaking about, then perhaps it's not the sort of thing you should be saying to someone else in their absence. And if you're not the kind of person who would stick up for a friend being spoken poorly of when they're not present, then perhaps it's time to consider what it means to be a friend.

Real friends may give each other shit — and often do — but they also don't let others speak poorly of their friends in their absence. Having integrity means sticking up for what you believe in, even when it isn't easy. And sometimes this means refusing to take part in conversations aimed at putting people down.

Learn to let people make up their own minds about others without trying to bond by creating a common enemy.

"You just want attention."

Wanting attention is *not* a bad thing. But if you want attention, you better know what to do when you get it. Because if what you want attention for isn't worth the attention it gets, then expect to get negative feedback. Although, you should expect to get negative feedback regardless.

Talking shit

Remember, we judge ourselves by our intentions, but we judge others by their actions. Because of this discrepancy, it's important to exercise restraint when one feels the urge to criticize people.

From our limited perspective, we often have very little understanding of what other people are truly thinking or what motivated them to do what they did. We only have our interpretation of other people's motivation and our interpretation isn't always an accurate reflection of the truth.

If you must talk about people, talk about what you *learned* from your experience with that person and use *that* to teach others how to beware of similar situations. Let others make up their own minds as to how to use the knowledge and insight you share. What you observe with other people isn't always true. But what you learn from experiences with other people can't be disputed.

Remember that what you choose to say and how you choose to say it when talking about other people says a lot about you. We all make mistakes. It's what we learn from experiences that's important, not directly disparaging and talking shit about others because they taught us a lesson we didn't want to learn.

Conversations come back

People have a natural tendency to talk about things that they've previously discussed with a person — especially people who are only acquaintances and not good friends.

If you speak about the weather with an acquaintance, the chances are good, the next time you see that person, the weather will be a topic of discussion. If you talk about your love of cars, cars will be a recurring topic of discussion. If you talk about something you're working on, the person you talk to will likely check-in on your progress later.

If you want to talk about something *new*, then you'll need to add something new to a conversation.

CHAPTER 24

ROLE MODELS & THE MEDIA

Propaganda (noun): 1. information, especially of a biased or misleading nature, used to promote or publicize a particular political cause or point of view.

⚡ We give assclowns and bad news the most press and then wonder why there is so much bad news and so many assclowns in the world.

Propaganda

Any source of information that has a consistent, opinionated narrative, *isn't* news, it's propaganda. *True* news delivers details *without* spin and leaves it up to consumers to form their own opinions based on the information provided.

Propaganda manipulates information by repeatedly focusing on a single point, perspective, or person or by intentionally leaving out key details in order to promote a particular agenda.

If you wish to be intelligently informed, it's important to recognize when you're being misled, misdirected, and manipulated by the media and to not simply take everything at face value. Always remember to fact check and resist relying on only a single source of information (or meme). Know that there is always more than a single side to a story and that even if something is repeated often by the media, it doesn't make it true.

Refuse to let the media pit you against people or causes you know nothing about except for what they've told you. Form your own opinions, don't let your opinions be formed for you.

> *"How many legs does a dog have if you call the tail a leg?*
> *Four. Calling a tail a leg doesn't make it a leg."*
> — *Abraham Lincoln*

A higher standard

Liars. Cheaters. Drug addicts. Racists. Homophobes. Wife beaters. The selfish. The narcissistic. The willfully ignorant. Just because someone is on TV, in movies, or records popular music doesn't make them a good role model.

The fact that someone has a lot of money in their bank account and is considered "successful" by that standard doesn't mean their life is a blueprint worth following or that their words are worth listening to.

The folks most worthy of emulating and drawing attention to are far more likely to be those who live modestly and with integrity than they are to be those who do whatever outrageous things they can to get attention. They're people doing the right things regardless of who's watching, not those who only show up to get paid.

They're people who do whatever needs to be done whether they get attention or credit for doing it or not. They're folks who far more likely to be your neighbor, a coworker, or a random person you cross paths with than someone who shows up on television, a billboard, or the cover of a magazine.

Resist the urge to simply accept the commercially driven role models that are marketed to the masses. Their prominence is more likely the result of a desire to make someone money than a desire to add value to the world or to set a good example for others to follow.

We owe it to ourselves to have truly positive role models, not assclowns on TV and on the covers of the magazines in the magazine rack. Hold your idols to a higher standard than simply being famous for being famous. Find people worth admiring, whether they are famous or not.

Yesteryear's heroes

Yesteryear's heroes: Explorers, envelope pushers, record breakers, the exceptionally talented... They represented many of humankind's greatest ideals. Integrity, honor, resourcefulness, respect, curiosity...

We believed in such things. We cared about such things.

Today's heroes: Millionaires, billionaires, corporations, celebrities, sell-outs... People who are far more concerned with their status and their bank accounts than whatever it was that allowed them to gain what they got.

Yes, there *are* exceptions. People acting unselfishly and adding value to the world. These are the people who deserve to be seen and heard because we deserve a better example to follow than the status quo.

We deserve better than politicians who sell themselves to the highest bidder, regardless of the evils that bidder represents. We deserve better than a media that cares more about ratings and spin and sponsors and the next election cycle than the truth. We deserve better than corporations that sabotage each other and impede progress and growth to simply make their stockholders happy.

We deserve people with integrity that we can trust. We deserve companies racing into the future with advancements that will benefit *all* people and not just the elite. *These* kinds of people and companies deserve the headlines every day. Not some celebrity having a baby. Not some singer releasing a remix. Not some deranged killer. Not another unfaithful, outrageous, drug-addicted, alcoholic, or corrupt politician.

Where are the heroes? Where are the people with integrity? Where are the people we can trust? Where are the people we can believe in?

Yes, they *do* exist, but we rarely see them because the media believes that we would rather hear about celebrities acting badly than "the crazy ones" trying to change the world. No wonder people are cynical. We are bombarded with the worst of humanity 24 hours a day, 7 days a week. Sickness, greed, killing, war. A corporate agenda.

The fact that a fast food item is *ever* back *isn't news*, it's advertising. We should be appalled that it passes for journalism. The fact we are striving for Mars and the stars *is news*. The fact that some envelope-pushing companies could use your support *is news*.

We deserve organizations striving for peace and harmony, not companies trying to perpetuate wars for the military complex that profits from them. War is a business and, unfortunately, business is booming. We owe it to ourselves to find better heroes than those who simply use our attention for profit rather than for the betterment of humanity. We deserve heroes that don't need to highlight their accomplishments every time they make a media appearance for us to believe in them. We deserve heroes that seek to inspire more heroes and not just inspire people to follow them.

We *deserve* better. And we can *do* better. *Not* tomorrow. *Today*.

A super day

Just imagine if once a year the media, retailers, and the general public devoted as much time, money, energy, and resources to doing something positive and productive as they do hyping and discussing two teams made up of multi-millionaires trying to get a ball from one side of a field to the other.

- A day highlighting the individuals and companies making a positive difference.
- A day spotlighting positive role models.
- A day giving visibility to good causes.
- A day encouraging people to be good to each other and the world at large.
- A day educating people on what they can do to enhance their lives and the lives around them in meaningful ways.
- A day focusing on friendship-making and tolerance instead of an "us vs. them" mentality or fear-mongering.
- A day that leaves a long-lasting positive impact and not just the aftertaste of buffalo wings and beer.

Supergood Sunday.

Greatness doesn't shout

Beware of any person or organization that constantly reminds you of qualities they would like you to believe they have. Those who are *truly* great don't need to frequently remind others of their greatness because their greatness is either self-evident or already an established part of their reputation.

If you're great at something, people will see it by what you do and the reputation you establish as a result.

The more one seeks to convince others of their greatness through words instead of actions, the less great they probably are.

CHAPTER 25

MISCELLANEOUS

⚡ Even some of the most reliable, most cared for, and most loved people in your life are only passing through. Always appreciate what you have when you have it. You never know when you won't have another opportunity.

Little by little

A little lie is still a lie.
A little abuse is still abuse.
A little racism is still racism.
A little bullying is still bullying.
A little infidelity is still infidelity.
A little nepotism is still nepotism.
A little negativity is still negativity.
A little immaturity is still immaturity.
A little narcissism is still narcissism.
A little name calling is still name calling.
A little discrimination is still discrimination.
A little sexual assault is still sexual assault.
A little mental instability is still mental instability.
A little disregard for the environment is still disregard for the environment.

Evil doesn't just show up and announce itself as evil. It might even look like something good at first. And it will certainly try to convince you that it is. But little by little it works in ways that end up having major negative consequences if you continue to turn a blind eye to the damage it's doing, in what it wants you to believe, is in your own best interest.

Good vs. popular

It should go without saying, but not everything that is good is popular. And not everything that's popular is good. And yet, people often judge their own work or others' work based on how much attention it gets. Never forget that there are always ways to game the system and some people have advantages that others don't.

While some things become popular naturally, many things that become popular only do so after money is spent to get those things enough exposure that word of mouth takes over. There is always a tipping point — and if your work isn't being seen by the right people in the right place at the right time, you could easily have something amazing and newsworthy still go unnoticed.

The future looking forward

Just because an abuser feels justified being abusive and has a vocal support group doesn't excuse their actions or make them right.

It can be difficult holding your ground in the shadow of forces that seek to stifle logic, tolerance, honesty, and common sense, but it's important that you do. This is especially true in a chaotic political climate.

If those who are meant to represent us are not leading us to a better and brighter future, it is important that we elect those who do. The future should be something we all look forward to, not just a select few. Regardless of our ethnicity, cultural background, political or religious beliefs, or sexual preferences, our leaders should inspire us all to be better people, better to each other, and better for the world.

Earning a reputation

If you frequently get caught doing things you're not supposed to do and you finally stop doing them, don't be surprised if no one notices.

People earn a reputation by how they consistently act. And if one of the things you consistently do is get caught for doing things you're not supposed to do, it will take a lot more than just starting to do what you're supposed to be doing to change people's impression of you.

 Your life is a Do-It-Yourself project. But if you're lucky and you're kind, you might just find a few people who will be more than willing to help you along the way. Because you would do the same for them.

Sweet little lies

Be very careful about putting your trust in someone who lies. Even if it's just once and it's in your favor. Lies have a way of coming back to haunt those who were involved with them. And people who place their trust in liars, particularly repeat offenders, will eventually be betrayed by one.

The same goes for putting faith in those who abuse their power. Even if it works in your favor today, it can easily come back to haunt you later.

Studies

Always keep in mind that studies show trends, not 100% effectiveness. Studies nearly always report results that are significant for *some people*, not *everyone*.

Even if a study suggests that an alternative to something that works for you works for other people, it doesn't mean it will work better. The point is, if something works for *you* in your life and *you're* happy with it, keep doing it.

"Less is more"

"Less is more." is a popular expression, but it should be known that like many popular expressions, it isn't always true. Sometimes less *is* more, and sometimes it's *not*.

Always remember that clever sayings may contain wisdom, but they are not without their exceptions and are not rules that were never meant to be broken. Sometimes the answers in life are counter intuitive. Ancient wisdom or conventional thinking don't apply to *every* conceivable situation.

Sometimes *less is just less*.

"I just tell it like it is"

Because no two people perceive or experience things in an identical fashion, anyone who says, "I just tell it like it is" is really saying, "I just tell it like I interpret it."

Perception may be reality — and there may be a great deal of agreement on shared experiences — but every one of our realities is unique. What one person considers normal, another may consider "alarming" or "extraordinary" depending on personal experience, beliefs, education, age, race, gender, sexual orientation, health, fitness level, energy level, timing, intelligence, their emotional state, and above all, *interpretation*.

Because we are prone to making mistakes in judgement, what we consider to be "true", based on our senses alone, is not a guarantee of accuracy. This can have a dramatic effect on our lives by allowing us to live according to false and self-limiting beliefs. As Alfred Korzybski put it, *"The map is not the territory."*

What we experience in life is an interpretation of events, not an absolute reality. Use this knowledge accordingly.

Productive boredom

Rather than take the time to tell anyone who will listen that you're bored, why not think about a problem in the world and imagine ways to solve it — because at least that's productive.

The world doesn't care if you're bored, but if you focus on a problem and try to fix it, you may just pique the interest of others who not only want to help you solve it, they might have crazy enough ideas to do it.

Remember: *Conventional thinking doesn't change the world, crazy ideas do.*

You don't have to be an expert to find a solution to a problem that has escaped those whose expertise is precisely the reason they can't see it.

You can't measure love

You can't measure love. You can't measure the impact you have on a person's life. You can't measure imagination or knowledge or creativity. You can't measure an instinct or a gut feeling. You can't measure synchronicity or serendipity. You can't measure a memory.

You can't measure some of the most important things that matter most in the world. And yet, this has no impact on the tremendous value these things provide to our lives. Not everything needs to be measured to be valued. And many of the best things can't be.

When in doubt, write it out

Sometimes you won't know what you *really* think or how you *really* feel about something until you write it down.

- ✓ Write down your goals
- ✓ Write down your fears
- ✓ Write down your desires
- ✓ Write a letter to someone you have unfinished business with even if you never send it
- ✓ Write down your feelings about anything that isn't resolved
- ✓ Write down your problems and potential solutions to those problems

The process of writing something down activates parts of the brain that allow it to be considered in ways that don't present themselves when it only exists in one's mind. *When in doubt, write it out.*

Afterword

Day 2,193:
Success takes time

Two thousand, one hundred and ninety-three days.

Exactly six years.

That's how long I've spent exploring a path that has taken me far from the place I thought I was heading when I started.

And in that time, I've discovered that arriving at a place you didn't expect to end up *isn't* failure. *It's life.* And it isn't the end of one's journey, it's simply a part of it.

Always remember that not ending up where you thought you wanted to go, doesn't mean you won't end up in a place you want to be. In fact, the most unexpected journeys are often those with the most valuable lessons to teach.

Sometimes not getting exactly what we want exactly when we want it is exactly what we need.

In a society that increasingly seeks safety, comfort, shortcuts, magic pills, and instant gratification, we often forget that almost anything worth having takes time. And it most certainly takes effort.

Ultimately, the journey of life isn't so much about how hard or easy one's path is or how quickly a person gets to where they want to be, it's about who they become along the way.

Successes are certainly sweet, but failure is the best teacher. Don't deny yourself the opportunity to evolve by refusing to see the lessons in hardship. Give yourself the time to work through mistakes and failures in order to ultimately succeed.

And remember, success is not only objective, it changes as we do. I may not have gotten exactly what I set out for exactly when I wanted it, but I think it was exactly what I needed.

Day 3,129:
Hang on

Two and a half years have passed since I wrote the entry on the previous page. That entry was written while I was working on what would ultimately evolve into the book you're reading. It was intended to be the last page and the last bit of new content I would add before the book was published.

While I still had some editing to do and the book still needed to be proofread, I could see the light at the end of the tunnel. And I was about to be a real, bona fide author.

That *isn't* what happened.

Because, well, things don't always play out as we expect them to. It's a lesson I keep learning.

And in the time that has passed since that last entry, this book went from an almost sure-thing, to something I wasn't sure was ever going to see the light, to — in just a few minutes — finally being completed.

And, as disappointed as I was when life saw fit to challenge me in a way that kept me from completing this book, I can tell you with absolute confidence that the book you're holding is *far better* because of it (there's a lesson there).

I will leave you with this... if there is something you *truly* want to do, and life keeps making it difficult, don't just let it go because it's hard. ***Hang on***.

Don't give up on things just because they are hard. Or just because they don't happen when you want them to. Or just because they don't seem likely. Because the moment you let them go completely is the moment that they're truly gone.

Hang on to the things that are truly important to you.
Success *really* takes time.

[control/option+s]

Thank you for being a part of my journey.

If you find value in this book, I'd love it if you told someone. Your positive word of mouth — in person or on Amazon, Goodreads, and social media — is not just welcome, it is absolutely essential in ensuring that this book gets into the hands of more people whose lives might be changed by it.

I promise to continue working on myself as well as my mission to make a positive difference in other people's lives. This includes learning from my mistakes, being open to feedback, and forever seeking ways to better myself as a person and help others in the process.

You have my sincerest thanks in helping me do that.

— Zero Dean

ABOUT THE AUTHOR

I think writing in the third person as a way to make one's self sound important is both deceptive and manipulative. So I'm not going to do it. As a result, this may be the most awkward "about the author" page you've ever read, but let's embrace it.

First things first, **_yes, my real name is Zero_**. And it is, in fact, written on my birth certificate. While there's a lot I could say about my name, this probably isn't the best place for it. Instead, I'll refer you to zerodean.com where you read more about it.

The lessons in this book stem from experiences I've had since embarking on a multi-faceted journey beyond my comfort zone in 2010. Although the initial phase of my journey led me to criss-cross the United States on an epic road trip covering over 60,000 miles, my geographical travels are far eclipsed by the inner journey they led to.

To be frank, some of the experiences I had were nearly the end of me. Not because anything I did on my journey was inherently dangerous (I _love_ adventures, but I'm not an adrenaline junkie), but because battling one's inner demons is likely the hardest battle one will ever face. Until a person learns to take control over how they think, one's mind can run rampant with thoughts that do little more than abuse its host. But hey, this probably isn't the best place to go into that. Awkward!

Prior to my journey, I was a professional 3D computer graphics artist, working at computer gaming companies like Rockstar Games in San Diego, California and Big Huge Games in Baltimore, Maryland.

And although I didn't know what I would be getting when I started on my journey, I am a wholehearted advocate of stepping beyond one's comfort zone as a means for personal growth.

I currently reside in north county San Diego, California. And if you're wondering if I am _still_ living beyond comfort as I did when I started my journey nearly a decade ago… the answer is yes.

Made in the USA
Columbia, SC
31 December 2019